ROBERT KING

Purcell

With 103 illustrations, 13 in color

 THAMES AND HUDSON

HALF-TITLE PAGE: *Godfrey Kneller's portrait drawing of Purcell.*
TITLEPAGE: *Detail from the map of London in 1690 reproduced on p. 164.*

© 1994 Thames and Hudson Ltd, London

First published in the United States of America in 1994 by
Thames and Hudson Inc., 500 Fifth Avenue,
New York, New York 10110

Library of Congress Catalog Card Number 94-60279
ISBN 0-500-01625-9

Printed and bound in Slovenia

CONTENTS

PROLOGUE

'*A greater musical genius England never had*' (ROGER NORTH, 1726)

'*If Purcell had lived, he would have composed better music than this*' (GEORGE FRIDERIC HANDEL, *c*.1752, of his own music)

'*He was superior to all his predecessors, that his compositions seemed to speak a new language; yet, however different… it was universally under-stood*' (CHARLES BURNEY, 1776)

'*I had never realised, before I first met Purcell's music, that words could be set with such ingenuity, with such colour*' (BENJAMIN BRITTEN, 1945)

For over three hundred years, Purcell's genius has been acknowl-edged. And yet history has still not finally placed this extraordi-nary figure in his rightful place amongst the truly great composers. Born and raised amidst the veritable explosion of culture that greeted the Restoration of the British monarchy, in the field of English music Henry Purcell stands as a colossus. Hugely prolific in his composition-al output, a consummate setter of words as able as Mozart or Schubert to turn even an ordinary text into music of spell-binding originality, admired and adored by his contemporaries, his is an astonishing story. Purcell wrote with equal skill and imagination for the opera house, the church, the theatre, for his royal patrons and for small domestic forces. Yet vast tracts of his music, although available for those who wish to hunt through library shelves, have for decades been unjustly ignored by all but the most ardent of his champions. How typical that British reserve should once again manifest itself in underplaying one of its national jewels.

Whilst much of Purcell's music has survived, we know far less of the man himself. Even the bare bones of his career have to be assembled from bare references in official contemporary records. To reveal his character there are few letters and no personal diaries; if Purcell was unfaithful to his wife, or caused scandals, history has failed to carry such information to the twentieth century. There are only a handful of surviving portraits. But we can nonetheless glean much about the life of this unique musical giant by setting him and his work into its colourful historical context.

The last four decades of the seventeenth century were a time when a constant stream of political and national events affected every intelligent creative figure. Purcell lived all his life in London: the capital was busy, dirty, crowded, unpredictable but always buzzing. As a child Purcell lived through the plague and the great fire of London: tragedy struck at the age of only five when his father died. The young Purcell learned his musical craft as a boy chorister at the Chapel Royal. As an adult he served in the court of Charles II and witnessed the lascivious behaviour and wanton excess that gave such excellent fodder to contemporary diarists, watched as King James dug his own political grave and looked on as the Glorious Revolution brought William and Mary to the throne. When opportunities for court musicians waned, he turned his attention to the world of the theatre: here too his output was constantly affected by events and the politics behind them. But, whatever his and the country's fortunes, Purcell constantly and prodigiously composed; the music that he wrote is amongst the greatest of the whole baroque era.

So it is by a study of the short life of Henry Purcell in the wider historical context that we can learn more about this remarkable figure, setting his wonderful, daring music into the events of the age. And by performing all Purcell's works – not just the small smattering that convention has led us to believe are representative of his whole output – we can judge the true greatness of the finest composer Britain has ever produced. Not without justification did his contemporary, Thomas Tudway assert that Purcell 'was confessedly the Greatest Genius we ever had'.

A NOTE ON YEAR NUMBERING

In seventeenth century England the year changed towards the end of March, rather than on 1 January. Throughout the text all years have been modernized (i.e. Purcell's '15 February 1683' has been transcribed as '15 February 1684').

Ciuitatis Westmonasteriensis pars.

Parlament House   the Hall   the Abby

W. Hollar fecit, 1647

CHAPTER I

A Restoration Childhood, 1659-1668

On 22 April 1659, with the dissolution of Richard Cromwell's Protectorate parliament, nearly twenty years of republicanism in England finally crumbled. Oliver Cromwell's government 'by a single person' had been a surprisingly effective form of rule but, after two decades, the English were moving, albeit chaotically, towards the belief that monarchy was, after all, the most stable political solution. Richard Cromwell hastened the decision, for he was a political failure who possessed none of his father's acumen. Oliver had managed to maintain a balance between civilians and military men, radicals and conservatives, whilst still achieving support from those outside the republican ranks, whereas Richard had alienated the army and the civilian radicals. The army, rapidly splitting itself into self-interested factions, demanded political autonomy, with a Commander-in-chief distinct from the Protector; when Richard refused their request (which would have meant virtual abdication of power) they set about destroying the very post they had helped create.

On 7 May 1659, the old Rump Parliament, consisting essentially of those members of the Long Parliament who had been left sitting in 1648, resumed power. On 24 May they induced Cromwell to abdicate as Protector, and the following day he did so. The political year that followed saw utter confusion. The army generals, whilst trying to satisfy the public call for a parliament, seemed intent on securing their own careers and political independence. The civilian parties, on the other hand, were determined to reduce both the numbers and the political aims of the army.

From this political mess emerged one figure who proved able to bring some sense to the proceedings. By doing so he saved the Stuart monarchy. George Monck was one of Cromwell's most trusted

OPPOSITE: *two views of London before 1660 by Wenceslaus Hollar.* Above: *Westminster from the river, showing St Stephen's Chapel (called Parliament House because parliament met there), Westminster Hall and Westminster Abbey.* Below: *the City of London from the north, with Old St Paul's in the centre.*

General Monck, the man largely responsible for Charles II's restoration, painted by Samuel Cooper about 1670.

lieutenants who had commanded the English army in Scotland since 1654. After the Protector's death he became increasingly unhappy about the course of political events and, encouraged by royalist agents, decided to take matters into his own hands. On 1 January 1660 Monck led his army across the River Tweed into England.

Amid such political uncertainty it is hardly surprising that the birth of Henry Purcell went, as far as historians can ascertain, almost completely unnoticed; no birth or baptismal records have yet been discovered, and indeed there is no incontrovertible evidence of Purcell's parentage. We do not know when during 1659 Henry was born, though it is safe to assume this was before 20 November, as the memorial tablet in Westminster Abbey states that he died on 21 November 1695 'in his thirty-seventh year'. From the will of John Hingeston, Henry's godfather and formerly state organist for Oliver Cromwell, later appointed 'tuner and repairer of his Majesty's wind instruments', we read that Henry was the son of Elizabeth Purcell: if we take this statement to be true, we can assume that the composer's father was the musician Henry Purcell. Scholars have in the past sometimes proposed Thomas Purcell, brother of Henry senior. Henry, who had married Elizabeth (surname unknown) some time before 1656 (when their first son Edward was born) appears only in one pre-Restoration document, being mentioned as having alternated the role of Mustapha with Thomas Blagrave in William Davenant's *Siege of Rhodes*, itself first published in 1656. It appears that Henry senior was living in London towards the end of the Commonwealth, working

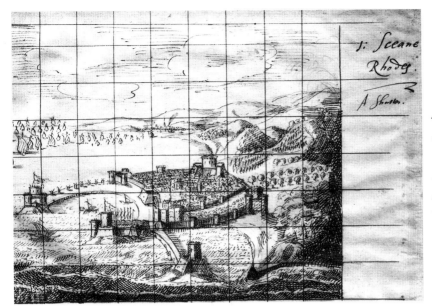

John Webb's backcloth for William Davenant's play The Siege of Rhodes, *in which Purcell's father Henry is listed as having played the part of Mustapha.*

with a group of musicians in Westminster: although we do not have firm evidence that the Purcell family were in the area when their son Henry was born, they are known to have been living in one of the houses on the south side of the Great Almonry later in 1659. Assuming that the Purcells didn't move house whilst Elizabeth was in the last stages of pregnancy, we can presume that their third child, Henry, was born just south of Tothill Street, a few hundred yards west of Westminster Abbey.

The population of England and Wales in 1659 was around 5.5 million, of whom nearly a tenth lived in the conurbation of London. No other city in Britain was of a similar size: Bristol and Norwich were the next largest with populations of just 30,000 people, each acting as a regional capital. Britain was still essentially an agricultural country, sparsely populated and with villages remote from even their near neighbours. Half the population were agricultural labourers, and one and a half million people lived in towns (of whom a third lived in the capital). Only about 10,000 of the population were reckoned to be merchants, matched by roughly the same number of clergy. There were also some 10,000 public servants and officials, and nearly 15,000 lawyers. The arts were reckoned to employ nearly 9,000 people. After a bad harvest or a poor year's trade, nearly sixty per cent of the population lived in poverty. 'Fewness of the people is the real poverty', noted Sir William Petty in 1662; the country could support twice its population 'were they rightly employed.'[1]

The country's financial centre was the strongly independent City of London, an entity of its own which fiercely guarded its rights and had always been capable of asserting its will against crown and parliament by virtue of the great wealth contained within its walls. In the Civil War the City had strongly supported the parliamentarians from the outset: although the initial military advantage had lain with the royalists, King Charles's supporters had failed to consolidate their successes in the field. As the war dragged on, economic realities gradually asserted themselves, and it was largely with funds supplied by the great merchants from within the City of London that Cromwell's army was raised, trained and, above all, paid.

The official entrance to the City of London in the west was at Temple Bar, the gateway that stood at the junction of Fleet Street and the Strand. The walls had long since ceased their original function, of protecting the City against siege and attack, and seventeenth-century London was expanding in all directions. The City proper was densely populated, with narrow streets and medieval wooden buildings blotting out the sky with overhanging storeys. A mass of small shops sold

Panorama of London before the Fire: the City with its dense mass of houses and church steeples dominated by Old St Paul's, the river crossed by Old London Bridge and thronged with boats, and on the near side the church of St Mary Overy, now Southwark Cathedral.

goods of every description. Noise was everywhere, with hawkers and apprentices bawling the merits of their wares, and the wheels of coaches and carts creating a constant rattle on the cobbled streets. Hackney coaches abounded, and their drivers would often brawl with each other and aggravate the footmen of the richer residents. Traffic congestion was terrible, beaten only by the smell of the city. Sanitation was primitive in the extreme.

But amongst the bustle of the City were majestic buildings. In the Royal Exchange merchants from around the world gathered daily to carry out large-scale business, to hire shipping and to discuss the latest news: it was as much a social centre as a centre of trade. Towards the west end of the City stood the largest church in England, St Paul's Cathedral. Its spire had burned down a century before, and the nave was partly in ruins after years of neglect during the Commonwealth: trading stalls were now set up in the aisles and the church was used as a meeting place and gossip centre as well as a place of worship. But it was a majestic edifice which dominated the skyline. At the east end

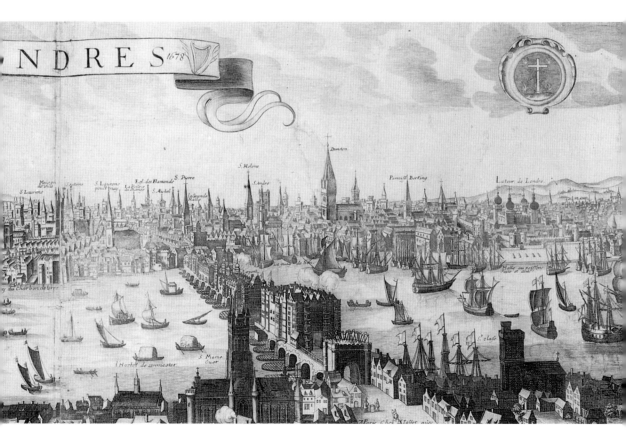

Detail of the previous plate showing traitors' heads exposed on spikes at the end of London Bridge.

Opposite: two views of Whitehall from the river. In both, Inigo Jones's Banqueting House of 1619–22, nucleus of a vast palace never to be built, stands out among the lower buildings.

was a smaller but older building, the Tower of London, which had been constructed nearly 600 years earlier by William the Conqueror. It was still used as a state prison and place of execution. Standing on the banks of the Thames, the Tower had become the showplace of London, famous for its menagerie which contained lions and other wild beasts.

The river Thames was the main highway for London. Whilst the City's streets were narrow and dirty, the river was wide and relatively clean. Boats travelled constantly up and down, manned by the Thames watermen who were renowned for their coarse manners and bad language. Boats could be hired near Palace Yard in Westminster and would take their passengers up and down the six miles of the river that linked the City and its outskirts. On the south bank was Southwark, built around the main road that led from London Bridge through to St George's Fields and the countryside that lay beyond, and to its west sat the wastes of Lambeth marshes and, directly across the river from Westminster, the small settlement of Lambeth. Since the thirteenth century, one bridge only linked the two banks of the Thames: the watermen, much of whose trade lay in making crossings from one river bank to the other, were one of the principal obstacles against another being built. Built on eighteen arches, London Bridge was the finest in the land. Lined with a double row of shops and houses, some of them six storeys high, it was one of the most imposing structures in the capital. Less graceful were the heads of traitors which were displayed on the turret at the southern end as a macabre warning to others who might attempt similar follies.

The seat of government at Westminster lay to the west of the City in an area housing probably 100,000 residents. The kings of England had held their court in the Palace of Westminster in its various forms for five hundred years. During the reign of Henry VIII the court had moved to a collection of buildings a few hundred yards down the road at Whitehall: Charles I had planned to replace the half-mile sprawl of these buildings by modern ones, but the Civil War put paid to such grand plans. In the event, only Inigo Jones's imposing Banqueting House was completed and still stands in modern London's Whitehall: contemporary illustrations show it towering above its sixteenth-century surroundings. In his Whitehall Palace, King Charles I had established one of the most formal and cultured courts in Europe. Some of the best artists had found patronage there, and the result had been one of the greatest collections of art in Europe. Courtly

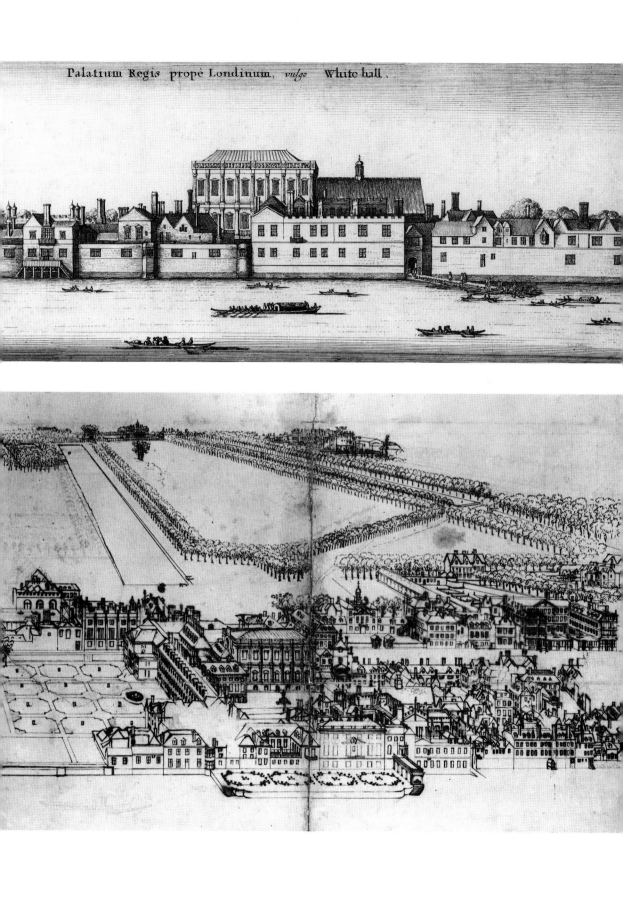

Palatium Regis propè Londinum, *vulgo* White hall.

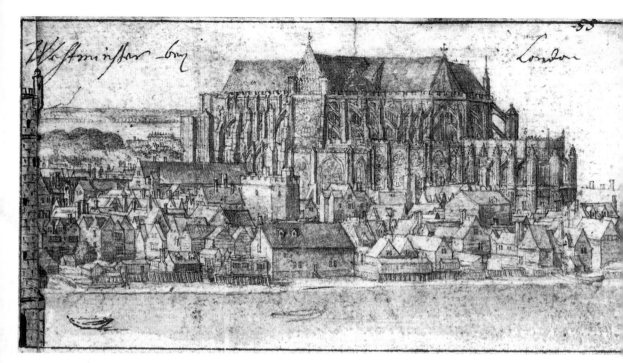

Westminster in Purcell's time, houses clustering round the Abbey and along the river bank. The Abbey's west towers were not built until the early eighteenth century.

splendour had vanished abruptly at the beginning of 1642 when, succumbing to pressure from his rebellious subjects, Charles I had left London with his family. He returned only as a prisoner for a few weeks, and was held in St James's Palace before finally being taken to the executioner's block in Whitehall on 30 January 1649.

Parliament, so much as King Charles had dared allow it to function, had met in Westminster in St Stephen's Chapel, which became known as the Parliament House. During the Protectorate, Whitehall Palace, a rambling collection of buildings, was used by the Republicans as their administrative headquarters but, over seventeen years, the Palace's former glory was lost. The fabric was neglected 'with cobwebs hanging on the wall',[2] and even when Cromwell assumed quasi-royal power as Lord Protector in 1653 and took over Whitehall as his residence, the building remained in a sad state. Nearby, in the parish of St Margaret's and suffering from neglect as well, was the splendid abbey church of St Peter, begun by Henry III in 1245, on a site that had housed an abbey since the days of Edward the Confessor around 1050. Though structurally Westminster Abbey survived the interregnum fairly well, by 1660 almost every item needed for worship had disappeared, and the internal decorations were in sore need of regeneration. In 1643 Roundhead soldiers were quartered in the Abbey, and caused terrible devastation to fixtures and fittings, destroying the organ and pawning the pipes to buy beer. In contrast, the other main building in the area, Westminster Hall, was a hive of activity. By now a large covered market, whose main entrance opened onto a large, bustling square full of people and carriages, the Hall housed a wide variety of traders offering anything for sale from toys to law stationery, and haberdashery to books.

On 3 February 1660 General Monck completed his march from Scotland, entered London with 7,000 troops and took control of the Government. On 21 February Monck re-established the Long Parliament, insisting that the moderate members who had been lately excluded from parliament be readmitted. When parliament refused to comply, Monck forced it to dissolve, which it did on 16 March. Meanwhile, in exile in Flanders, Charles watched with growing interest: his hopes had been raised before, only to be dashed, and Monck had not proved totally reliable in the past. On 4 April, guided by the careful diplomacy of Hyde, now his Lord Chancellor, Charles issued a declaration now widely known as the Declaration of Breda.

This Declaration, complete with its promises of a lawful parliamentary settlement, a general pardon to all except those named by parliament and a measure of religious liberty, was taken back to Monck by Grenville. On 25 April, Monck summoned a Convention Parliament, and on 1 May that gathering voted to restore the monarchy. Messengers were despatched to the continent, and exactly a week later came the formal Restoration. A proclamation was issued from both Houses of Parliament that Charles II was 'lineally, justly and lawfully next heir of the royal blood of this realm, and that by the goodness and providence of Almighty God he is of England, Scotland, France and Ireland the most potent, mighty and undoubted king'.[3] Parliament voted £50,000 to His Majesty (though he is reckoned by this stage to have been in debt by at least £80,000) and messengers delivered the news to Charles in Breda on 9 May.

Charles speedily prepared to return to Britain. His change in circumstances brought rapid financial results: Holland made an immediate gift of £30,000, fourteen important London citizens sent £10,800 in gold and even the City of London contributed £10,000. The navy, which had already declared for Charles, sent thirty frigates to bring back the king. Amongst those on board the king's boat, rapidly rechristened the 'Royal Charles', was the fleet commander, General Edward Montagu, and his cousin and secretary, Samuel Pepys, who had begun his famous diary on 1 January 1660. On 25 May Charles landed at Dover, and was greeted by Monck, who handed him a

Samuel Pepys, eminent civil servant and Secretary to the Admiralty under Charles II. His private diary, not published until the nineteenth century, gives a uniquely intimate glimpse of life at the Stuart court.

sheathed sword, the Mayor, who presented a Bible, and 50,000 people, who rejoiced noisily. The procession rested for the weekend at Canterbury, where Charles wrote to his youngest sister, Henriette, that 'My head is dreadfully stunned that I know not whether I am writing sense or nonsense'[4] and then proceeded towards London.

The celebrations in the capital on 29 May 1660 were the largest ever seen. The diarist John Evelyn described 'above 20,000 horse and foot, brandishing their swords and shouting with inexpressible joy; the ways strewed with flowers, the bells ringing, the streets hung with tapestry, fountains running with wine, the Mayor, Aldermen and all companies in their liveries, chains of gold and banners: lords and nobles clad in cloth of silver, gold and velvet: the windows and balconies well set with ladies: trumpets, music and myriads of people flocking even so far as from Rochester'. At Whitehall Charles gave a formal speech, but then cancelled a thanksgiving service at Westminster Abbey, preferring to spend the first night of his Restoration with his mistress, Barbara Palmer: it was, after all, the King's thirtieth birthday.

Charles was faced with the enormous job of reconstructing court and governmental life, and trying to balance the books. The finances of the country and of the crown were in a parlous state. The army and

navy had not been paid properly for some time, and there was now an additional queue of people claiming redress for wrongs that they had suffered during Cromwell's time, or wanting repayment of favours given during Charles's flight. Parliament was a major headache: it had never been summoned by the king and so was unconstitutional. With such mountainous tasks facing him, that of reviving music at court must have seemed a minor consideration for Charles, but he nonetheless acted decisively, rapidly making his first appointments. It is untrue to say that Cromwell had put a stop to all official music-making – he had maintained his own small group of performers who played for his private entertainment – but in church the Puritans had held that only the singing of Psalms and biblical cantatas would be permitted. Complex music, and certainly all instrumental music, was prohibited: cathedral choirs had been disbanded all over Britain, and consequently musical standards throughout the country had fallen. No children were starting their musical training as choristers. A petition presented to the authorities on 19 February 1656 by John Hingeston (the leader of Cromwell's band of musicians) had summed up the situation:

The restoration of Charles II, 1660. The king arrives at the Banqueting House, Whitehall, in front of which his father had been executed over ten years before.

by reason of the late dissolucion of the Quires in the Cathedralls where the study & practice of the Science of Musick was especially cherished, Many of the skilfull Professors of the said Science have during the laste Warrs and troubles dyed in want and there being now noe preferrment or Encouragement in the way of Musick Noe man will breed his Child in it, soe that it needes bee that the Science itself must dye in this Nacion, with those few professors of it now living, or at least it will degenerate much from the perfeccion it lately attained unto.[5]

At the Restoration there was no choir at the Chapel Royal. Indeed, as far as we can tell, there were only two official boy choristers in Britain at any one time during Cromwell's reign. Part of John Hingeston's salary of £100 per annum had been to supervise Cromwell's two singing boys, though the repertoire which they were allowed to perform was very limited. Charles needed to make rapid appointments in all areas of his musical establishment, aiming, initially at least, to restore the musical establishment to the scale and size which his father had enjoyed. Within ten days of entering London, he had made his first musical appointments, who were sworn into the royal household by Edward, Earl of Manchester, appointed Lord Chamberlain on 1 June. Thanks to exhaustive researches into Chancery accounts, now held in the Public Record Office, first by the musical historian Lafontaine[6] and, more recently, by Dr Andrew Ashbee[7], we get a surprisingly clear picture of the king's secular musical establishment: from his appointments we can greatly enhance what are often otherwise sketchy accounts of court musical life. During June 1660 the Lord Chamberlain's department made no less than forty-eight musical appointments (many replacing former employees of Charles I who were now dead) and commissioned several new instruments. The record books include entries such as:

June 16.
Mr Henry Lawes, Composer in ye Private Musick for Lutes & Voices in Mr Tho: Ford's place.
David Mell, a Violin, his owne place & in Woodington's place for the broke Consort also.
June 19.
Mr Gybbons approved of by ye King at Baynards Castle, and an organ to be made for him'. (We know from Pepys that the King dined at Baynards that day).

June 23.
Matthew Lock, composer in ye private musick in ye place of
Coperario (deceased).
14 July.
Patent for John Hingston as tuner and repairer of his Majesty's
wind instruments; £60 a year, from Midsummer 1660, for life.
Paid from the Treasury Chamber.[8]

Ten musicians were appointed to 'do service in Chapel Royal,
whose salaries are payable in the Treasury of His Majesty's Chamber':[9]
amongst these appointments was Henry Cooke as Master of the
Children of the Chapel Royal (also created, on 29 June, 'master of ye
boyes in ye private musick').[10] Maintaining a boys' choir is at the best
of times a major task, as any modern choir-trainer can testify: building
one from nothing, especially when there was no recent musical tradition on which to draw, must have been a monumental challenge.
Cooke had achieved a high reputation during Cromwell's rule as a
teacher, and possessed one of the vital ingredients for a successful
choir master, a good voice of his own. Pepys, writing in typically
enthusiastic style a year after the Chapel Royal reopened for business,
described Cooke as having 'the best manner of singing in all the
world',[11] and John Evelyn had reported him on 28 October 1654 as
the finest singer in England. Playford too mentions him in the preface
to his *Musicall Banquet* of 1651 as being one of the 'excellent and able
masters' for the voice and viol; we know that Cooke performed the
role of Solyman (in the same cast as Henry Purcell senior) in
Davenant's *The Siege of Rhodes* in 1656, also writing some of the songs
for it.

Of Cooke's early efforts with the choir we know very little, not
even having a full list of who were his choristers. But we do know that
amongst the first batch were four boys who went on to become
notable musicians in later life. Two of them would have been thirteen
years old in 1660: Pelham Humfrey, the nephew of a prominent
London Parliamentarian, Colonel John Humfrey, and a chorister who
probably came from Salisbury, Michael Wise; we know him as a rather
wild character later in life and we can perhaps surmise that he was not
one of Cooke's easier pupils. Two more known choristers would have
been eleven or twelve years old: of Robert Smith's origins we know
nothing, guessing that he was born in 1648; John Blow, baptised on
23 February 1649 (so probably born early that year), came from quite

humble beginnings in Newark, Nottinghamshire. One other famous chorister, William Turner, born in 1651, began his training at Christ Church Oxford, so it is safe to assume that he joined the Chapel Royal a year or two later. As with all choirs, the occasional service went awry, and Pepys notes on 14 October 1660 that the anthem was a mess: the king was amused. We know too that at Westminster Abbey from 1661 to 1667 a cornett player was salaried, and John Evelyn also records this fact:[12] his function would have been to double the upper voices, a system that Roger North suggests was duplicated at the northern cathedrals of Durham, Carlisle and York.

In the main sphere of politics too, much was also happening. On 2 October the army was disbanded, all but for about 5,000 men. In parliament Charles insisted on bringing a Bill of Indemnity and Oblivion which granted immunity to those who had been his enemies. Parliament spent a month adding names to the list of those who were to be exempted but the Lords were less certain. Charles had to explain to them himself that 'this mercy and indulgence is the best way to bring men to a true repentance … It will make them good subjects to me and good friends and neighbours to you.'[13] The bill, granting a general pardon for all treasons and felonies committed since 1637, was granted the Royal Assent on 29 August. Forty-nine named people were however exempted from the pardon 'for their execrable treason in sentencing to death … or being instrumental in taking away the precious life of the late sovereign Lord Charles'. Nineteen had already given themselves up and were granted clemency; of the remainder, only ten were eventually sentenced to death. Pepys went to see one such execution and wrote: 'I went to Charing Cross to see Major-General Harrison hanged, drawn and quartered – which was done there – he looking as cheerfully as any man could do in that condition. He was presently cut down and his head and heart thrown to the people at which there was great shouts of joy.'[14] Charles did not enjoy these executions, and passed a note to the Earl of Clarendon during one meeting of the Privy Council stating that 'I am weary of hanging, except on new offences'.[15] But the people of London found the whole process to be excellent entertainment. On 29 December 1660, Charles dissolved parliament and ordered fresh elections. The new Cavalier Parliament was heavily royalist. The time was right to stage a grand coronation.

The date was fixed, symbolically, for 23 April, St George's Day, 1661 and the preparations, supervised by a special commission headed by Clarendon, were considerable. Music was to play a large part in the ceremony, and composers, players and the newly reconstituted choirs of both Westminster Abbey and the Chapel Royal worked overtime. In January a 'commission from his Majesty' had been issued by the Signet Office 'authorising Henry Cooke, Master of the Children of his Majesty's Chapel Royal, and Private Music, to take children and choristers out of any cathedral or collegiate church, or any other place within his Majesty's realm of England, to breed them up and make them fit for his Majesty's service in the said Chapel Royal'.[16] On 21 January it was backed up by a patent issued to Cooke 'giving authority to him to take up boys for his Majesty's service in the Chapel Royal'.[17] Later in the year Cooke received a back payment of £23 7s 9d 'for fetching five boyes from Newarke and Lincolne for his Majesty's service'[18] and, at the same time, received £2 14s to cover the cost of 'Torches and Lights for practiceing Musicke against his Majesty's Coronacion'.[19] Clearly late-night rehearsals took place, and we may wonder if the travel payment made to Cooke for his northern chorister foray resulted in the young John Blow being brought down from Newark. Or perhaps Blow was already showing himself to be such a useful chorister that Cooke had returned to raid the Magnus Song School for further vocal talent!

Cooke's counterpart at Westminster Abbey was now Henry Purcell senior, for on 16 February 1661 'Henry Purcell, Edward Bradock, William Hutton, Richard Adamson and Thomas Hughes were installed singing-men, and the aforesaid Henry Purcell, Master of the Choristers also'.[20] Undoubtedly Purcell and Cooke worked together on the music for the coronation, for their choirs combined for many of the musical items. So busy was Purcell with his preparations that he was one of the few well-known musicians in London who did not take part in the lavish cavalcade which captivated London on the eve of the coronation. John Evelyn reported that a 'magnificent train on horseback proceeded through the streets strewed with flowers, houses hung with rich tapestry, windows and balconies full of ladies, the London militia lining the ways, and several companies with their banners and loud music in their orders'. The king also appeared 'in a most rich, embroidered suit and cloak', looking 'most nobly' and made the journey from Whitehall to the Tower of London by barge. 'So glorious was the show with gold and silver', wrote Pepys, 'that we were not able to look at it – our eyes at last being so overcome with it'.[21]

The morning of the coronation was fine, and people were up very early to get the best possible positions to view the processions. The king too was up early: he changed in the House of Lords and then moved on to Westminster Hall where, at 9.30 a.m., a short ceremony took place with the choirs of Westminster Abbey and the Chapel Royal, the king and the nobility. The twelve Children of the Chapel Royal were spruced up for the occasion too. On 6 April a Warrant had been issued from the Lord Chamberlain to the Great Wardrobe authorizing 'twelve suits of apparel for the twelve children of the Chapel Royal to be delivered to Captain Henry Cooke, master of the said children'[22] and two days later a similar document authorized 'coronation liveries for the Chapel Royal 12 children and 20 gentlemen'.[23] An original receipt now held in Oxford's Bodleian Library finds Cooke being reimbursed for expenditure on the extra parts of the choristers' uniforms: twelve pairs of shoes (seven pairs costing £1, three further pairs 9s, and the last two £1 6s 6d – why were these two last pairs so expensive?), two dozen bands and cuffs, twelve pairs of gloves and 13s worth of 'ribon for garters & shoeties'.[24] Cooke's total shopping bill came to £4 19s: by comparison the Duke of Buckingham spent £3,000 on the coronation. The full twenty-four violins were present at the service, their names carefully recorded in the Chamberlain's records, along with those of the eight 'musicians for the wind instruments'.[25]

The coronation service contained much music: although the surviving records do not always list the names of the composers, much of the form of the service is known. As the king entered the Abbey the Westminster choir sang a setting of 'I was glad', and after Charles was presented to the people as king the Chapel Royal choir sang 'Let thy hand be strengthened'. After the sermon came the hymn 'Come, Holy Ghost' and, for the anointing, a setting by Henry Lawes, now in his sixty-fifth year and one of the few musical survivors of Charles I's court, of 'Zadok the priest'. The combined choirs sang a setting, possibly by William Child (another survivor from before Cromwell's rule who was now back in his post as organist at St George's Chapel, Windsor and also had the previous year been appointed one of the 'musicians to his Majesty's private musick in ordinary' where he played the cornett) of 'The King shall rejoice' and then the 'Te Deum', and the Gentlemen of the Chapel Royal performed 'Behold O God our defender'. Some of this music seems to have been in the Venetian 'cori spezzati' style: the layout of the choirs and instrumentalists on both the north and south sides of the Abbey would have made this most effective. The sermon was preached by the Bishop of Worcester on a text from the Book of Proverbs. During the communion service that followed the coronation Henry Cooke's specially-written setting of the Creed was performed. Two more anthems completed the service: 'Let my prayer come up' and 'O hearken unto the voice of my calling'. The procession left the Abbey and a magnificent banquet was held in Westminster Hall to a musical accompaniment performed by the royal violins.

A week later London celebrated May Day by erecting the tallest maypole in England: it stood 130 feet high. In parliament there were rather more serious matters to consider. Charles's first properly constituted assembly, the Cavalier Parliament, first met on 8 May and started to enact a series of repressive measures. Charles was slow to realize that parliament was going to erode the crown's powers substantially, and that his declaration at Breda of 'a liberty to tender consciences' was already being countered: twenty years of republican rule had moved control of the army, navy, church and foreign trade, all formerly in the king's power, to parliament. The civil service had gained greatly in power, and groups such as the City merchants had also tasted direct experience of government. None of them were likely to relinquish such control easily. The Anglican Church was established, and over the next three years a series of measures were enacted which placed impossible restrictions on the Puritans and their clergy. All acts of Cromwell's parliaments were annulled, numerous penal laws were passed, the temporal power of bishops was restored, and a crime of high treason established: even to plan rebellion would result in death. The Corporation Act was passed at the end of the year effectively ensuring that all members of municipal bodies, including those who selected prospective members of parliament, had to be members of the Church of England.

A vital duty of the monarch was to ensure the continued succession and, even before the coronation, Charles was considering all the possible marriages. His amorous exploits were well known: an earldom was suddenly found for Roger Palmer, whose wife became Lady Castlemaine. 'Everyone knows why', noted Pepys. But mistresses and illegitimate children could not supply the nation with a queen or an heir to the throne. There was no shortage of candidates for the job, but diplomatic and financial needs were paramount. Spain and France were on fairly good terms with the English, and Brandenburg and Denmark were the subjects of long-standing treaties. Relations with

Holland were deteriorating, so that country certainly showed diplomatic possibilities. But Portugal proved the most interesting: politically the situation was right, the country being a pawn in France's struggles against Spain for European domination, and the twenty-three-year-old daughter of the King of Portugal, Catherine of Braganza, appeared to fit Charles's own bill. Charles had only seen her portrait and noted 'that person cannot be unhandsome', but the huge advantage came with her dowry: in return for permission to enlist English troops for her defence, Portugal would offer a cash sum of around £300,000, the island of Bombay and the port of Tangier together with trading privileges in Brazil and the East Indies. On 23 June a Treaty of Alliance (a marriage treaty) was agreed with Portugal. The warrant books register that eight 'able and sufficient trumpeters'[26] were commanded to be sent with the royal fleet to that country 'to attend the Queen's Majesty'.[27] In the event, the fleet departed from England on 15 January 1662, and it was another four months before the princess actually arrived in Britain.

Charles's musical appointments at court continued to increase, and so too did the wages bill. There were three principal musical posts. The Master of the Children of the Chapel Royal, as we have seen, was in charge of the music that was performed in the king's chapel; Nicholas Lanier, also Marshal of the Corporation of Westminster Musicians, was the Master of the King's Musick, responsible for supervising and preparing performances of music at court, and Jervaise Price was the Sergeant Trumpeter. Just glancing at one block of official receipts from 1661, we can see salaries paid to Jervaise Price, his sixteen Ordinary Trumpeters and the official Kettle Drummer, Hans BeryHosky [Barney Hosky] – a total of £1120. In the same batch are payments to fourteen members of His Majesty's Musicians for the Violins, two Composers for the Violins, various wind players, three official lutenists, a 'Musition for the Virginalls' (Christopher Gibbons, son of Orlando, who also held the posts of organist at Westminster Abbey and at the Chapel Royal) and John Hingeston, 'Tuner and Repairer of His Majesty's Wind Instruments'.[28] Hingeston must have been kept busy! Rehearsal premises were needed, and on 3 July the Treasurer to the Chamber was ordered to pay out £50 to the Master of His Majesty's Music 'for the hiring of two large rooms for the practise of music and for keeping the instruments in'.[29] Davies Mell took delivery from the 'coffer maker' of three chests 'for his Majesty's musical instruments'.[30]

All these musicians were under the overall control and discipline of the Lord Chamberlain (and were immune from arrest unless by warrant from their employer). On 31 May 1661, not long after the royal violins had been formed, musical standards were deemed to be not up to scratch, and an official slap was administered by the Chamberlain:

Whereas his Majesty hath been graciously pleased to entertayne diverse persons in his service for his Band of violins, and that there hath been Complaint made to mee of diverse neglects in their practize and performance to doe his Majesties faithfull service. These are therefore to will and command all persons concerned that are of his Majesties said band for the violins to take notice that I have ordered George Hudson and Davies Mell to give orders and directions from tyme to tyme to every perticuler person herein concerned for their practize and performance of Musick to prevent their former neglects, and if any of the said Musick shall refuse to obey this my order, he is to answer his Contempt before mee upon complaint of the said George Hudson and Davies Mell.[31]

Charles I had maintained a band of fourteen string instruments, and at the Restoration Charles II re-established this ensemble, enlarging it to imitate the Vingt-quatre Violons that he had so admired at the court of Louis XIV during his exile. Charles had also seen Lully directing the 'petite bande' of sixteen players, and ordered a parallel, equally select ensemble to be formed in England. In 1662 John Banister was given 'full power to instruct and direct' the new group who, the State Papers of 3 May 1662 tell us, were intended to provide 'better performance of service, without being mixed with the other violins, unless the King orders the 24'. The Vingt-quatre Violons continued to play dance music day-to-day in public at Whitehall, but soon smaller groups from it were also playing in the Chapel Royal and in the king's private apartments. Over the next decade the violins rendered the other court ensembles obsolete: fashions changed to favour string music, led in no uncertain manner by the king who, according to Roger North, 'had an utter detestation of Fancys'. The only exceptions to this change were provided by the ceremonial groups of musicians, such as trumpeters, drummers and fifers, who maintained an independent existence. The violins not only played before the king in London, but also accompanied the monarch on various travels around England. For these services, such as the visit to Portsmouth in May 1662 to welcome the new queen to England, they received extra fees which enhanced their basic annual salary of around £40 – £50 some-times by as much as £15, though such a sum included the 'subsistence' payments still received by touring orchestral musicians today.

Thomas Purcell, young Henry's uncle, was rapidly advancing in his musical importance at court. On 8 August 1662 he was appointed Composer-in-ordinary to the violins: on 10 November, along with his brother Henry, he was appointed to the Private Music as a singer/lutenist, succeeding Angelo Notari and Henry Lawes. Henry had been assisting the extremely aged Italian musician since 1660 due to Notari's 'unabilities to execute that employment without an Assistant'.[32] The Exchequer list of 6 January 1663 records that Purcell's salary was payable 'to the longer liver' of Purcell and Notari but makes no official note of the fact that Notari was 96 years old![33]

By now the musical establishment seems to have become more set-tled, and the Chamberlain's accounts give a clear record of the month-by-month series of appointments: many of the initial musical appointments at court had been of older musicians who had attended Charles I, and these were rapidly dying off. One of the most pleasing events for the Chapel Royal singers during 1662 was the result of a pay enquiry: 'It appearing by the Report of ye Lord Steward of his Majesty's Household (to whom it was referred) that their present Salaries not amounting to £40 p. ann. and is too little and that he con-ceives the said sume of £70 will be a competent allowance for them.'[34] Rather more depressing would have been the knowledge that royal payments were already in serious arrears. Parliament had voted the king an annual grant of £1,200,000 in 1661 but the taxes it was trying to raise never allowed it to pay more than three-quarters of that amount. The money coming into the royal coffers was simply not ser-vicing all the bills, of which wages made up a large part. Pay cuts were ordered throughout the royal household, but the choir, perhaps after protests, were eventually exempted in 1663 by a warrant: '22 December. Warrant to continue the allowances granted to the mem-bers of the Chapel Royal, notwithstanding the retrenchments ordered by warrant.'[35] As well as trying to balance the books, the Chamberlain had also to deal with some problems of discipline amongst the ranks of his musicians: orchestral psychologists will note that in several cases a percussionist was involved. Among the records, we find:

A Warrant to apprehend John Wright, he being intreated by his Majesties Kettle Drumme[r] to carry his Banner, refuseth now to

Queen Catherine of Braganza. A devout Catholic, she is depicted here by Jacob Huysmans in the character of her namesake St Catherine of Alexandria. She was only twenty-three when she married Charles and with difficulty adapted to the free manners and lax morals of his court.

deliver the same.[36] [14 January 1662]

A Warrant to apprehend John Mawgridge, Drumme Major, for abusing the sergeant Trumpeter and giving abusive language in his Majesty's pallace [22 March 1662].[37]

Warrant to apprehend Humphrey Dance and Robert Ostler, sergeant-at-mace, for seizing and assaulting Gervase Price, sergeant-trumpeter [7 June 1662].[38]

John Mawgridge was clearly a persistent offender, for his name reappears regularly over the next decade in the lists of official complaints for failing to pay his musicians and for using 'ill language'.[39]

Charles's bride-to-be, Catherine of Braganza, arrived at Portsmouth on 13 May. Their wedding took place there eight days later, secretly using the Roman Catholic rites, and then publicly in an Anglican ceremony conducted by the Bishop of London. Charles had not seen his bride before. To Clarendon he wrote: 'her face is not so exact as to be called a beauty, though her eyes are excellent good, and not anything in her face that can in the least shock one'.[40] The queen was twenty-three, frail, convent-educated and spoke very little English. Her upbringing might not have prepared her for the lively behaviour of Charles and his courtiers, but she had, it would appear, been warned about Charles's mistress, Barbara Palmer, who had recently produced her second child by Charles. Once the royal couple were back at Hampton Court, the queen made it clear that Barbara would not be allowed in the royal presence. Barbara had other ideas and forced Charles to appoint her one of the new queen's Ladies of the Bedchamber, while having Catherine's Portuguese lady courtiers dismissed. Catherine was furious and threatened to return to Portugal, the king protested that he had not touched Barbara since the marriage in Portsmouth, and the court watched on in consternation. Clarendon exercised his best diplomatic skills to solve the stalemate and, already becoming increasingly lonely and isolated, the queen was forced to concede Barbara's presence at court. Charles's earlier liaison with Lucy Walter had produced James Crofts; on 10 November 1662 Charles, with no inkling of the problems his son would cause him in later life, created him Duke of Monmouth.

Barbara gathered together around her a clique including Henry Bennet, later made Earl of Arlington, Anthony Ashley Cooper (the Chancellor of the Exchequer, later elevated to Baron Ashley), the Earl of Lauderdale and her own cousin Buckingham.

The year 1663 started badly in parliament for the king: when the Declaration of Indulgence (which would have relaxed the rules of religious uniformity) had been announced on 26 December 1662, parliament had been aghast. If passed, Catholics and Dissenters would have been able to take advantage of the suspension of the penal laws by royal prerogative. In February 1663 Charles was forced to withdraw his plans. Gilbert Sheldon, the most able of all contemporary statesmen, headed the opposition; he was an energetic administrator who had led the reconstruction of the Church of England (which had been virtually ruined during the Interregnum). On 31 August 1663 he was promoted from Bishop of London to Archbishop of Canterbury: his longest-remaining legacy was a liturgy and prayerbook which remained in use in the Church of England until the mid-twentieth century.

The start of the year must have seemed just as bad for the king's irascible Drum-Major: we can only guess at what he had done to cause 'A warrant to apprehend John Mawgridge, drume Major, and Tertullian Lewis, Drummer, and to bring them before mee [Lord Chamberlain] to answer to such Crimes as shalbe objected against them &c'.[41] Four days later John, together with his brother Richard, was again before the Chamberlain, but this time appointed 'keepers of his Majesty's stables at Greenwich… 8d a day'.[42] Trouble seems never to have been far away, and on 28 November we see two separate petitions served against Mawgridge by members of the drummers: one by Devereux Cloathier, and the other by four members of the corps.[43]

In the world of London theatre all eyes were on Drury Lane: the king had in 1662 granted Royal Letters Patent giving a monopoly of the London theatres, closed by Cromwell, to William Davenant and Thomas Killigrew. On 7 May London's first theatrical season for two decades opened with *The Humorous Lieutenant*. Pepys went to the second night and thought it 'a play that hath little good in it'.

There was major building work at the Chapel Royal. On 20 August a warrant was made to the Surveyor General 'to make and erect a large organ loft by his Majestys Chappell at Whitehall, in the place where formerly the great Double organ stood, and to rebuild the roomes over the bellowes room, two stories high, as it was formerly, the lower story for the subdeane of his majestys Chappell, and the upper story with two rooms, one of them for the organist in waiting and the other for the keeper and repairer of his Majestys organs, harpsichords, virginalls and other Instruments, each room to have a Chymney, and Boxes and shelves for keeping the material as belonging to the organ, and the organ books.'[44] John Hingeston, the 'keeper and repairer', was now to have his own premises, which was just as well. A warrant of 6 November finds him being remunerated for a whole host of jobs carried out in the six months from 25 March 1663, including: 'taking down the organ in her Majesty's Chapel at St. James's, and remounting the same in the new music room; for mending the organs and harpsichords; also for mending her Majesty's harpsichord that stands in her own chamber; for mending a claricon; for erecting an organ in the Banquetting House at Whitehall against Maundy Thursday, and for diverse other things'.[45]

Of interest too from the Chamberlain's records is the first of many slightly sad entries that are made documenting the voice breaking of one of the Chapel Royal choristers: 'Warrant to deliver to Henry Cooke, master of the children of his Majesty's Chapel, clothing [a list follows] for Thomas Price, one of the children, whose voice is changed and who is to go from the Chapel.'[46]

Cooke had to perform that task many times, but it is clear that the establishment took surprisingly good care of its choristers when their voices broke: Cooke was usually given an allowance of £30 to 'keep' the boy concerned: for Thomas Price[47] we find Cooke claiming £2 15s 6d as the cost of '4 paire of shows, 4 paire of stockins, 4 paire of gloves, half a peece of riban for his first sute'[48] which made up his outfit. Later in Charles's reign we find a record of the complete set of clothes that was provided for a departing Chapel Royal child: 'Two suites of playne cloth, two Hatts and Hatt-bands, foure whole shirts, foure half-shirts, six bands, six paires of Cuffes, six handkerchiefes, four paire of stocking foure paire of shooes & foure paire of Gloves'.[49] The records show that many boys took advantage of their musical training and eventually found employment in the royal service, at the Chapel Royal as adult singers, or as instrumentalists.

Cooke was responsible, as Master of the Children, not only for the boys' choral training, but for all aspects of their education. We find frequent payments to him for arranging or giving music lessons ('£30 for the children of the Chapel learning the violin, £30 for the children of the Chapel learning the organ'[50]), for their general tuition ('£45 expended by him to masters for teaching the said children to write, learn and speak latin'[51]), for their books and paper[52] and also for their day-to-day domestic arrangements. Cooke arranged the boys' clothing ('materials for liveries for the 12 children'[53]) and ensured that it was washed and repaired, that the boys were housed, cared for when they were sick ('for nursing three boys that were sick of the small pox'),[54] were fed, and that their premises were heated properly ('£20 for fire in the music room').[55] In winter the outfit for each boy was 'one cloak of bastard scarlett cloth lined with velvett, one suit and coat of the same cloth made up and trimmed with silver and silk lace after the manner of our footmen's liveries, and also to the said suit three shirts, three half shirts, three pair of shoes, three pair of thigh stocking, whereof one pair of silk and two of worsted, two hats with bands, six bands and six pairs of cuffs whereof two laced and four plain, three handkerchers, three pairs of gloves and two pieces and a half of rebon for trimming garters and shoe strings' and at Easter the cloak was swapped for one lined with satin, and the 'suit and coat' changed for 'one doublett of sattin with bastard scarlett trunk hose made and trimmed up as aforesaid'.[56]

*This anonymous portrait of Purcell shows him at an earlier age than others
extant. More than any other portrait of Purcell it conveys
the impression of an inspired composer.*

Claude de Jongh: London Bridge about 1650. For centuries this was the only bridge across the Thames at London and over the years had become crowded with houses and shops. We are looking east, with the Tower of London on the left and Southwark on the right.

London from Southwark, a painting of about 1650. It was probably copied from an earlier original, which accounts for some of the anachronistic features. A curious error is the way the Thames seems to bend abruptly to the north after the Tower of London.

St Paul's in flames is at the centre of this vivid scene, clearly painted by an eye-witness to the Great Fire. In the foreground people are trying to salvage their possessions with carts and boats. The viewpoint is opposite the Tower, glaring red in the flames, with London Bridge on the left.

Abraham Hondius: Frost Fair on the Ice at Temple Stairs, 1683/84. *A row of booths stretches across the frozen river; two ships are imprisoned in the ice and there are horses, coaches and sleds.*

The church on the right is that of the Temple. The Thames was wider and shallower then than now, and Old London Bridge created a barrier that made it not so unusual for it to freeze.

Obtaining reimbursements of the money that Cooke frequently laid out himself from the royal purse was no easy task: clothing twelve boys was an expensive business, and as the court finances became more strained the financial bureaucrats would pass documents back and forth between their various departments – a very effective delaying tactic. On at least one occasion Cooke engaged an attorney in his attempt to receive arrears due to him from the Exchequer.[57]

By 1664 the Dutch Republic's growing strength was beginning to challenge England's position in many of the most important centres: the East Indies, the West Indies, the east coast of North America, the African coasts and the Mediterranean. On 9 February Pepys reported a conversation, where he heard 'great talk of the Duch proclaiming themselfs in India lords of the Southern Seas and deny traffique there to all ships but their own, upon pain of confiscation – which makes our merchants mad'.[58] The country looked towards the king for a lead, and in April 1664 parliament presented Charles with a petition which demanded action and promised its support. Certainly the navy was a strong one, with a fleet numbering around 130 vessels, 21,000 men and some 4,200 guns, but war would be an expensive business, and full-scale hostilities against the Dutch would push England's finances to the point of bankruptcy. Charles wisely did not yet commit himself.

At the Chapel Royal and the court financial shortages were reflected in the rising numbers of petitions from members owed salaries. On 30 April the composer in ordinary, Matthew Locke, requested settlement of arrears of salary going back one and a half years,[59] and during September a special warrant was issued to various of the financial officers authorizing 'payment to the Gentlemen and Master of the Children, for their diet, lodging, washing and teaching'.[60] But their musical standards remained high, especially in comparison with other London choirs. On 28 February Pepys went to a service at St Paul's and 'was most impatiently troubled at the Quire, the worst that ever I heard'.[61] He was rather more impressed in August to have Henry Cooke send a letter to him recommending as a potential clerk Cooke's former chorister Thomas Edwards, whom he met, and took good references from Cooke and Mr Blagrave.[62] On 27 August Tom Edwards arrived after having been 'bred in the King's chapel for these four years'. Pepys found the youngster 'a very schooleboy that talks inocently and impertinently'[63] and immediately took to him. His musical training from Cooke had clearly been thorough, for on

OPPOSITE: *Charles II, by John Michael Wright. Charles was a generous patron and lover of music. Purcell became one of his court composers in 1677. Apart from works for the Chapel Royal, Purcell had to write odes and welcome songs when the king returned to his capital from such places as Newmarket and Windsor.*

4 September Pepys wrote that 'it is a great joy to me that I am come to this condition, to maintain a person in the house able to give me such pleasure as this boy doth by his thorough understand of music, as he sings anything at first sight'.[64] Tom Edwards was not the only chorister to leave the Chapel that year: on 26 May Michael Wise's voice had broken,[65] though if Wise's later exploits are anything to go by, Cooke might have been relieved to see this chorister depart. Wise later became a lay clerk at Windsor and Eton, then organist of Salisbury Cathedral (where there was almost immediately trouble between him and one of the lay vicars) and returned in 1676 as a Gentleman of the Chapel Royal: he was constantly in trouble with the authorities, accused of negligence, neglect of duty, profanity, drunkenness 'and other excesses in his life and conversation', but despite this poor record was finally appointed organist at St Paul's Cathedral in London on the direct recommendation of James II. He was unable to take up that appointment as on 24 August 1687 he 'was knocked on the head and killed outright by the night watch at Salisbury for giving stubborn and refractory language to them'.[66]

On 11 August tragedy struck in the Purcell household. Henry senior (now the father of five sons, Edward, Charles, Henry, Joseph and Daniel, and one daughter, Katherine) died – quite suddenly, we presume, as he is mentioned in records right up to his death – and was buried two days later in the east cloister of Westminster Abbey. We do not know the cause of death, although Nathaniel Hodges[67] mentions that there had been isolated outbreaks of the plague in London since the summer.

Quite what effect the death of his father would have had on young Henry, probably just five years old at the time, has to be surmised. At an age when the boy's immediate family was his entire world, the loss of his father would have left him, at least temporarily, profoundly affected and traumatized. It is possible that he could have carried some unresolved grief and sadness for the rest of his life. The wistfulness that is so prevalent in Purcell's music could therefore be seen as the manifestation of a little boy still crying for his lost father.

Henry senior's widow Elizabeth was granted 'Letters of Administration' on 7 October[68] and fairly rapidly she moved herself and her six children to Tothill Street South, for her annual payment of 4s for the poor-rates is entered in the overseer's accounts of St Margaret's Westminster from 1665.[69] Elizabeth would have struggled on the meagre widow's pension: she certainly had to take in lodgers such as Frances Crump.[70] Just as with any other musician who died, Henry Purcell's position as 'Musician in ordinary for the voice and lute' was taken by another musician, John Goodgroome.[71] To make matters worse, the winter was a hard one, and in November parts of the river Thames froze, some not thawing until March 1665.

During that winter the Dutch threat continued to be the talk of London and it was no surprise when war was officially declared in March; it was widely assumed that the British forces, under the command of the Lord High Admiral, the Duke of York, would easily defeat the enemy. Pepys recorded on 1 April that the navy had cost above half a million pounds in the previous six months, and would cost double that over the next seven: the Lord Treasurer was in a state of desperation, and was not being helped by the 'ignorant asse' and Treasurer of the Navy, Sir George Carteret. The two fleets jockeyed for position, and on 2 June they engaged off the coast at Lowestoft. The next day 'by all people upon the River and almost everywhere else hereabout, were heard the Guns' and on 8 June he wrote that 'we have totally routed the Dutch'.

But, as Clarendon recorded in his memoirs: 'There begun now to appear another enemy, much more formidable than the Dutch, and more difficult to be struggled with; which was the plague, that brake out in the winter, and made such an early progress in the spring, that though the weekly numbers did not rise high, and it appeared to be only in the outskirts of the town, and in the most obscure alleys, amongst the poorest people; yet the ancient men, who well remembered in what manner the last great plague (which had been near forty years before) first break out, and the progress it afterwards made, foretold a terrible summer.'[72]

On 30 April Pepys noted 'Great fears of the Sicknesse here in the City, it being said that two or three houses are already shut up' and on 24 May 'the plague growing upon us in this town'; June 7 was the hottest day Pepys had ever known, and 'much against my Will, I did in Drury Lane see two or three houses marked with a red cross upon the doors, and 'Lord have mercy upon us' writ there – which was a sad sight to me, being the first of that kind that to my remembrance I ever saw'. On 10 June he noted the first cases within the City itself, in Fenchurch Street.

Those who were able to get out of London did so, and many of the first to leave were physicians and higher clergy. It is calculated that by the end of July 10,000 houses were deserted: maybe as many as 200,000 people had left the capital.[73] The court too was quick to move out of town, and took with it many of its musicians: on 29 June the royal party travelled to Syon House in Isleworth, and then on to Hampton Court on 9 July (where they were joined by many of the musicians), moving to Salisbury on 1 August. When parliament began its fifth session, it held it in Oxford: the entire court moved there on 23 September, remaining there until 27 January 1666. Pepys's Navy Office moved out to Greenwich, and he and his wife relocated to Woolwich (although he regularly commuted back to the City to do business).

In the height of one of the hottest summers in memory, the infection spread wildly through London, carried by fleas which were themselves carried by rats. In May some 43 deaths had been reported from bubonic plague. In June there were over 600 fatalities, and by July the figures were in their thousands. By September, a thousand people were dying each day. The remaining population was panic-stricken.

Houses which were infected had their doors daubed with a red cross, and the bodies of the dead were carried away, mostly during the hours of darkness, on carts to mass graves which could hardly contain the numbers of dead. Those who were confined to their infected houses could then get no provisions: 'No drop of water, perhaps, but what comes at the leisure of a drunken or careless halberd bearer at the door; no seasonable provision is theirs as a certainty for their support. Not a friend to come nigh them in their many, many heart and house cares and complexities. They are compelled, though well, to lie by, to watch upon the death-bed of their dear relation, to see the corpse dragged away before their eyes.'[74]

Cures of all sorts abounded: that provided by the College of Physicians was imaginative:

> Take a greate onion, hollow it, put into it a fig, rue cut small, and a dram of Venice treacle; put it close stopt in wet paper, and roast it in the embers; apply it hot unto the tumour; lay three or four, one after another; let one lie three hours.[75]

Another contemporary remedy was equally bizarre:

> If there doe a botch appeare: Take a Pigeon and plucke the feathers off her taile, very bare, and set her taile to the sore, and shee will draw out the venom till she die; then take another and set too likewise, continuing so till all the venome be drawne out, which you shall see by the Pigeons, for they will die with the venome as long as there is any in [the tumour]: also a chicken or henne is very good.[76]

King Charles, albeit rather too late, attempted to bring order to the chaos. Examiners were appointed to every parish in London whose job was to report any infected person to the constable who then authorized that person's house be shut and guarded. To prevent the plague spreading outside the city, the authorities insisted that a pass must be obtained from the Lord Mayor's office. When it was rumoured that the authorities intended to put turnpikes and barriers on the roads leading out of London within hours 'there was hardly a horse to be bought or hired in the whole city'.[77] Early in September Pepys witnessed the great bonfires which were set alight in the streets, on the Lord Mayor's instruction, in a futile attempt to purify the air of infection. Other instructions were, with hindsight, more sensible, and were the first steps towards public health regulations; they also give an indication of the appalling conditions that must have existed before revolutionary ideas such as cleaning the streets were proposed. Each householder was commanded 'to cause the street to be daily prepared [kept clean] before his door, and so to keep it clean swept all the week long'. The 'sweeping of filth of houses' was to be 'daily carried away by the rakers'.

In October, as the temperature dropped, so did the death count. The plague had ravaged centres besides London, including Norwich, Southampton, Salisbury, Portsmouth, Sunderland and Newcastle, but it was the capital which had suffered most. By the end of the infection some 70,000 people had died. On 16 October Pepys walked to the Tower and was horrified by the desolation of the City: 'But Lord, how empty the streets are, and melancholy, so many poor sick people in the streets… in Westminster there is never a physitian, and but one apothecary left, all being dead'. Evelyn found 'the shops universally shut up; a dreadful prospect.'[78]

But throughout this troubled year, life had continued for the working musicians, albeit often on the move. The drum-major, John Mawgridge, maintained his poor disciplinary record and on 16 February 1665 orders were issued to the Knight Marshal, Sir William Throckmorton, to take Mawgridge into custody because he 'hath behaved himself rudely and abusively within the palace of Whitehall':[79] he was released from jail eleven days later. On 17 May the customary allowances were granted to three boys whose voices had broken and were leaving the Chapel Royal, Pelham Humfrey, John Blow and John Blundivile. The calibre of Cooke's training was by now evident, for Humfrey was immediately granted a special allowance in connection with his work 'for his Majesty's extraordinary service'; we know that he went to France and studied the court music there.[80]

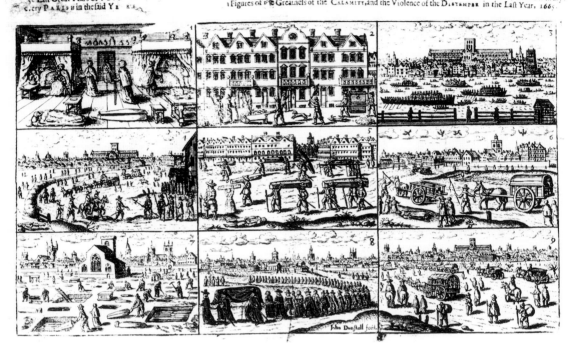

A[...] for th[...] City of LONDON, And Parishes Adjacent:
[...]e Laft Great Years of Past [...] 1655. bein[...] [...]rue Account [...] how many Perfons died Weekly in every of thofe Years, alfo how many [...]
[...]ery Parifh in the faid Y[...] R[...] [...] Figures of the Greateafs of the Calamity, and the Violence of the Distemper in the Laft Year, 166[...]

John Dunftall fecit.

Blow was to return to the court and the chapel a few years later and become one of the most important musical figures of the century.

It was not until 1 February 1666 that it was deemed safe for Charles and his whole entourage to return, via Hampton Court (where improvements to Cooke's lodgings and schoolroom, ordered on 16 July 1665,[81] had presumably by now been carried out), to Whitehall. The temporary removal of the establishment out of London had been very expensive, and the warrant book finds Henry Cooke owed nearly £700 as the 'said Chapel have been at great charges for themselves in their extraordinary attendance upon his Majesty in his progress for 141 days',[82] John Banister owed £464 for his eight musicians being on the road for 232 days and Jervaise Price £410 for the trumpeters.[83] Nevertheless, the Chapel Royal was now to be furnished with a brand new organ, and on 11 April John Hingeston was authorized to spend the considerable sum of £900. Robert Dallam was commissioned to make the instrument for £650, Peter Hartover was budgeted £130 for 'painting, guilding and beautifying the Said Organ', and Thomas Kinward's casework and joinery was to cost £120.[84] On 20 May 1666 young Pelham Humfrey, departed from the Chapel Royal as a chorister for only just over a year and

The young Purcell had to live through two horrific events before he was seven years old. The first was the plague, which raged through the summer of 1665 and killed 70,000 people in London. These illustrations are from a broadsheet published at the height of the epidemic giving details of deaths and burials in the parishes of the City. They show the dying in a hospital, funeral processions through the streets and burials in the communal graves hastily dug on the outskirts.

47

probably still absent from Britain on his French travels (these funded, according to the nineteenth-century musicologist, Edward Rimbault quoting a document now lost, from Secret Service payments),[85] received official confirmation of his first appointment, as a 'Musician in Ordinary to his Majesty for the Lute'.[86] Keeping up the family tradition of causing trouble at court, it was now the turn of Richard Mawgridge who was the subject of a petition on 24 June.[87] On the same day Henry Cooke was provided with a warrant to defray the expenses of another journey searching for choristers, on this occasion travelling to the cathedrals of Gloucester, Worcester and Hereford.

As if plague and war had not brought enough problems to the capital, on Sunday 2 September another catastrophe arrived. Early in the morning a baker's oven in Pudding Lane set fire to his house and burned it down: such an event was nothing new. But suddenly the wind changed direction and spread the fire into neighbouring Thames Street. Here in the merchants' warehouses were stored tallow, oil, spirits, hemp, timber and coal. The area was swiftly ablaze and the nearby church of St Magnus the Martyr was gutted. London's firefighting equipment was primitive in the extreme – effectively just buckets of water – and those attempting to fight a fire that had grown out of control were helpless. Pepys was wakened at three in the morning by his maid, looked out of the window and went back to bed. By seven in the morning the news was that three hundred buildings had been destroyed. Pepys went to the area and saw the devastation: worse still, he could see 'nobody to my sight endeavouring to quench it, but to remove their goods and leave all to the fire…the wind mighty high and driving it into the city, and everything, after so long a drought, proving combustible'. He went to the palace at Whitehall with the news, and was summoned before the king, stating 'that unless his Majesty did command houses to be pulled down, nothing could stop the fire… the King commanded me to go to my Lord Mayor from him and command him to spare no houses but to pull down before the fire every way'. On his way back, Pepys met the exhausted Mayor, who complained that 'People will not obey me. I have been pull[ing] down houses. But the fire overtakes us faster than we can do it'. By nightfall, the fire was completely out of control. 'As it grew darker, appeared more and more, and in Corners and upon steeples and between churches and houses, as far as we could see up the hill of the City, in a most horrid malicious bloody flame we saw the fire as only one entire arch of fire from this to the other side of the bridge, and in a bow up the hill, for an arch of above a mile long. It made me weep to see it.'

By Monday the king realized that he had a major catastrophe on his hands and launched into action, summoning the Privy Council and calling in the militia from four neighbouring counties. He appointed his brother James to take charge, but seems to have directed operations personally. With the royal presence on hand the 'tenacious and avaricious' merchants that Evelyn records could no longer prevent their properties being felled but much of the damage was already done. With fears that the gunpowder contained inside the Tower of London might go up, properties all around it were demolished. Evelyn reckoned that the pall of smoke from the City now stretched fifty miles. Once again Londoners were fleeing for their lives, and the cart and boat owners were making huge profits: 'The riches of London and the substance of the inhabitants thereof were as well devoured by suburban thieves and by the countrymen's exhortation for their carts and conveyances as by the Fire'.[88] The king rode up and down on his horse, frequently dismounting to lend a hand: with James he 'stood up to the ankles in water, and playing the engines for many hours... which, people seeing, fell to work with effort, having so good fellow labourers'.[89]

By dawn on the Tuesday Cheapside was on fire and St Paul's Cathedral, the spiritual centre of the City, was threatened. Finally in the evening St Paul's itself succumbed to the flames. Evelyn wrote that 'the stones of St Paul's flew like grenades, the mealting lead running downe the streets in a streame, and the very pavements glowing with fiery rednesse, so as no horse nor man was able to tread on them, and the demolition had stopp'd all the passages, so that no help could be applied. The Eastern wind still more impetuously driving the flames forward. Nothing but the Almighty power of God was able to stop them, for vaine was the help of man.'[90]

On the fifth day the fire burned itself out. Charles ordered a survey and learned that 13,200 houses in 4,000 streets had been destroyed, along with 87 parish churches. In an area about a mile and a half wide some 373 acres had been devastated. Within the City only 75 acres lay relatively undamaged. A member of Lincoln's Inn wrote that 'you may see from one end of the City almost to the other. You can compare London (were it not for the rubbish) to nothing more than an open field.'[91]

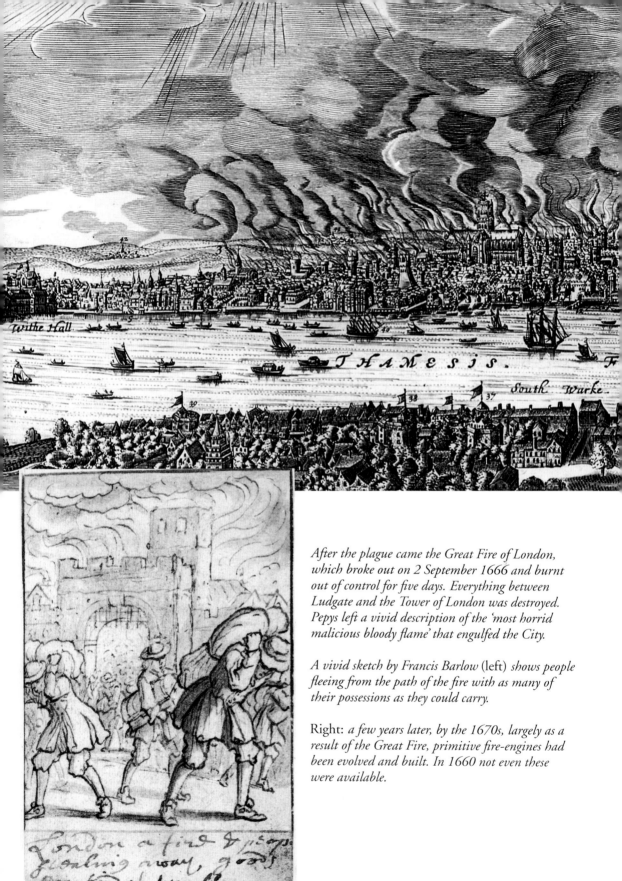

Witte Hall

THAMESIS.

South Warke

London a fire & people dealing away goods you kind of tumult

After the plague came the Great Fire of London, which broke out on 2 September 1666 and burnt out of control for five days. Everything between Ludgate and the Tower of London was destroyed. Pepys left a vivid description of the 'most horrid malicious bloody flame' that engulfed the City.

A vivid sketch by Francis Barlow (left) shows people fleeing from the path of the fire with as many of their possessions as they could carry.

Right: a few years later, by the 1670s, largely as a result of the Great Fire, primitive fire-engines had been evolved and built. In 1660 not even these were available.

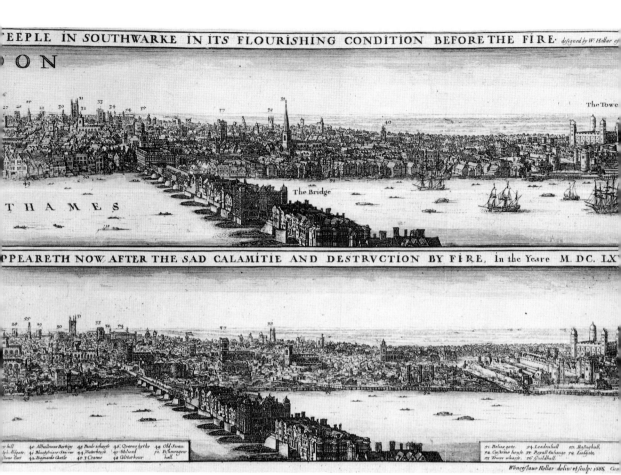

ON

The Towe

THAMES

The Bridge

PPEARETH NOW AFTER THE SAD CALAMITIE AND DESTRVCTION BY FIRE, In the Yeare M.DC.LX

hall   40 *Allhallowes Berking*   43 *Puils wharfe*   46 *Qveene hythe*   49 *Old Swan.*
ph Aldgate.   41 *Blackfriars Staires*   44 *Waterhouse*   47 *Stilard.*   50 *Bishansgate*
hane East   42 *Baynards Castle*   45 *3 Cranes*   48 *Glitarbour*   *hall*

51 *Belins gate.*   54 *Leadenhall*   57 *Bassinghall.*
54 *Custome house.* 55 *Royall Exchange* 76 *Ludgate.*
55 *Tower wharfe.* 56 *Guildhall.*

Wenceslaus Hollar delin: et sculp: 1688. Com

Wenceslaus Hollar's two
engravings of London before
and after the Fire (above)
give an idea of the
devastation, confirmed by
the map, where the burnt
area is left white. It
includes almost everything
within the City wall and
some parts beyond it to the
west. The great Gothic
cathedral of St Paul's was
among the casualties.

A MAP or GROVNDTLOT
of the City of London and
the Suburbs thereof that is
to say, all which is within the
Jurisdiction of the Lord Ma
yor or properly call'd London

A GENERALL MAP
of the whole Citty of London
with Westminster & all the
Suburbe In which may bee
computed the proportion of
that which is burnt with
the other parts standing.

THE   RIVER   THA   MES

Part of Southwarke

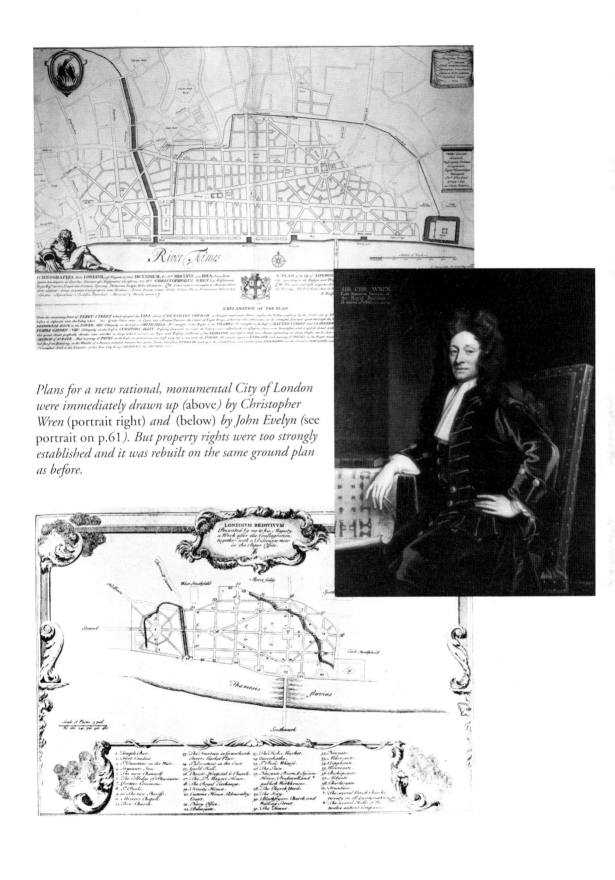

Plans for a new rational, monumental City of London were immediately drawn up (above) by Christopher Wren (portrait right) and (below) by John Evelyn (see portrait on p.61). But property rights were too strongly established and it was rebuilt on the same ground plan as before.

For Charles, the most important task now was reconstruction. Within six days of the fire being out, Christopher Wren, the Deputy Surveyor of His Majesty's Works, had submitted a spectacular town plan. John Evelyn too submitted his own ideas and was greatly peeved that Wren narrowly beat him in the race. Wren's plan showed an orderly pattern of streets and an approach road to Ludgate that would be ninety feet wide, leading to a triumphal arch commemorating the king. Directly east of the arch would be a grand piazza and the new St Paul's Cathedral. The Fleet ditch, formerly a sewer, was to be transformed into a canal, and the banks of the Thames were to be raised three feet to prevent flooding; a walkway, forty feet wide, was to be built alongside the river. Around the Royal Exchange were to be the other main state buildings. The complete replacement cost was estimated at £7,370,000 and the general population and Charles were in favour of the grand design. But the plans were never approved by parliament, and the City, anxious that construction on such a large scale would result in considerable delays and hence loss of revenue, blocked the ideas as much as they could, informing the authorities that they had 'no common stock, nor revenue, nor any capacity to raise within itself anything considerable towards so vast an expense'.[92] The Government's accounts were by now in even deeper trouble and, to make matters worse, the Customs House had been destroyed in the fire, making the collection of taxes even more difficult. Over the following months Charles attempted to stop the piecemeal redevelopment of the City and a proclamation was issued containing general building regulations. Charles also forced through parliament an Act 'for the better paving and cleansing of streets and sewers' which appointed a Commissioner for Sewers to take responsibility for the maintenance and planning of drainage. Nathaniel Hobart, Master in Chancery, wryly remarked that 'the rebuilding of the City will not be so difficult as the satisfying of all interests'[93] and his cynical outlook proved to be entirely correct. Nothing of Wren's street plan was ever utilized, but his magnificent churches and St Paul's Cathedral stand as tantalizing monuments to London as it might have been.

For the musicians of the Chapel Royal and of the Court, finances were getting worse. One of the wind players, John Gamble, 'pleaded for payment of £221 10s 4½d, arrears of his salary over four and three-quarter years. All he possessed he had lost by the dreadful Fire, and he had contracted a debt of £120, for which one of his sureties had been sent prisoner to Newgate. Twenty-two musicians on the violin made similar plaint, having had houses and goods burnt in the Fire.'[94] Cooke was owed amounts totalling £599 7s for a variety of expenses and services stretching back as far as 1662 and still unpaid by the Treasurer.[95] John Hingeston was owed £77 5s for his instrument repair services going back an equally long period of time.[96]

In June 1667, a huge Dutch fleet, led by fifty-one men-of-war, sailed up the Thames, overrunning Sheerness and Canvey Island and hoisting their own flag. Britain was totally unprepared, and the Duke of Albemarle (George Monck) found 'scarce twelve of eight hundred men which were then in the King's pay, in His Majesty's yards, and these so distracted with fear, that I could have little or no service from them'.[97] The Dutch fleet continued up the Thames, snapping a secret chain that had been laid to prevent such an attack, destroyed the embankments of the Thames at Sheppey to flood the land, captured one frigate and sank another, and then seized the flag-ship 'Royal Charles' 'with a boat of nine men who found not a man on board'. Albemarle ordered that other English boats in the vicinity be scuppered to prevent the Dutch capturing them, and the raiders completed their devastation by setting fire to the rest of the fleet as it

One of Charles II's most humiliating defeats came in June 1667 when the Dutch sailed up the Thames, sacked and burnt naval installations along the shore and captured the pride of the king's navy, the 'Royal Charles'.

lay at anchor. Edward Gregory, the Clerk of the Check at Chatham, remembered it as 'the most dismal spectacle my eyes ever beheld. And it certainly made the heart of every true Englishman bleed.'[98] Now Charles, who had not wanted war in any case, had to negotiate for peace, and on 21 July the Treaty of Breda ended the war. Charles felt that he had been badly advised and realized that if he was to preserve his position as monarch, he would in future have to be firmer and more devious in government. He replaced the single advisory figure of Clarendon with a Cabinet centred around five ministers, known by their initials as the Cabal: Sir Thomas Clifford, the Earl of Arlington, the second Duke of Buckingham, Lord Ashley and the Duke of Lauderdale. Over the next years Charles played each of them against the others in a complex web of duplicity, political intrigue and tangled diplomacy. Government was now to be along lines that most suited the monarch.

At court there was scandal brewing too amongst the musicians. On 29 March 1667 a group of violinists petitioned the King, complaining that John Banister had failed to distribute money owing to his players: he 'hath kept sometimes five or six of us out of wayting, according as hee is pleased or displeased, and three of us he hath turned out of his Band, his Majesty's pleasure not being knowne therein, nor the Lord Chamberlaine's, by this meanes, hee thinks to put all our arreares in his owne purse, whereby the Kings service is abused, and his poor servants utterly ruyned.'[99] It also emerged that this was not the first time that Banister had pocketed his colleagues' fees; perhaps they had been too scared to protest before but, now Banister had apparently been sacked in favour of the foreigner Louis Grabu[100] (and was, according to Pepys, 'mad that the King hath a Frenchman come to be chief of some part of the King's musique'),[101] his previous sins were coming out into the open. In August the Lord Chamberlain ruled that the sums owed must be paid.[102]

It almost goes without saying that one of the Mawgridges was yet again in trouble with the authorities: this time there were three separate petitions lodged with the Lord Chamberlain against Richard Mawgridge by Alice Hebburne, Thomas Cooke and his wife, and Elizabeth Rose.[103] We are not certain what the trouble was, but Mr Justice Newman was asked by the Chamberlain to sort out the problem 'in a friendly and amicable manner or else report the same unto mee'. Proving equally troublesome, but far more talented, was Pelham Humfrey, freshly returned from his stay in France and now busily informing everyone at court of their limitations. Pepys, on his way back from parliament (where the Houses were debating whether they could sequester the Earl of Clarendon on grounds of treason), called in at his tailor, and found 'little Pellam Humfrys, lately returned from France and is an absolute Monsieur, as full of form and confidence and vanity, and disparages everything and everybody's skill but his own. The truth is, everybody says he is very able; but to hear how he laughs at all the King's music here, as Blagrave and others, that they cannot keep time nor tune nor understand anything, and that Grebus the Frenchman, the King's Master of the Musique, how he understands nothing nor can play on any instrument and so cannot compose, and that he will give him a lift out of his place, and that he and the King are mighty great, and that he hath already spoke to the King of Grebus, would make a man piss.'[104] Bumptious or not, this former chorister was a prodigiously talented musician: he had already been appointed 'Musician in Ordinary for the Lute' in 1666 during his absence abroad,[105] and on 26 October 1667 started singing tenor at the Chapel Royal. He had also begun to compose, and on 1 November Pepys had noted 'a fine anthem...of which there is great expectation, and indeed it is a very good piece of musique'. Although after this point we know little more about Humfrey for the next five years, he composed church music and songs for entertainments at court and plays in the City, and that he taught choristers at the Chapel Royal the violin, lute and theorbo; he may have taught composition to some of them as well.[106]

The cornerstone of Charles's international politics over the next three years involved an agreement with the most powerful of all Britain's neighbours, France. Charles realized that such an alliance would not be welcomed by parliament nor by the nation, who could see in France not only a potential threat to Britain, but also an instrument of the Catholic Church. Charles skilfully manipulated one of his Cabal, Lord Arlington, into negotiating a treaty with the Dutch against the French which promised hostilities if France did not stop the highly successful war she was waging against Spain. The treaty, signed in The Hague in January 1668, also included the Swedes, and was known as the 'Triple Alliance'. When in May Louis XIV accepted a general peace with the Treaty of Aix-la-Chapelle, the Triple Alliance was seen in England as a diplomatic triumph.

CHAPTER II

Learning the Trade, 1668-1679

It was, presumably, around 1668 that the young Henry Purcell became a chorister at the Chapel Royal, probably at the age of eight or nine. We know tantalizingly little of his early life: it seems that, on the death of Henry Purcell senior, his brother Thomas (who had been one of the Gentlemen of the Chapel Royal since 1661 and a member of the Private Music since the next year) had apparently stepped in part at least into the role of father (in 1679 he refers to the then nineteen-year-old Henry as 'my Sonne').[1] Living so close to the court, and with his uncle singing and playing daily, Henry must have been surrounded by music: it would have been an obvious step to propose him as a chorister. Elizabeth Purcell was a single mother on a limited income (the Precentor's Books at Westminster Abbey show that she intermittently received sums, such as £20 on 20 May 1668 and the same amount again on 8 July)[2] so the opportunity for one of her boys to be given a decent education, clothed and fed must have been most welcome. Henry's older brother Edward was already a 'gentleman usher daily waiter assistant'.[3]

We can only guess the time at which Henry might have begun his career as a chorister but, as today, a place as one of the twelve choristers would only fall vacant when one of the senior boys left the choir because his voice had broken. We know that choristers in the seventeenth century, again as today, began their training at around the age of eight or nine. Richard Hart's voice is registered as having broken early in 1688, with the customary 'retirement' payments beginning on 25 March,[4] and Thomas Tudway (who went on to become a distinguished organist at King's College Cambridge) is noted as having left at Michaelmas 1668.[5] Henry Montagu and John Farmer also left

OPPOSITE: *Henry Purcell, a sensitive drawing by John Closterman.*

❧ 59

around the same time as Master Tudway. So perhaps it was at the start of the Michaelmas term 1668, or possibly a few months earlier, at Easter, that the eight (or possibly nine) year-old Henry Purcell took his place as a Child of the Chapel Royal.

The financial situation at court was by now dire. Even when a Treasury Warrant was granted, there was often not any money to hand out. On 24 January 1668 Cooke had refused to let the boys attend the Chapel. When summoned before the authorities he had stated that the boys' clothes were in such a bad state he had been forced to keep them indoors.[6] Now, two years later, the same thing happened again. In June 1670 Cooke submitted a petition to the king which read: 'The Children not receiving their liveries as usual, are reduced to so bad a condition that they are unfit to attend his Majesty, or walk in the streets. Begs an order for their liveries, the charge not being great.'[7] On 30 June came the reply: 'Order on the above petition that the Children of the Chapel be for the future entertained and clothed as they were before the late retrenchments'.[8] On 6 July 'Mr. Newport and Mr. Reymes called in with Captain Cooke about the clothes for the Children of the Chapel. That the King will have them made as formerly. The officers of the Wardrobe say they have no money. My Lords desire Captain Cooke to furnish the money by loan on the funds on which the Wardrobe has orders; which he promised.' On 12 July came the official warrant: 'Chapel boys; warrant for £214. 4s. 0d. to complete £300. They have had £85. 16s. To be employed and laid out for provision of liveries for the said children in full of the estimate dated 16 May last.'[9] Captain Cooke was now having to take out loans on behalf of His Majesty's treasury so that the king's choristers could be properly clothed. Eventually the bills were paid out of the revenue earned from selling wine licences but Cooke was constantly owed large sums of money by a desperately over-stretched royal purse.

At the Chapel Royal we can only piece together the education which young Henry Purcell was receiving. His choir master, Henry Cooke, was a fine singer and an especial champion of the Italian style. Pepys had frequently paid compliments to Cooke's musicianship, noting once a performance when 'Capt. Cooke and his two boys did sing some Italian songs, which I must in a word say I think was fully the best Musique that I ever yet heard in all my life.'[10] We know that the boys learned the violin, the bass viol, the theorbo, virginals and the organ, as well as the theory of music. In later life, Purcell was known principally as a keyboard player; the contemporary writer Anthony à

John Evelyn pursued a variety of interests – the volume he is holding here, Sylva, is 'a discourse of forest trees' – but is chiefly remembered for his Diary. It is less gossipy than Pepys's but covers a longer period and is one of the primary sources for the reigns of Charles II, James II and William and Mary.

Wood states that Purcell was 'Bred under Dr. Chr. Gibbons' while Thomas Ford wrote that Purcell was 'Scholar to Dr. Blow and Dr. Christopher Gibbons'.[11] Gibbons was himself a former chorister who had studied under his distinguished father Orlando; he was, according to Evelyn, a 'famous Musitian' and undoubtedly an excellent player who for a while was organist and subsequently Master of the Choristers at Westminster Abbey. The young Purcell might also have found his keyboard lessons entertaining for Gibbons was, in the splendid words of Wood, 'a grand debauchee' who 'would sleep at Morning Prayer when he was to play on the organ'.[12] John Blow would certainly have been a major influence on Purcell's composition: he was a former chorister at the Chapel, and only ten years older than Henry. The two men certainly became close personal and professional friends in later years. Two supposedly authentic paintings, now lost, were said to have pictured Purcell in later life with a viola, and it would seem perfectly plausible that Henry learned a string instrument at school: competent choristers have for centuries learned both a keyboard instrument and one other, and there was no shortage of string-players around the corner at court who would have welcomed the extra fees for instrumental tuition for which we frequently find Cooke requesting payment from the Treasury.[13] As well as their music, the boys were certainly taught Latin and reading, writing (we know that Robert Moore had an outstanding debt of £22 10s in 1677 'for teaching the Children of the Chapel Royal to write'),[14] and arithmetic.

The Chapel boys were also encouraged to compose and, if we are to believe Tudway (who had himself come through the ranks of choristers and left probably just as Henry was coming to the Chapel), the king was an especial enthusiast of their compositions. 'His Majesty who was a brisk & Airy Prince, coming to the crown…Order'd the Composers of his Chappell to add symphonys &c. with Instruments to their Anthems…In about 4 or 5 years time some of the forwardest & brightest Children of the Chappell, as Mr. Humfreys, Mr. Blow, &c. began to be Masters in a faculty in Composing. This his Majesty greatly encourag'd by indulging their youthfull fancys, so that ev'ry month at least, & afterwards oft'ner, they produc'd something New of this Kind. In a few years severall others, Educated in the Chappell, produc'd their Compositions in this style; for otherwise it was in vain to hope to please his Majesty.'[15]

No composition by Purcell has survived from his choir school days, though Rimbault claimed to have owned a copy of 'An Address of the Children of the Chapel Royal to the King, and to their master, Captain Cooke, on His Majesty's birthday, A.D. 1670, composed by Master Purcell, one of the Children of the said Chapel'. If the manuscript ever existed, it has certainly since disappeared without trace. One other song, published in *Catch that catch can* (1667), has occasionally been attributed to the young Henry Purcell, but it is more likely that this is the work of his father. Budding composers also learned their craft by copying out the works of other composers. Purcell himself stated in his preface to the 1694 edition of Playford's *Introduction to the Skill of Musick* that 'the best way to be acquainted with 'em, is to score much, and chuse the best Authors',[16] and in the earliest of the three large volumes written out by Purcell[17] we find that he copied older works by Thomas Tallis, William Byrd, Orlando Gibbons, William Mundy, Thomas Tomkins, Nathaniel Giles,

Adrian Batten and Matthew Locke, as well as more contemporary compositions by Locke, Blow and Humfrey. But the biggest influence on Henry's compositions would have been regular performances of a range of music in the Chapel Royal, at court, and in the theatre: a chorister with a good ear and a quick mind will pick up musical traits from actually performing music far faster than anyone, or any theory book, can teach them.

In his patent of 1626 'for taking up boys' the choirmaster Nathaniel Giles had been ordered that 'none of the said choristers or Children of the Chapel…hall be used or employed as comedians, or stage players, or to exercise or act any stage plays, interlude or tragedies; for it is not fit or decent that such as should sing the praises of God Almighty should be trained or employed in lascivious and profane exercises.'[18] Now, in the more relaxed court of Charles II, boys from the Chapel Royal started to appear again in the London theatres. Choristers, used to public performance, often make superb actors, and it seems more than likely that Purcell too would have taken his place on the stage for performances with William Davenant's company at the new theatre in Dorset Garden, which opened on 7 November 1671. Such experiences on the stage may have been not only thoroughly enjoyable for Henry but formative in the development of a composer who as an adult was to have such an important influence in the London theatres.

But while the fortunate were enjoying all the entertainments that London could bring them, King Charles's financial problems were being felt at the Chapel Royal. From May 1670 we see that, of the fifteen available string players, just five were now scheduled each month to 'wayte & attend in his Majestys Chappell Royall'. The list explained that each player should 'attend every third moneth as they will answere the contrary'.[19] There were evidently attendance problems again too amongst the musicians – hardly surprising in view of the arrears of some of their payments – with a threat that any person who 'shall refuse or neglect their attendance there…shall forthwith be suspended his place'.[20] Cooke was still having to leave London to scour the country for new singing talent, being reimbursed on 25 June 1670 'for fetching of boys from Rochester, Lincoln, Peterborough, Worcester and other places'.[21] He might well have had mixed feelings about the chaos that the building works that were authorized on 8 February 1671 would cause, with a warrant to the Surveyor General 'to cause the music room in his Majesty's Chapel Royal to be enlarged

3½ feet in length towards his Majesty's closet'.[22] By 21 March the work had evidently been completed, for three 'crimson damask curtains' were ordered, 'the music room being enlarged'.[23] But there were bonuses too, no doubt especially looked forward to by the choristers, when the court moved out of town: in May 1671 king and court moved to Windsor for part of the summer, taking the full choir for two weeks in May 1671.[24]

The summer of 1672 must have been traumatic for the choristers. Henry Cooke, now in his late fifties and choirmaster for the past twelve years, was seriously ill. On 24 June he resigned his post as Marshall of the Corporation of Music 'by reasons of sickness', and on 6 July, 'weak in body', he made his will.[25] Exactly a week later the official records note 'Capt. Hen: Cooke departed this life, the 13 day of July, 1672'.[26] He had been a much loved figure, indefatigable in his dealings with the authorities, and especially with the treasury: he noted in his will that he was still owed £1,600, and carefully itemized each amount. His eye for picking musical youngsters was clearly unsurpassed. He turned his charges not only into good choristers but almost single-handedly produced a superb second generation of post-Restoration musicians. At the news of his death his colleagues and choristers must have been desolate. According to his wishes he was buried, four days after his death, in the east cloister of Westminster Abbey. Certainly Gentlemen of the Chapel Royal were present at the service, for Cooke thoughtfully left 10s in his will 'To those gentlemen of the Chapell shall be at my burial'. This must have been a fee that they would much rather not have collected.

Within two days of Cooke's death his son-in-law, Pelham Humfrey, was made Master of the Children of the Chapel Royal.[27] Humfrey was clearly in favour at court, for on 10 January 1672 he and Thomas Purcell had been made 'composers in ordinary to his Majesty for the violin, without fee, and assistant to George Hudson, and upon the death or other avoidance of George Hudson, to come in ordinary with fee'.[28] Humfrey was also appointed to be 'composer in his Majesty's private musick for voices'.[29] Cooke would have been especially pleased to find one of his earliest and most promising choristers, William Turner (already singing countertenor at the Chapel Royal), taking his place as 'musician in ordinary in his Majesty's private musick for lute and voice'.[30] We must assume that Humfrey had matured in personality during the five years since his savaging from Pepys, but he may nonetheless have enjoyed the clerical error that ordered, just in time for the winter of 1672, the Great Wardrobe to provide 'summer liveries' for the choristers![31] Like his predecessor, he had to account regularly for the expenses he ran up educating his charges. He was especially careful to have noted by the Treasurer of the Chamber in his half-yearly account of 2 May 1673 that 'In this warrant was nothing for fetching of Children from several Cathedrals, as is sometymes',[32] though we know that during the year he had lost two choristers, Henry Hall and Thomas Heywood.[33] We can suppose that they were replaced by boys from within London.

In March 1672, as part of his complicated manoeuvres to achieve a French alliance, Charles had issued his Declaration of Indulgence which granted toleration to Catholics and Dissenters. Now he needed parliament to vote him more money, but knew that it was furious about a war against the Dutch which had been declared in its absence and a Declaration of Indulgence which had been published without consultation. When Charles finally could no longer delay recalling parliament, his fears were confirmed. The Commons would not vote money to the king until he withdrew his Declaration. Trapped, Charles had to give way, and parliament, knowing that many of the king's closest colleagues were Roman Catholics, added insult to injury and rushed through a Test Act which stated that all public servants had to be active members of the Church of England. A bill for the ease of Protestant Dissenters was added. Though Charles quickly adjourned parliament, it was too late to stop the damage: Lord Clifford resigned after the doors of his carriage were thrown open to reveal a Catholic priest inside. Those members of the Cabal who knew of a secret treaty signed at Dover dumped all their incriminating documents on Clifford, who buried them in his garden at Exeter (where they were not discovered for 250 years) and then apparently poisoned himself. On 12 June James, Duke of York, resigned as Lord High Admiral. His conversion to Catholicism was now clear for everyone to see and, as heir apparent to the throne, there was much depression at the prospect of an unending Catholic succession. James made matters worse by deciding it was time to remarry: there were two choices, the fifteen-year-old Mary of Modena or her aunt Leonora, both Catholics, and both of whom wished to become nuns. James was so uncertain that when Lord Peterborough went to France to complete the transaction, there was a blank in the space on the documents where the name was to be filled in. When Mary was eventually selected and, later in the year, arrived in London, she met with a stony reception from citizens and the Lord Mayor, who declined to welcome her with the customary bonfires. Court gossip began to mention the name of the young, heroic Monmouth as a possible successor to the throne.

In the context of complex European diplomatic wrangles, the moves within the court, and especially the Chapel Royal, must have appeared quite tame, although a copy of an Order in Council noted on 14 November 1673 shows that the religious purge was felt at court too: 'No person who is a Roman Catholicke or reputed to be of ye Roman Catholicke Religion doe presume after the Eighteenth day of this instant November to come into His Majesties Royall presence or to His Palace or to ye place where his court shalbe.'[34] Thomas Purcell and Pelham Humfrey continued to add to their extensive lists of court musical appointments. On 15 July 1673 they were both named as composers for the violins, now (with the death of George Hudson) at a fee of £42 15s 10d per year:[35] nine days later Humfrey was also confirmed in his appointment as 'composer in the private musick'.[36]

During the summer of 1673 Pelham Humfrey could see that his chorister Henry Purcell's voice was, if not already breaking, certainly not going to last much longer, and it would have been largely on Humfrey's advice that Henry was ensured of an apprenticeship to take up once his treble singing days were over. On 10 June 1673 a warrant was sworn to 'admit Henry Purcell in the place of keeper, mender, maker, repairer and tuner of the regals, organs, virginals, flutes and recorders and all other kind of wind instruments whatsoever, in ordinary, without fee, to his Majesty, and assistant to John Hingeston, and upon the death or other avoidance of the latter, to come in ordinary with fee.'[37] To be assistant to the supervisor of the royal instruments was an important post, for it ensured that Purcell would come into regular contact with most of the important musicians at court: it also guaranteed that when his godfather eventually died – Hingeston was now in his late sixties – Henry would take his place. We do not know precisely when Henry's voice broke, but such a warrant would surely only have been ordered when a chorister was no longer able to be of use in the Chapel. The other main reference to Henry's voice breaking at the age of only fourteen – an unusually early age in the seventeenth century, when voices often lasted to sixteen or more – is dated 17 December 1673, when we find the customary warrant 'to provide the usual clothing for Henry Purcell, late child of his Majesty's Chapel Royal, whose voice is changed and who is gone from the Chapel'.[38]

An annual £30 allowance is mentioned in Treasury documents which state that the payment to Purcell commenced at Michaelmas 1673.[39]

Once again we know precious few precise details of what Purcell did during the next few years of his musical training. He had regular contact with Pelham Humfrey, and may well have had formal or informal composition lessons with him. Certainly Purcell would have been aware of the growing quantity of music being added to performances in the increasingly fashionable London theatres. He may have seen the 'French opera' *Ariadne* produced at the theatre in Bridges Street for which Christopher Wren was commanded to deliver 'such of the scenes [i.e. scenery] remaining in the theatre at Whitehall as shall be useful'.[40] The opera seems not to have been too successful – though it is not clear why – but the return of the loaned scenery had to be requested a month later.[41] The increasingly popular trend to perform Shakespeare too was noted at court, with a royal decree being issued on 16 May 1674 on the subject of 'Chappell men for the theatre'. It shows a generously lenient attitude to time being taken away from salaried court work: 'It is his Majesties pleasure that Mr. Turner & Mr. Hart, or any other men or Boyes belonging to his Majestys Chappell Royall that sing in ye Tempest at His Royal Highnesse Theatre doe remain in Towne all the weeke (during his Majesty's absence from Whitehall) to perform that service, Only Saterdayes to repair to Windsor and to returne to London on Mundayes if there be occasion for them. And that [they] also perform ye like service in ye Opera in ye said theatre Or any other thing in ye like nature where their helpe may be desired upon notice given them thereof.'[42]

Henry's younger brother Daniel may well have started as a chorister of the Chapel Royal at about this time, in which case he would have felt the benefit of Humfrey's contribution to court architecture: 'October 7 1673. to Dr. Wren, surveyor general of his Majesty's works. These are to signifie unto you of his Majestys pleasure that you cause to be made & opened a Doore out of ye present Dwelling house of Mr. Pelham Humfryes into the Bowleing green for the perticuler use of Him and ye Children of his Majestys Chappell.'[43] In the event, the choristers' new access to their recreation area was not to be used for very long, and Humfrey's house was soon occupied by the Earl of Oxford.[44] Thomas Purcell, Henry and Daniel's uncle (and apparent adoptive father) received his sixth simultaneous court appointment, that of musician-in-ordinary in the Private Music,[45] and was rich enough to live in fashionable Pall Mall.

Pelham Humfrey's tenure at the Chapel Royal did not last long. On 23 April his health must have been deteriorating, for a copy of his will was lodged in the court records[46] and on 14 July 1674, while he was at Windsor with the Court, the same records note that 'Mr Pelham Humfries departed this life.'[47] He was only twenty-seven years old. His place as 'master of the children of his Majesty's Chapel Royal and composer in his Majesty's private musick for voices in ordinary'[48] was taken by John Blow who seems, perhaps already prepared for Humfrey's death, to have taken over immediately at Windsor. Blow had been organist at Westminster Abbey since 1668 (when he was only nineteen years old), musician in ordinary to His Majesty for the virginals since 1669, and a Gentleman of the Chapel Royal since March 1674. For the first time the records tell us the names of the eight children of the Chapel who were in attendance, and whose education Blow now took over: William Holder, William Sarell, John Waters, Gilbert Conisby, Augustus Benford, Francis Smyth, Bartholomew Isaack and William Goodgroome (son of the Chapel Royal singer John Goodgroome, who had replaced Henry Purcell's father).[49]

Henry Purcell too was now musically under the principal supervision of John Blow; Blow's memorial in Westminster Abbey states that he was 'Master to the famous Mr H. Purcell'. Though we have little more information than that, we do know that Blow was the writer of two instruction books on music, *Rules for Playing of a Through Bass upon Organ and Harpsichon* (now held in the British Library)[50] and *Rules for Composition*.[51] Watkins Shaw has suggested that these books may have been written to instruct Purcell, but Blow would have had more pupils than Purcell: perhaps they all used these text books. We do know that Blow was a well-respected teacher, and that he and Purcell remained close colleagues and friends for the next twenty years. In his capacity as assistant to the royal instrument technician Purcell was under the supervision of John Hingeston, at least part of whose workload would by now have been falling to his young apprentice. Hingeston's extra expenses, mostly the transport and cleaning of various organs and harpsichords, are carefully itemized for 1674 and 1675.[52] On 3 September 1674 we find a record of Purcell authorizing the supply of two new violins for use in the Chapel Royal.[53] He clearly quickly picked up his skills as an organ tuner, for the Westminster Abbey payment records of 1675 show him receiving £2 as a fee for tuning the organ; we presume that Hingeston was confident enough in Purcell's abilities to leave his young assistant to get on with the job

Dr. John Blow.

April y 23 : 74

Be itt knowne to all people whomso-
- ever itt may Concerne that I leave my
Deare wife my sole executrix and Mrs:
of all I have in the world after those
few Debts I owe are payd:
I only desire that 3 Legacyes may bee given
that is to say to my Cousin: Betty Gelfe:
to Mr: Blow, and to Bess Gill: each
of them twenty shillings to buy them
Rings :

Pelham Humfrey

30 Aprile July 1674

himself.[54] In the same Abbey accounts the following year we also find Purcell being paid £5 'for pricking out two books of organ parts': as part of his training the young student was being given organ parts to copy by Blow, a responsible and quite skilled job which involved musical judgement and well-developed keyboard skills. The parts that Purcell copied were probably for contemporary, post-Restoration works and not anthems by the great composers of the past – Gibbons, Byrd, Tallis and the like. Though these copies by Purcell have not survived, contemporary ones at the Chapel Royal include, amongst sixty-five works (nineteen services and nearly three times that number of anthems), only four by pre-Restoration composers: the remainder are works by composers such as William Child, Michael Wise, William Tucker (himself a prolific music copyist), John Blow and Pelham Humfrey.[55] Back at the instrument room Purcell would have heard one side of the problems that John Hingeston was encountering with the distinguished organ maker Bernard Smith who, demanding £196, petitioned Hingeston on 8 March 1676 and was ordered to appear 'at common law' on 15 June.[56] We can assume that Father Smith was having to go to law to recover his dues for work done for the court. One can sympathize with Hingeston's predicament, for on 16 April 1674

During the young Purcell's years as a chorister, two men were Masters of the Children of the Chapel Royal and must have strongly influenced his musical training. Pelham Humfrey was appointed in January 1672, but died, aged only twenty-seven, in July 1674, after making a will (right) witnessed by John Blow (left). Blow succeeded him at the Chapel Royal and remained an important figure in English music for the next thirty years.

the General Wardrobe had noted that arrears of £112 17s 6d were due to him for no less than seven years' liveries.[57] Purcell and Hingeston might have been more amused to hear of the document, relating to another instrument, which passed from the Lord Chamberlain's department to the Jewel House early in 1676: 'Whereas his Grace the Duke of Monmouth hath informed mee that one of his Majestys silver Trumpetts in the Custody of Symon Beale, one of his Majestys Trumpeters, was lately lost and stole from off the Horse Guard and cannot be heard of, and that there is a Trumpet wanting for his Majestys service.'[58] Beale's ceremonial trumpet was only six years old[59] and, containing 39 ounces [1.1 kg] of silver, would have been well worth melting down!

Money too, but on a rather larger scale, was still a major concern for King Charles, despite the industrious attempts of his new political captain, Thomas Osborne (shortly to be made Earl of Danby), to restore some semblance of order to the chaotic royal finances. Even with the increased revenues that a fortunate expansion of trade was bringing to the royal coffers – taxes which came directly to the king – he still needed the support of parliament to try to balance the books. Danby had done his best, by placing judicious bribes amongst the members, to ensure that the king could rely on a majority in parliament, but even so the two sessions in the spring and autumn of 1675 were unpleasant for Charles. When parliament met on 13 April the opposition, led by Shaftesbury, refused to vote him funds to pay off past debts, granted less than he needed to build new warships and appropriated all his existing customs revenue for the navy. Shaftesbury's supporters led their public opposition from the Green Ribbon Club at the King's Head Tavern in Fleet Street, creating the first political club.

Whatever the political temperature, the court made its annual recesses to Windsor, taking with it much of the musical establishment, and life in the London theatres continued to develop. Away from the court there were exciting discoveries and developments: the Restoration had seen a huge flowering not only in the arts, but in science and technology too. On 28 November 1660 fifty-five people had gathered together at Gresham's College in London, agreeing to pay a subscription of one shilling each week with the aim of furthering their understanding of the world around them. King Charles was genuinely interested in their work and on 15 July 1662 presented them with a mace and incorporated their society as 'The Royal Society for the

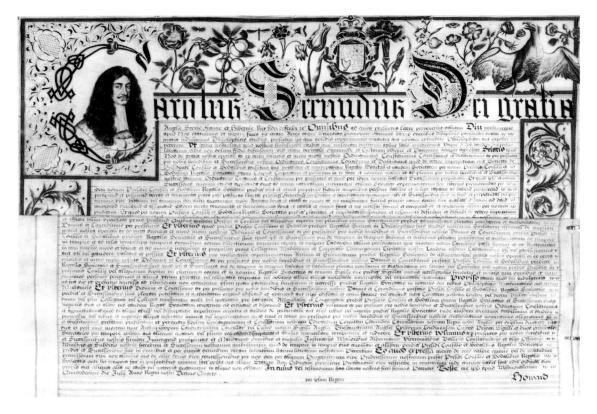

Improvement of Natural Knowledge by Experiment'. The Royal Society, taking a fresh approach to the problems of a post-Restoration world, represented a vigorous age of scientific discovery. The committees they formed encouraged and disseminated scientific knowledge, investigating pharmacy, agriculture, antiquities, chronology, history, mathematics, ship-building, travel, mechanics, grammar, chemistry, navigation, architecture, hydraulics, meteorology, statistics, longevity, geography and even monsters.

Parliament reconvened on 15 February 1677 in some indignation. Shaftesbury led the attack on Charles, assisted by Buckingham, claiming that an interval of fifteen months automatically made for a dissolution and thus fresh elections. Parliament, siding for once with the king, voted Charles the money he required but demanded that he go to war with the French, who were still battling with the Dutch. Charles tried a more diplomatic approach, prompted by Danby, and proposed that William of Orange should marry Princess Mary, the fifteen-year old daughter of James, Duke of York. When Mary finally met her future husband, prematurely old, small and serious, she burst into tears, but she was nonetheless married on 4 November 1677, infuriating the French king Louis.

The charter of the Royal Society, founded by Charles II in 1662 for 'the Improvement of Natural Knowledge by Experiment.' It was the beginning of science as an academic discipline in England.

Matthew Locke died in August 1677, when Purcell was seventeen. Locke belonged to an earlier generation of composers, a survivor from the age of Charles I, but Purcell revered him, and his ode 'on the death of his worthy friend' (opposite) seems to be deliberately modelled on the older musician's style.

For the musicians of the court a far sadder event was the death, during August 1677, of the eminent musician Matthew Locke. Locke was one of the last surviving composers who had come through the Civil War, and his influence on English music had been great, maintaining the peculiarly individual style which distinguished English writing from that of the rest of Europe. He had been a friend and colleague of Thomas and Henry Purcell senior, and had held posts as composer at court, private composer to the king, composer for the wind music and composer for the violins, of whom he also became assistant leader. His support for English music had been great: he had written, in the introduction to his first publication, the *Little Consort in Three Parts* (1656) that 'I never yet saw any Forain I[n]strumental Composition (a few French Corants excepted) worth an English mans Transcribing'.[60] It had probably been through the two older Purcell

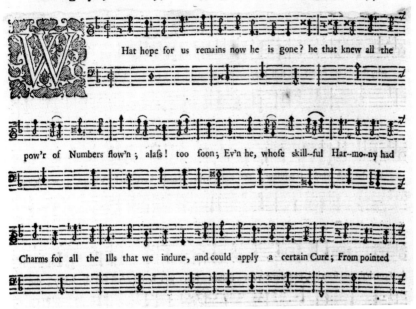

On the Death of his Worthy Friend Mr. MATTHEW LOCKE,
MUSICK-Compofer in Ordinary to His Majefty,
And Organift of Her Majefties Chappel, who Dyed in Auguft, 1677.

What hope for us remains now he is gone? he that knew all the

pow'r of Numbers flow'n ; alafs! too foon; Ev'n he, whofe skill--ful Har--mo--ny had

Charms for all the Ills that we indure, and could apply a certain Cure; From pointed

brothers that Locke had met Henry Purcell: as a chorister Purcell would have sung some of the dozens of anthems written by the composer – a number of which he eventually copied into his own manuscripts – and in later life he would certainly have heard much of Locke's ever-adventurous music for a series of theatrical productions in the 1670s, perhaps including the movements (especially the 'Curtain Tune') that he contributed to Shadwell's famous 1674 production of *The Tempest.* When working at court Purcell could hardly have avoided hearing Locke's chamber and instrumental music, his songs and his keyboard music. Thus Locke's direct musical influence on Purcell must have been great, whether or not one chooses to believe the theory, put forward by Cummings and Rimbault[61] that Purcell may have been a formal pupil of the composer. That indebtedness of musical style is shown in the touching Ode Purcell set 'on the death of his worthy friend Matthew Locke', titled 'What hope remains for us now he is gone?' In this case the deliberate similarity in style may have been Purcell's tribute to a fine composer.

CHAPTER III

Rising Star: Purcell at the Court of Charles II, 1677-1685

The death of Locke brought Henry Purcell his first salaried court appointment. On 10 September 1677 the Lord Chamberlain's department sent a warrant to the Gentlemen Ushers 'to swear and admit Henry Pursell as composer in ordinary with fee for the violin to his Majesty, in the place of Mathew Lock, deceased'.[1] With the bureaucratic delays that were now a part of court life, the signet office only finally issued its warrant to pay Purcell his salary of 20d per day and a yearly livery of £16. 2s. 6d. to be paid from the Treasury Chamber in December 1679,[2] but the eighteen-year old Purcell must have set about his new task with enthusiasm, including carrying out his task to 'order & direct them in his course of wayting'.[3] Fifteen years previously the principal function of the composer for the violins had been to write instrumental dances and airs which were played at court, but as increasingly late payments had forced musicians to seek work elsewhere, so the numbers of performances of this sort at court had dropped: the numbers of compositions required had diminished accordingly. Additionally, Nicholas Staggins, the Master of the Music, seems to have taken upon himself much of the composition of this type of music: his work was not highly regarded by his contemporaries, and much of his output appears to have been destroyed in the huge fire which gutted Whitehall Palace in 1698. Instead, Purcell's professional attention was turned towards producing ceremonial odes, together with anthems and other sacred works for performance in the Chapel Royal. And here he excelled beyond almost all comparison.

It is not possible to date many of Purcell's church compositions with total accuracy, but there are a handful of works which scholars believe were written before February 1679; effectively during (or

OPPOSITE: *Henry Purcell in 1683: an engraving published in* A Collection of Ayres.

maybe even before) Purcell's first year of office. Examination of three of the best of these shows why his contemporaries may have been awe-struck by what they were hearing from this newly-appointed, teenage composer. What they also show is that Purcell must have been practising his art for some time: these are in no way the compositions of a novice.

On stylistic grounds, perhaps the earliest of these works (and maybe Purcell's earliest surviving church anthem) is a verse anthem setting Psalm 8, 'O Lord our governor, how excellent is thy name in all the world'. The solo and verse writing is wonderfully responsive to the text, highly individual, and the overall effect quite majestic, but Purcell's youthful desire to show his skills in maintaining strict coun-terpoint does lead him into some unusual harmonic moments in the choruses. The opening five bars demonstrate Purcell's characterist-ically wistful melodic instrumental writing in a passage, high in its register, for the bass violin, leading to an extended section for solo bass extolling the majesty of the Lord in expansive style. Maybe looking back to his days as a chorister in the same choir for which he was now writing, Purcell scores the music for the 'babes and sucklings' for three solo trebles, who innocently still 'the enemy and the avenger' in charming three-part harmony. We can be sure from this writing that the Chapel Royal must have had three excellent solo trebles: would that we knew who they were. Later in the anthem they are joined by two solo basses who consider the creation of matters celestial and mankind's good fortune. The chorus take on the role of the animals that inhabit the world, the sheep and oxen in thoughtful style, and 'the fowls of the air and the fishes of the sea' in joyfully bizarre coun-terpoint. Purcell's contrapuntal ingenuity is clearly demonstrated when the music of the opening returns: this time he repeats the same music, but now ingeniously occupies two basses in exact imitation. After such technical skill, the Gloria seems quite old-fashioned in its style, but blossoms beautifully at 'world without end' and closes with a serene and harmonically individual 'Amen'.

More astonishing is Purcell's setting, in ten parts, of three verses from the Book of Joel, 'Blow up the trumpet in Sion', in which the mastery of large-scale vocal textures would be extraordinary by any composer, let alone one still in his teens. The text was traditionally a Lenten one, and so the work could have first been performed in February or March 1678. Purcell's opening is anything but penitent, with ringing fanfares thrown between seven solo voices: once again three of these solo lines are for trebles. At 'Sanctify a fast' the key changes from C major, and Purcell's rich harmonic language comes to the fore: a 'solemn assembly' is called, and there is a compelling build-up through the vocal entries of 'and sanctify the congregation'. The chorus interrupt briefly, restating the joyful opening music and ending on a marvellous ten-part chord of C major which must have rung spectacularly through the Chapel Royal. Next Purcell contrasts groups of lower and upper voices, the lower voices portraying the elders and the bridegroom, the upper voices children and the bride. There is daring augmented harmony at 'Let them weep', but even this pales into insignificance when set alongside the devastating harmonic shift at 'Spare thy people, O Lord' which must rank as one of the most striking moments in Purcell's church music.

It seems likely that Purcell's earliest anthem for the Chapel Royal which required the participation of the royal violins (for whom he had been employed by the king to write), as well as the choir, was his setting of the expressive, graphic text from the Song of Solomon, 'My beloved spake'. Over the centuries since Purcell's version these verses have been memorably set by a number of British composers (including a twentieth-century setting by the under-rated Patrick Hadley) but none has been more original than Purcell's. With a text full of references to spring, the anthem is remarkable in almost every aspect: for its freshness, its word-painting, its novel harmonic language and for its glorious string writing. The single-section symphony contains music of enormous individuality, and the writing for solo quartet treats the excitement of the coming of spring with rapturous lyricism. The passing of winter and the instrumental ritornello that takes over from the voices produces more delicious discords before the arrival of spring is celebrated by soloists, orchestra and chorus. But the most remarkable harmony is reserved for 'And the voice of the Turtle is heard in our land', where Purcell creates one of the most breathtaking tonal shifts of the era. A solo tenor, accompanied by a winding solo violin, imitates the fig tree tortuously growing her 'green figs' and the vines slowly putting forth their produce before the anthem ends with an ecstatic return of the opening mood and a joyful 'Alleluia'.

During 1678 we gain a puzzling insight into Purcell's education. He was then eighteen or maybe even nineteen years old, generally regarded as the most promising musician of his generation and already a court composer. Suddenly he appeared on the lists of Westminster School as a 'Bishop's Boy' (formerly known as a 'Lord's

Westminster School as a 'Bishop's Boy' (formerly known as a 'Lord's Scholar'). His cousin Charles had been a scholar there since 1670, but in 1678 the Westminster Abbey treasurer's accounts show that Henry was one of four boys awarded £25: Purcell continued to be given this annual stipend up to Michaelmas 1680. We can only assume that the famous headmaster of that school, Richard Busby, had noted Purcell's talents and, in the same way that he educated John Dryden, Christopher Wren, Henry Aldrich and many others, took him under his wing. We know that Busby bequeathed Purcell a gold mourning ring in his will, so we can assume that he was fond of the young musician, as well as being an important influence on his intellectual development.[4]

At around the same time Purcell copied a series of works by his contemporaries and immediate predecessors including anthems by Adrian Batten, John Blow, William Byrd, William Child, Orlando Gibbons, Nathaniel Giles, Pelham Humfrey, Matthew Locke, William Mundy, Thomas Tallis and Thomas Tomkins.[5] The collection, which he is believed to have started copying in 1679 or 1680 and finished in 1682, would have been compiled both for Purcell's own 'library' of works, and also as part of his study of the music of other composers.

Developments, but of a far more sinister nature, were taking place at court. On 13 August 1678 Christopher Kirkby, a chemist in the royal laboratory who was known as an anti-papist fanatic, approached King Charles and told him of a plot against his life. The king was used to such rumours and dismissed them, especially as he was due to go to Windsor the next day, but the problem did not go away so easily. Kirkby was found to be only an intermediary, working for Dr Israel Tonge, a cleric who Antony à Wood remembered as being 'cynical and hirsute, shiftless in the world'.[6] He was known to be fanatically anti-Jesuit, and the plot he described (covering forty-three main articles) involved London being fired, Catholics rising in Ireland, the conquering of England by French and Irish forces, and the murder of Charles. The story did not convince the king, but Danby believed that rumours of the plot might assist Charles in obtaining more money from parliament for the maintenance of the English army against French invasion or, equally likely, that it would strengthen Danby's precarious standing with parliament. The plot thickened, for Tonge now revealed that the author of the forty-three articles was one Titus Oates. Much against Charles's wishes, on 28 September Oates and

Tonge were brought before a meeting of the Privy Council. The articles had increased now to eighty-three but Oates, a professional perjurer in the days when (without a police force or anything but the crudest form of detection) courts relied on the sworn testimony of witnesses to convict criminals, gave a convincing performance. His tale was a tall one, and Charles found it so unbelievable that, having asked a few pertinent questions (the answers to which showed the story to be a fabrication) he left for Newmarket. Unfortunately, during his absence, two incidents occurred which gave some credence to Oates's lies. The first was the discovery of secret letters, in code, between Edward Coleman, a former secretary to the Duke of York, and a series of prominent Catholics abroad; coupled with an unusually hot summer and various ill-omens in the form of eclipses of the sun and moon, it brought near panic to London. The tension was further increased by the mysterious murder of the magistrate to whom Oates

Titus Oates became famous for spreading lurid rumours of a Catholic plot against Charles II. For a while he was believed but was later convicted of perjury and set in the pillory outside Westminster Hall.

and Tonge had sworn their evidence: Sir Edmund Godfrey was found, stabbed through the heart, on Primrose Hill. Mobs marched through London, ladies carried loaded pistols in broad daylight and innocent suspects were put in jail. Charles was powerless to stop the panic, and others who may also have realized the fiction of it all maintained silence as such a public outcry could only strengthen the case against the Catholic succession of James. All Charles could do was wash his hands of the whole affair, leaving it to the topsy-turvy course of law: innocent people were sent to the gallows, and the loathsome Oates was given a pension of £1,200 and a luxurious apartment in Whitehall Palace. With the opposition smelling victory, parliament met and demanded a new Test Bill which would have prevented James succeeding to the throne. Danby, using all his influence, had it quashed but fell foul of the machinations of the French King Louis who, bribing Ralph Montagu, a former ambassador to Paris, ensured that various secret treaty documents fell into the hands of the Speaker of the House of Commons. Before they could impeach Danby, Charles prorogued parliament and then, for only the second time in his reign, on 24 January 1679, dissolved it.

Charles's new parliament was not of the colour he had hoped: the majority, mostly made up of Shaftesbury's Whigs, was hostile to him and his ministers. Danby remained in the Tower of London (though he seems to have had a fairly comfortable existence there, and was regularly consulted by the king). James was advised to flee to Flanders, and parliament introduced an Exclusion Bill. Meanwhile the trials of Papists continued, many of them overseen by the awful Chief Justice, Scroggs: Roger North described him as a man whose 'course of life was scandalous' and 'his discourses violent and intemperate'.[7]

At home the king was suffering. Shaftesbury was eroding Charles's closest supporters. Charles's mistress Louise de Keroualle (later created Duchess of Portsmouth), scared by Shaftesbury's threats to proceed against her as a 'common whore', sided with the earl and promised to use her influence with the king in favour of James's exclusion but, worse still, the king's eldest, illegitimate son, the handsome Duke of Monmouth, swayed by Shaftesbury's dangling carrot of legitimacy and the throne, defected. And at the end of August, Charles was suddenly taken feverishly ill: for a time he was close to death, and his advisers and ministers were thrown into a panic. 'Good God,' wrote Henry Savile, 'what a change would such an accident make. The very thought of it frightens me out of my wits.'[8] James was hastily recalled from Brussels but, by the time he arrived, Charles was better again. The shock served a useful purpose, for a body of thinking people began to realize that the king's essentially reasonable views were much better than the other options currently available. They also perhaps saw how close the country had just come again to civil war. Charles persuaded James to leave the country once more, deprived Monmouth of many of his honours and commissions and sent him to Holland. The king fought hard to counter Shaftesbury's growing anti-Papist movement, which was spreading rapidly throughout the country. In October, seeing that the electorate had returned a parliament favouring exclusion, Charles prorogued it for twelve months before it could even meet.

In 1679, Henry Purcell received his next important appointment. Tradition has related the story that John Blow, seeing his pupil's brilliance, stepped aside to allow Purcell into the post of organist of Westminster Abbey. There is no actual historical evidence to support that theory, but it would seem more than possible that Blow found that being a Gentleman and one of three organists at the Chapel Royal, Master of the Children of the Chapel Royal, a teacher, a father to five children and a prolific composer was a little too much when added to the tasks of organist at Westminster Abbey. Perhaps an overworked Blow did suggest to the authorities that his former student would do a good job. All the treasurer's accounts of Westminster Abbey actually show is that from Michaelmas 1679 Blow's name gives way to that of Purcell. Like the lay-clerks at the Abbey, Purcell received just £10 per year, plus a further £8 towards the rental of a house. With court musical salaries starting at four times that rate, we can assume that the Abbey post was not considered to be a full-time job. The Purcell family also increased their presence at court, for around this time we find Purcell's younger brother Daniel first mentioned as one of the eight senior boys of the Chapel Royal.[9]

Purcell's compositions were not restricted to works for the church. In the second book of John Playford's *Choice Ayres and Songs to Sing to the Theorbo-lute or Bass-viol*, published (after some delays) during 1679, five of the young composer's songs were published; he was also credited with two others which are of less certain authorship. Four songs ('Since the pox', 'Amintas, to my grief I see', 'Scarce had the rising sun appear'd' and 'I resolve against cringing') were small-scale, but also included was the affectionate ode that Purcell had written on

Archlute: a multitude of different sizes and designs of plucked instruments were in use. Far easier to transport than a harpsichord or organ, their ease of portability meant that they could be used in all situations.

A portrait by Sir Peter Lely of a lady of the Lake family playing a guitar c. *1660.*

the death of Matthew Locke, 'What hope remains for us now he is gone?'. These were probably the first compositions of Purcell's to go into print. Authors have previously suggested that Banister and Low's *New Ayres and Dialogues* (1678) contained six of Purcell's compositions, but the attribution has been convincingly questioned by recent scholarship. In particular, 'Sweet tyranness, I now resign' had been published in *Catch that catch can* in 1667, attributed to 'Mr. Henry Purcell' – hardly the correct title for a child of eight years old. It is more likely that Henry Purcell the elder had been the composer.

These works aside, it was still in the field of church music that Purcell was excelling himself. It is difficult to tell which of his compositions may have been written for performance at Westminster Abbey, and which were performed at the Chapel Royal, and it is equally hard to date many of his works with complete accuracy. But from the period around 1679-80 comes a host of fine compositions, many of them unreasonably neglected.

The craftsmanship of the anthem 'Behold now, praise the Lord', especially its string writing, is exemplary. The opening of the string symphony is ravishing in its daring harmonic and melodic lines, highly attractive in its desolate beauty. The verse writing (the sections for

Playford's collections of songs, in which a large number of Purcell's works were first published, were aimed primarily at the private music-lover wishing to entertain himself and his friends. This engraving after Francis Barlow was used as the frontispiece to Musick's Delight on the Cithren, *1666.*

soloists) is exuberant, with themes expressively picked up in string ritornelli, and in the only surviving manuscript (found in the second volume of William Flackton's three-volume collection, now held in the British Library) the young composer's pride in his work emerges at the large-scale Gloria where he heads the section '10 parts', showing that he could confidently handle two blocks of voices and an independent string section, before florid writing and some characteristically inventive modulations end the anthem in great opulence.

Another astonishing anthem from around 1679 is 'Hear my prayer, O Lord', apparently intended as part of a larger piece that Purcell did not complete. In the autograph manuscript (now held in Cambridge's Fitzwilliam Museum) the anthem is followed by a number of blank pages; Purcell's concluding barline (through the staves but not through the intervening spaces) is of the type which usually indicates another section is to follow, and there is no sign of the elaborate flourish with which he usually marks the end of a piece. The setting is in eight parts, and takes as its text the despairing first verse of Psalm 102. The melodic material is, on its own, quite simple. The first phrase ('Hear my prayer') uses only two melancholy notes a

Purcell's autograph of his anthem 'Hear my Prayer', preserved in the Fitzwilliam manuscript book. The way it ends, without the usual flourish, suggests that he meant to continue the composition.

minor third apart, but the turning chromaticism of 'crying' provides great plangency. The harmonic language, after the opening phrases always in at least six parts, is exceptional, but the most extraordinary feature of the anthem is the build-up which Purcell orchestrates from the outset – an inexorable vocal crescendo lasting over three minutes, culminating in a monumental discord at the start of the last bar – which marks this anthem out as one of his greatest.

During this period Purcell wrote the first of his devotional songs. These are works, often for smaller forces than those utilized at the Chapel Royal or the Abbey, that have non-biblical texts, often by contemporary or recent poets. (The early devotional songs were all for small consorts of voices, as opposed to works composed after 1685 which, though still given the same generic label, are largely for solo voice.) Purcell was clearly struck by the work of the poet John Patrick, setting over half a dozen of his Psalm paraphrases by 1680. The four-part setting 'Early O Lord, my fainting soul' is full of novel harmony and subtle illustrations of the text. Purcell must have had two particularly fine boy trebles on hand. The characterful writing immediately catches the supplicatory mood of the text, illustrating words such as 'fainting' and 'implore', and setting the tenor high in its register, allowing it to cross with the two intertwining treble parts. 'Dangers, whilst thou art near to me, Do threaten me in vain' brings sensuous vocal suspensions and daring harmony, with the four voices moving to within only a fifth of each other at 'when I keep close': a perfect Purcell miniature.

Equally notable is another setting of a Patrick Psalm paraphrase 'Lord, I can suffer thy rebukes', which is desolate in mood and full of anguish, with the two trebles consumed with grief in intertwining vocal lines, mournfully passing their 'weary days in sighs and groans'. Completely different in mood, yet taking a text by the same author and probably written at around the same time as 'Lord, I can suffer' is 'O, all ye people, clap your hands', where the Psalm text allows Purcell to indulge in busy running passagework and jubilant trumpet-like calls as the four soloists proclaim God's goodness and 'high perfections'.

It is not beyond the realms of possibility that Purcell chose the text for another verse anthem with his royal employer's parlous state in mind. 'Who hath believed our report' took a section from the Book of Isaiah (much of it also selected sixty years later by Handel's librettist Jennens for Part 2 of *Messiah*) and in doing so found a tool with which to demonstrate his mastery of text-setting. A strong text invariably fired Purcell's imagination, and Isaiah's stark picture of a person dejected and rejected by men, full of sorrows and griefs, 'stricken and smitten', may have drawn some parallels with Charles's own situation at that time. Zimmerman[10] has suggested that the anthem may have been written for the anniversary of the execution of Charles I which would have been commemorated on 30 January. The writing is at times highly Italianate in its strong declamation, and always rapidly responsive to the changing emotions of its text.

To Charles's fury, at the end of 1679 Monmouth reappeared in London, probably encouraged to do so by Shaftesbury. Charles banished him from the country and stripped him of all his offices. Monmouth refused to go, and Shaftesbury distributed pamphlets which 'can only serve to manifest the factious and seditious spirits of those who promote them' and 'raise tumults and disorders in the city and discontent against his Majesty's government'.[11] But Charles reacted courageously. He announced on Christmas Eve that he would not allow parliament to meet until at least the following November, and set about clearing out his advisers who had favoured appeasement or had spoken against James. When Shaftesbury's principal supporters threatened their resignations in retaliation, Charles delightedly accepted. An ambassador sent to Holland reported back that William, a staunch Protestant with a far stronger claim to the throne than had Monmouth (William was the grandson of Charles I), possessed 'an abundance of good qualities'.[12] Charles, more confident, invited James back to London and the Aldermen of the City, also starting to tire of Shaftesbury, held a feast to celebrate the reunion. Charles, greatly pleased, retired to Newmarket, but had to return to London when rumours were spread that deeds had been found showing that he had married Lucy Walter, Monmouth's mother. The king categorically denied that the marriage had ever taken place. He spent the summer at Newmarket and Windsor, returning to prepare for his next battles with parliament on 9 September 1680.

For the king's return Purcell composed the first of twenty-four odes and welcome songs that he was to write over the next fifteen years. Of these works, seventeen were composed for royal occasions – mostly royal birthdays and returns from summer retreats. Often the standard of the text (usually anonymous) was not high, but Purcell never once failed to delight with his neat mixture of solos, duets, trios, choruses and splendid instrumental symphonies and ritornelli. 'Welcome, vicegerent of the mighty King', which painted Charles as God's representative on earth, was of a far higher musical standard than many of the efforts previously written for him, containing a fine opening symphony (ingeniously repeated and combined into the first chorus) and an especially appealing movement for solo tenor, 'Music, the food of love', whose tune is taken up by the chorus before the continuo modulates up a fourth and leads into a string ritornello of great charm and beauty.

It must have been a busy summer for Purcell, for the same period also saw the composition of at least nine of the string Fantasias and, quite possibly, various of the other remarkable instrumental pieces whose dates of composition are so tantalizingly vague to scholars – the 'Sonnata's of III Parts' (finally published in 1683), the 'Ten Sonata's in Four Parts' (posthumously published in 1697 but generally reckoned to date from around 1680), the two 'In Nomine' settings, five Pavans and possibly five more Fantasias. We know that Purcell worked fast, writing seven of the four-part Fantasias in just twenty days, probably while the court was in retreat at Windsor, where it had moved for the summer on 19 April. If any proof of Purcell's consummate mastery of

James, Duke of Monmouth, Charles II's dashing illegitimate son, whose ambitions were a constant threat and anxiety to his father and who was to perish as a rebel against his uncle James II.

counterpoint were needed, these instrumental works provided it. The way in which Purcell colours the music with every subtlety and surprise of harmony never fails to amaze. The neatness with which he copied out the Fantasias, meticulously dating each one, is an indication of a thorough, careful mind at work.

It was not only instrumental music and his first ode that took up Purcell's time: the first play utilizing his music was staged at the Dorset Garden theatre during 1680. The opening night of Nathaniel Lee's *Theodosius* is reckoned by some scholars to have taken place in September or October 1680, though Curtis Price and others have suggested the spring or summer. John Downes, the prompter of the Duke's Company, noted 'several Entertainments of Singing; Compos'd by the Famous Master Mr. Henry Purcell, (being the first he e'er Compos'd for the Stage)'. Downes's apparent assertion that already 'famous' may be explained by the fact that *Roscius Anglicanus* (in which his statement was printed) was published in 1708. Purcell's contribution – assuming that all the music is his, which is not altogether certain – included songs (the most famous being 'Ah, cruel, bloody fate'), choruses and instrumental music, a major portion of which have not survived. Purcell's music was obviously deemed successful, for later in the year he was asked to contribute a song to Nahum Tate's adaptation of Shakespeare's *King Richard the Second.* Unfortunately, the censors, sensitive to current events and seeing this was a play which dealt with the deposition of a king, refused it a licence. The work was revamped and renamed *The Sicilian Usurper.* Tate complained in the dedication that the plot was now 'render'd obscure and incoherent'.[13]

Charles's ride with parliament when it reassembled in October 1680 was bound to be a rough one, and Shaftesbury and his supporters did not disappoint. A second Exclusion Bill was presented to parliament. Only three members dared support their king and speak against it, and the bill was, quite literally, carried to the House of Lords. There Shaftesbury himself led the attack, supported amongst others by Monmouth, of whom Charles was said to have muttered, as his son rose to speak, 'The kiss of Judas'. Halifax, speaking on behalf of the king, rose to reply sixteen times, and to the amazement of the Commons, won the day by 33 votes. The threatened rebellions in the streets failed to materialize, and over the next weeks came signs that public opinion was finally turning in Charles's favour. When parliament reassembled in Oxford later in the year, the king was able to dissolve it and completely defeat the opposition.

On 9 July 1681 the baptismal register of the church of All Hallows the Less states that 'Henry son of Henry and Frances Purssell' was baptised there. The register of burials in the same set shows that the young child survived only a few more days, and was buried in the churchyard on 18 July. From this we can assume that Purcell must have married the previous year, perhaps during the summer. His wife, Frances, is thought to have been the daughter of J. B. Peters, a noted Catholic. We know tantalizingly little about her. Perhaps Purcell's short, four-part anthem 'Beati omnes qui timent Domini' (the text taken from Psalm 128, and one of only three Latin church texts which he is known to have set) was written for the wedding; a Latin text would have been quite suitable for a Catholic, and it was certainly well suited for such an occasion. Maybe the fact that the middle section of the anthem, 'Uxor tua sicut vitis abundans in lateribus domus tuae' ('Thy wife shall be as the fruitful vine upon the walls of thy house; Thy children like the olive branches round about thy table') is set for a solo bass is an autobiographical indication that when Purcell sang in the choir, he sang bass.

Compositions continued to pour out, particularly those for the Chapel Royal and, probably, Westminster Abbey. Purcell is known to have written the anthem 'O God thou hast cast us out' around 1680–82, and it is plausible to suggest that the text (from Psalm 60 and including lines such as 'Thou hast mov'd the land and divided it: Heal the sores thereof, for it shaketh') would have been eminently suited to the current political situation. The greater part of the anthem is for five-part choir, though there is an attractive verse section, 'O, be thou our help in trouble, For vain is the help of man'. The king might have especially appreciated the robust final chorus, confident in its solid belief that 'Through God will we do great acts: And it is he that shall tread down our enemies'.

Another anthem which is thought to date from this period, and which had an equally topical text, is 'Jehova, quam multi sunt hostes' ('Lord, how are they increased that trouble me'). Being in Latin, Purcell cannot have intended the work for use in Charles's reformed Chapel; instead, perhaps it was intended for performance in the private Roman Catholic queen's chapel at St James's. Whatever its origins, amongst the anthems written largely for choir (this one also contains two short solos) 'Jehova' is one of Purcell's most dramatic works, contrasting richly-scored polyphony with vivid solo and choral declamation. The section 'Ego cubui et dormivi; ego expergefeci me' ('I laid me down and slept; I awaked') is exquisitely scored, and a bellicose solo bass calls on Jehovah to save him, smiting his enemies on the cheekbone and breaking the teeth of the ungodly.

Other anthems which may come from around this time include a setting (for similar forces as 'O God thou hast cast us out') of 'Lord, how long wilt thou be angry', and two fine devotional songs set for two tenors and a bass. 'Plung'd in the confines of despair' was a setting of another doleful Psalm paraphrase by the poet John Patrick, with a striking opening section which plays falling chromaticism against the rising tension of the vocal entries, deeply responsive throughout to the text. 'When on my sick bed I languish', one of three works on the subject of death published in 1674 by the Winchester-educated poet and painter of miniatures Thomas Flatman (1637-88), brought an equally poignant setting from Purcell, colouring the mournful words (such as 'fainting, gasping, trembling, crying') in masterly fashion.

John Playford continued to publicize Purcell's secular work by including a selection of the composer's songs in the third book of *Choice Ayres and Songs*. Among them are 'Amintor, heedless of his flocks', a charming setting of 'How I sigh when I think of the charms of my swain', 'I take no pleasure in the sun's bright beams', a lutesong-like strophic setting of 'Pastora's beauties when unblown', 'Since one poor view', 'When her languishing eyes' and some of the songs he had written previously for the play *Theodosius*. From a manuscript in the British Library signed 'Charles Campleman his book, June ye 9th 1681',[14] we know that the poignant song 'Beneath a dark and melancholy grove' dates from around 1681. In a similar mould (and dated December 1682 in a manuscript copy now in the British Library)[15] is the song 'Urge me no more', whose text uses language and metre of eighty years earlier and appears to come from a play which may have been written around 1600 – perhaps one of the late choirboy plays. Purcell's setting is especially full of graphic word-painting: the colourful descriptions of the poet's low state and references to music and musical instruments clearly inspired the composer.

For the return of Charles to London after his annual autumn visits to Windsor and Newmarket Purcell wrote the second of his welcome odes, 'Swifter, Isis, swifter flow'. It is uncertain for which reception his ode was intended: the text refers to the river Thames and the royal barge, which would suggest a return from Windsor, but earlier scholars (including Vaughan Williams) have pointed out that Narcissus Luttrell, the Royal Historiographer, recorded in his diary on 12 October 1681 (after the return from Newmarket) that 'at night, for joy, were ringing of bells and bonefires in severall places': the ode's anonymous author, clearly familiar with such homecomings, makes references to them in his text. Whatever the occasion, Purcell took up the reference to bells, and the second half of his symphony is permeated by a six-note descending motif, as is the tantalizingly short instrumental ritornello which closes the attractive tenor solo, 'Hark, hark, just now my listening ears'. There is also some notable chromatic writing in the last chorus which presages moments in *Dido and Aeneas*.

At around the same time Purcell was commissioned by the King's Company to write at least one song for their production of Tom D'Urfey's *Sir Barnaby Whigg: or, No Wit like a Woman's*. If Purcell set the song in Act III which includes the couplet 'But still let the Town never doubt my condition; Though I fall a damn'd poet, I'le Mount a Musician', history has unfortunately lost what would have been an entertaining song! However, a good storm song survives from Act I, 'Blow, Boreas, blow'.

Without a parliament to irritate him and with no foreign wars to drain the coffers, King Charles entered into the autumn of 1681 in a more relaxed mood than his courtiers had ever seen. Thomas Bruce later wrote that 'He wanted not money. He was free from Parliaments that so greatly disturbed him, the succession was settled in the due line, he had a good ministry, he was out of intrigues with France... and he gave no countenance to loose and buffooning persons that flourished so in former years... his heart was set to live at ease, and that his subjects might live under their own vine and fig tree.' He systematically mopped up the remnants of Shaftesbury's opposition, and his policy of securing Tory control over local government proved highly successful. By the autumn of 1682 London had a Tory Lord Mayor and two Tory sheriffs. He had 'mastered this great beast, the City'. [16]

Charles began to enjoy life again, travelling outside London as often as possible. He especially enjoyed fishing and horse racing, and it was when he was at Newmarket that he relaxed most, as Sir John Reresby later wrote: 'The King was much pleased with the country, and so great a lover of the diversions which the place did afford, that he let himself down from majesty to the very degree of a country gentleman. He mixed himself amongst the crowd, allowed every man to speak to him that pleased; went a-hawking in the mornings, to cock matches or foot races in the afternoons (if there were no horse races), and to plays in the evenings acted by very ordinary Bartholomew Fair comedians'. [17]

At court, Purcell too must have breathed a sigh of relief, for the years of political uncertainty had been felt by the king's musicians, not least of all in the slowness with which they were paid (or, more usually, not paid). Purcell is recorded as having been amongst the musicians who attended the king at Windsor in May 1682. Later that month, to celebrate the return of the Duke of York (later James II) from Scotland he wrote his third ode. We are not certain exactly when the ode was performed, but it seems likely that 'What shall be done in behalf of the man' was performed as James returned to London on 27 May: Luttrell recorded that 'at night there were ringing of bells, and bone-fires in severall places, and other publick expressions of joy'. Once again, Purcell began his ode with a fine symphony, its stately, dotted opening nonetheless leaving room for the wistful harmonies which make the composer's string writing so appealing. The librettist was full of praise for the duke's success in defeating the rebellion of Monmouth, and took the opportunity to remind the assembled audience 'That York, royal York, is the next in succession'. The extended bass solo 'Mighty Charles, though joined with thee' was another example of Purcell's genius for word-setting, full of nobility and character, and led into a lilting chorus in which we see the composer's humour. Purcell throws a rather ridiculous list of the characteristics that James is advertised as possessing between the voices: perhaps the singers amused themselves by deciding which member of the ensemble should sing words such as 'obedient', 'grateful', 'just', 'courageous' and – best of all – 'punctual'. This was surely a performance where few of the musicians kept a totally straight face!

We still have little accurate information as to when the items of church music were written. Mostly a record book or manuscript simply gives a *terminus ante quem*. That is the case with Purcell's 'Service in B flat', a massive setting of ten canticles. Alongside a Magnificat and Nunc Dimittis (and their alternatives, the Cantate Domino and Deus Misereatur) for performance at Evensong were a Te Deum, Benedictus, Benedicite and Jubilate for Morning Service and Kyrie and Nicene Creed for Holy Communion. Such a 'Complete Service', though not unique, was a comparative rarity at this time, and must have been extremely useful to cathedral and other choirs: it appears, either complete or in part, in numerous manuscripts all over Britain and has featured on service lists almost ever since. Compared to the anthems, the B flat service settings appear conservative, usually remaining harmonically simple and often homophonic. However, they do contain a series of ingenious canonic devices in the glorias, and alternate their choruses with sections of verse, usually split into writing for three upper and three lower solo voices. A payment of 30s is registered in the accounts of Westminster Abbey for Michaelmas 1681 'for **writing** Mr Purcell's service and anthem',[18] though other scholars have indicated that it was completed 'before October 1682'.[19]

Also completed at around this time were yet more anthems. 'Remember not, Lord, our offences' is a masterpiece. Purcell's use of harmony and discord, his startlingly effective word-setting and his mastery of drama are all magnificently demonstrated in a piece lasting just over three minutes. The atmosphere is created with the first word, set as a simple block chord, and then reiterated as the phrase moves forward to 'offences': the text is repeated again, still in homophonic style, but this time in the relative major. Counterpoint appears at 'nor th'offences of our forefathers', and the tension begins to increase with 'neither take thou vengeance of our sins', always countered simultaneously in at least one voice with the rising phrase 'but spare us good Lord'. Gradually calls for mercy, to 'Spare us', begin to dominate, and the chromaticism and unbelievably daring use of discord increases: the music climaxes with a desperate plea, 'spare us, good Lord'. The mood quickly returns to supplication, and Purcell's harmony relaxes onto 'redeem'd' whilst the tenors' dominant seventh clashes exquisitely with a second inversion chord on 'precious'. It is the tenors again who have a wonderfully subtle inner line at 'for ever' as the anthem ends with a calm prayer for salvation.

Two works which date from around 1682 suggest that the Chapel Royal was blessed with a pair of especially fine boy trebles. We do not know who the boys were, but we do know that Purcell's younger brother Daniel was by this time one of the more senior choristers. Perhaps he was one of the pair for whom Henry wrote 'O Lord, rebuke me not in thine indignation', whose desolate text from the Psalms inspired Purcell to produce duet writing which made few allowances for its young singers, either technically or emotionally. Purcell's word setting of the darker moments is especially graphic as the soloists illustrate weary 'groaning', and poignant at 'Every night wash I my bed, And water my couch with my tears'.

Similarly, the writing for two solo trebles in 'The Lord is king, be the people never so impatient' again suggests that the Chapel Royal had a pair of top-rate choristers. Purcell's setting is Italianate and florid, at times almost instrumental – a vocal tour-de-force to which only two talented trebles could have done justice. The opening is extrovert, with Purcell lifting the voices exultantly through their upper registers at 'The Lord is great'. The Gloria is even more ornate, and culminates in a thoroughly violinistic outflow of notes before a simple choral Alleluia closes a unique verse anthem. Equally imposing, but for different reasons, is 'O Lord God of hosts', which shows Purcell's contrapuntal skills. The three choral sections are written in eight-part counterpoint, and are separated by two sections of verse: the second of these verses, 'Turn us again, O Lord of hosts', is especially appealing.

Purcell's younger brother Daniel followed him as a chorister at the Chapel Royal and had a successful musical career. At the end of Henry's life he contributed music to The Indian Queen *and after his death set a moving ode to his memory with words by Nahum Tate.*

In the summer of 1682 Purcell received a considerable further promotion when he was made one of the three organists of the Chapel Royal. The 'Cheque Book' of the Lord Steward's department records the issue on 14 July of a 'Certificate of admission for Henry Pursell, sworn and admitted as Gentleman of the Chapel Royal in place of Edward Lowe, deceased'.[20] Another entry, dated 11 July but formally written up some months later, records 'Mr. Edw Lowe, Organist of his Majesty's Chapel Royal, departed this life at Oxford the 11th day of July 1682, in whose place was sworn Mr. Henry Purcell, the 16th of September 1682, but to take place according to the date of his warrant, which was the 14th of July 1682'.[21] The 'Cheque Book', nearly some twenty years previously, had set out the way in which the three organists should share the job: 'Of the three Organistes two shall ever attend, one at the organ, the other in his surplice in the quire, to beare a parte in the Psalmodie and service. At solemne times they shall all three attend. The auncientest organist shall serve and play the service on the eve and daye of the solemne feastes, viz: Christmas, Easter, St. George, and Whitsontide. The second organist shall serve the second day, and the third the third day. Other dayes they shall waite according to their monthes.'[22] Perhaps as a result of the extra salary that this appointment brought Purcell, he and his wife, by now pregnant with their second child, moved to rather more grand quarters in Great St Ann's Lane, Westminster.

During the course of the summer it became apparent that Henry's uncle and father figure, Thomas Purcell, was unlikely to live much longer. In the spring the Lord Chamberlain's department sent the Gentlemen Ushers a warrant 'to swear and admit Dr. John Blow and Nicholas Staggins in the place of composer for the violins in ordinary without fee, to come in ordinary with fee upon the death, surrender or other avoidance of Thomas Purcell',[23] and on 15 May Thomas (in an original letter now in Japan's Nanki Library) appointed his son Matthew as his 'true and lawful attorney to receive all arrears and money which are or which will be due to him from his Majesty's Treasury Chamber, Exchequer, Coffery Office or any other place'.[24] On 4 June he wrote his will, leaving all his goods and his house to his wife Katherine, and on 31 July 1682, he died, and was buried three days later in the cloisters at Westminster Abbey. Thomas had collected an unusually large number of posts: as well as being a Gentleman of the Chapel Royal and a member of the Private Musick, he was a Groom of the Robes, a Composer for the Violins and Marshal of the Corporation of Musicians. Sadness at his death would, in part at least, have been softened by the birth of Purcell's second-born son. The exact date is not known, but he was baptised on 9 August, and so had probably been born a few days earlier. The boy was named John Baptista, perhaps after his mother's father (or maybe after the keyboard virtuoso and composer Draghi, from whom Purcell may have had lessons) but, like Purcell's first child, survived only a few weeks: he was buried on 17 October 1682.

We know that the astonishing five-part verse anthem 'Let mine eyes run down with tears' dates from around 1682; one of Purcell's greatest choral masterpieces, we may wonder if the desolate text, from the Book of Jeremiah, was an expression of his own grief at two recent deaths in the family. Purcell's rich harmonic and melodic language is at its most original, and word-painting abounds. The opening, downward melisma represents tears, 'broken' is desolately set, a 'great breach' is represented by a false relation and the 'very grievous blow' is illustrated by a scotch snap (a back-dotted rhythm) and jagged downward leap. The Italianate, recitativo-style 'If I go forth into the field' (with fine word-painting for the word 'sick') is given to the solo tenor and bass before the five voices unite for the doleful question 'Hast thou utterly rejected Judah: hath thy soul loath'd Sion?'. Purcell uses his five voices with consummate skill, passing short phrases such as 'Why hast thou smitten us?' mournfully, almost angrily, between them, and then uniting at moments such as 'And there is no healing for us'. The simplicity of the first chorus, 'We acknowledge O Lord', comes as a relief from such tensions but desolation quickly returns, with the pleading phrases punctuated with repetitions by each voice in turn of the word 'remember' and the desperate cry of 'O do not disgrace the throne of thy glory'. After the tenor's 'Are there any among the vanities of the Gentiles' a more optimistic mood emerges with 'Art thou not he?' before the final chorus, more hopeful in its mood of resignation, gives grounds for optimism and closes one of the most remarkable pieces of the age.

During the course of the year Purcell had been continuing to copy and write anthems into a now-famous manuscript held in the Fitzwilliam Museum in Cambridge. The works are not individually dated, but there is a much-quoted inscription at the end which reads 'God bless Mr Henry Purcell 1682 September the 10th'. Scholars and others have suggested all sorts of reasons for this remark – for instance that it was Purcell's birthday or his wedding anniversary – but all such theories are speculation. What we do know is that around this time Purcell stopped copying anthems into the volume: his new appointment at the Chapel Royal was taking more of his time and giving him extra responsibilities. The new job also provided exciting new opportunities for his compositions. With a group of string players regularly at his disposal, Purcell now switched his attention to writing church works which provided a prominent role for strings. Between late 1682 and 1685 the result was the composition of over a dozen of the finest accompanied anthems.

But other official duties also beckoned. At the end of October 1682 the return of the Duke of York and King Charles from their annual retreat to Newmarket was celebrated at court in London. The journey home had not been without incident, although what had happened was not fully discovered until some months later. The king had been busily mopping up the remains of Shaftesbury's disintegrating opposition and ensuring that most major cities now had a Tory council. The Duke of Monmouth had, unsuccessfully, been trying to raise support for another exclusionist parliament and Charles had had his troublesome son arrested for disturbing the peace (though he allowed him to be released on bail): Shaftesbury, hearing that new warrants were out for his arrest, fled the country in disguise, and died two months later in Holland. Monmouth managed to inspire another conspiracy against Charles: the plot was that the king and his brother were to be murdered as they travelled by coach from Newmarket to London. The site of the deed was to be a junction, overlooked by the house of a one-eyed drunk called Captain Rumbold, 18 miles (29 km) north of the city. Nearly fifty men, armed with blunderbusses, were meant to have taken part in the Rye House plot, but a fire at Newmarket meant that the king returned earlier than expected. The discovery of the plot launched rumours and tales almost as unlikely as those that Oates had manufactured, but Charles seized the opportunity to disgrace the Whigs and gain further public support. Many of those implicated fled or turned king's evidence.

On 21 October 1682, just four days after the burial of his infant son, Purcell's fourth ode, 'The summer's absence unconcerned we bear', was performed. Beneath its veneer of joyfulness the two-section symphony is one of his more introspective openings, leading directly into a virtuoso bass solo which covers a range of over two octaves. Later in the work comes another of Purcell's gems, the alto solo 'These had by their ill usage drove', set over a four-bar modulating ground bass, and leading into the best string ritornello of the ode.

Such delightful string ritornelli from Purcell's pen were now beginning to be heard at the Chapel Royal; before 1682 we know of the composition of only a handful of his anthems with strings. On stylistic evidence we may guess that 'O praise God in his holiness' dates from around this time. Its text takes the famous words of Psalm 150, which are full of references to music and musical instruments – a subject which always inspired Purcell. He separates each verse of the Psalm with a dancing instrumental ritornello, building up the work to its climax in a most compelling fashion. The harmony of the opening section of the symphony is unusual, even by the composer's individual standards, with the angular lines, complex rhythms and suspensions creating the melancholy mood that is so prevalent in Purcell's early writing. The second section of the symphony introduces a triple-time, dancing theme which continues through much of the anthem and is taken up by the four male soloists. To brighten the texture, and to provide a natural link with the orchestral ritornelli, Purcell writes a descant for the first violin throughout much of the verse sections. Each of the voices is given a solo 'break' as the different instruments on which the Lord is to be praised are introduced – the higher bass for the trumpet, the tenor for the 'cymbals and dances', the lower bass for the 'well-tun'd cymbals' (with an especially 'blue' harmony for the word 'tun'd' and covering a tessitura of over two octaves), and there is a striking harmonic shift from the full quartet for the 'lute and harp'. The build-up is inexorable, with Purcell holding the choir in reserve until the final section, 'Let everything that hath breath praise the Lord'. Gone here are the dotted rhythms, replaced with a huge sweep of sound as the instruments, the soloists and the choir combine in a magisterial, broad ending.

Another verse anthem with strings, 'In thee O Lord do I put my trust', is also thought to date from 1682. Although ground basses are found frequently in the odes, their use in the church music is far less frequent. The symphony to this anthem is based on a six-note, rising scale (similar to the bass used for the song 'O solitude, my sweetest choice') which is heard not only in its cyclical repeats in the bass but in a series of looser developments and inversions in the three upper string parts. The closing section too is anchored by a two-bar ground.

Around November 1682 (the exact date is not noted) the Lord Chamberlain's department issued a notice 'For Mr. Goslin at the Cathedral Church at Canterbury: His Majesty haveing Occasion of your Service you are imediately upon receipt of this to dispose of yor-selfe to come to Court, where you shall receive your further Order from yours. Arlington'.[25] The famous bass John Gostling had been noted as 'sworn and admitted as Gentleman of the Chapel Royal in place of William Tucker, deceased' on 28 February 1679[26] but was an irregular attender in London, for he simultaneously held a number of other appointments, including that of a minor canon at Canterbury Cathedral, vicar of Littleborne, Kent and, in the same county, rector of Hope All Saints. Over the next twelve years John Gostling's range ensured that Purcell composed a considerable number of demanding solos that made full use of both ends of his vocal compass. Gostling was a great favourite with King Charles, who one day is said to have presented him with a silver egg filled with guineas, telling him that 'he had heard that eggs were good for the voice'.[27]

Shortly after this entry comes one reimbursing £100 to Jervaise Price, covering four royal trumpeters and the kettle drummer 'for their losses at sea in their attendance upon his Royal Highness the Duke of York into Scotland and back again in May and June last, 1682: £20 to each of them'.[28] During that journey the royal ship, Gloucester, sank off the coast: 150 people went down with it on 6 May including, it would seem, one of the royal musicians, Walter Vanbright, for his place as 'kettle drummer in ordinary' was taken by Robert Mawgridge on 8 June 1682.[29] On 5 June another entry records £12 'for a new pair of kettle-drums…a pair…having been lately lost at sea'.[30] The trumpeters seem to have survived, albeit without their instruments: 'July 5 1682: Warrant to deliver to Jervas Price, his Majesty's serjeant-trumpeter, four silver trumpets of the same fashion, quantity and proportion as have formerly been delivered, to replace four trumpets lost at sea'.[31]

On Sunday 4 February 1683 Purcell publicly took the sacrament in front of four witnesses, Moses Snow (another court musician), one Robert Tanner, Giles Borrowdell (a churchwarden) and the officiating minister, Bartholomew Wormall. Tanner and Borrowdell also had to swear under oath at Westminster Hall on 16 April that they had seen Purcell take the sacrament, and the two churchmen had to sign the document. Why he had to undergo this rigmarole is unclear: perhaps the procedure was a formality resulting from his recent appointment at the Chapel Royal. Or perhaps suspicions had been raised of Purcell having Catholic leanings; his wife, after all, came from a Catholic family, and the authorities were very wary of Papists.

During 1683 Purcell composed what are assumed to be his first devotional songs for solo voice. These small-scale works were not intended for grand public performance in the Chapel Royal: instead they contained more personal, contemplative sentiments that made them suitable for intimate performances, perhaps in private chapels. The accompaniment was on a similarly small scale, probably played by a chamber organ, but much improved by the addition of a string bass and a theorbo. The author of 'Adam's Sleep' is unknown, but Purcell's 1683 setting displays the characteristics of skilful pictorialization and rapid changes of emotion, subtly controlled, which were to culminate ten years later in masterpieces such as 'The Blessed Virgin's Expostulation'. At the opening words, 'Sleep, Adam, sleep and take thy rest', Adam rests quietly, the voice low in its range but quickly rising as Adam awakes to see what God has done while he

The first edition of 'Adam's Sleep', one of Purcell's most moving devotional songs, published in 1683.

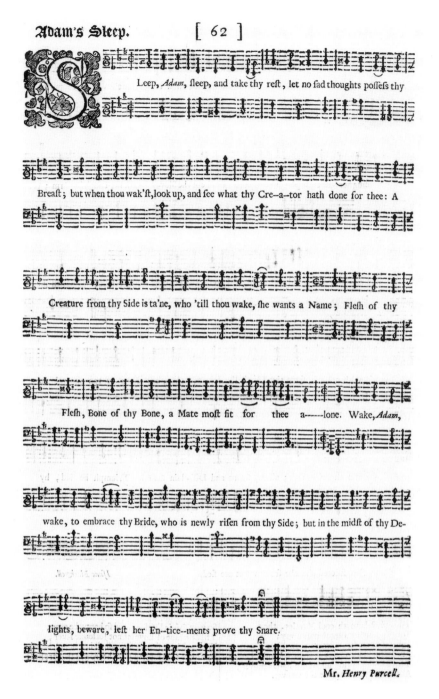

Leep, *Adam*, sleep, and take thy rest, let no sad thoughts possess thy

Breast; but when thou wak'st, look up, and see what thy Cre--a--tor hath done for thee: A

Creature from thy Side is ta'ne, who 'till thou wake, she wants a Name; Flesh of thy

Flesh, Bone of thy Bone, a Mate most fit for thee a-----lone. Wake, *Adam*,

wake, to embrace thy Bride, who is newly risen from thy Side; but in the midst of thy De-

lights, beware, lest her En--tice--ments prove thy Snare.

Mr. *Henry Purcell.*

slumbered. The key brightens as Eve is viewed for the first time: her appearance ushers in the brief seven bars of arioso 'Flesh of thy flesh'. 'Wake, Adam, wake' comes with more emphasis as Adam greets his new bride, but the caveat is delicious in its sinewy, serpentine lines for both voice and continuo lest the new-found joy 'prove thy snare'. 'Let

100

the night perish' (or 'Job's Curse') was a setting of a text by Jeremy Taylor (1613-67) which paraphrases one of the darkest moments from the Book of Job. Job is sitting in a desert, covered in sores and bitterly wishing that he had never been born: he longs for death to relieve his misery, and prays that the Lord will forget the day of his birth, shrouding 'its fatal glory in some sullen clouds'. Word-painting abounds: the music groans to illustrate unborn babies dying in the womb at the mere mention of that awful day; the desert finds 'no sun, no moon, no twilight stars', only 'gloomy darkness': there is a hushed silence before the 'midnight cry' rises up an arpeggio, only to be felled by a harmonic slide at 'oppression'. Job's vision of the calm that death brings to the weary soul, where the prisoner 'sleeps in peace', is illustrated in a short, sad triple-time aria and the desolation of the 'silent chambers of the grave' closes the piece.

Also contained in the same manuscript as 'Job's Curse' is another highly descriptive setting, this time of a 'Religious Elegy' by George Herbert (1593-1633). As well as a gifted poet and an influential academic figure before he turned to the priesthood, Herbert was a keen musician whose regular visits to hear the singing in Salisbury Cathedral he described as 'Heaven upon Earth'. Purcell coloured the ardent sentiments of 'With sick and famish'd eyes' with music of great intensity, enhancing the words with detailed pictorialization. The opening is doleful, the writer's spirit at its lowest ebb, eyes and bones weary to the point of exhaustion: his groans and cries rise with faint optimism through the scale, only for his hopes to be dashed at 'No end?'. His throat is discordantly hoarse, his heart withered at the lowest point of the scale, and his confused thoughts are represented in musical terms. 'Bowels of pity' are suitably discordant, and the singer calls to the 'Lord of my soul', hopelessness represented by reaching only the seventh note of the scale: 'love of my mind' hits a plangent false relation, and the music bows 'down thine ear'. Words 'scatter', sorrows are desolately harmonized, and the music rises as the flames of the furnace increase. The interval on 'griefs' sadly falls, and 'shames' again plunge to the bottom of the voice. The death of Jesus is coloured with mournful harmony. Desperation is replaced by the faintest of optimism as 'thy dust doth stir, it moves, it creeps to thee'. The poet pleads that his lowly prayers will be heard: 'Pluck out thy dart' and, with a monumental discord, 'heal my troubled breast' But the emotional outburst is to no avail: the writer, and Purcell's music, dies.

The verse anthem with strings 'I was glad when they said unto me' also dates from around 1682 or 1683. The text, from Psalm 122, is often associated with coronations (Purcell himself provided a new setting for that purpose in 1685) but would also have been suitable, with its prayers for peace and prosperity, for less formal occasions. Purcell's setting takes an understated line on the celebratory side of the text, picturing instead a contemplative scene of a country apparently at peace with itself. The symphony is ravishing, full of drooping melodic lines: the triple-time second section too has pastoral, even melancholy, undertones beneath its surface jollity, which continue into the opening solo for a high tenor. Purcell's glorious melodies (including two wonderful melismas on the word 'O') are continued in the concluding instrumental ritornello. At the middle of an anthem Purcell often repeats the triple time from the opening symphony, but here instead he introduces a new instrumental section in the tonic minor, after which the soloists quietly appeal for peace and prosperity for Jerusalem. The perfunctory chorus at the end suggests that the composer may have been in a hurry to complete the work.

The sentiments in the text of that anthem are perhaps more relevant than they might at first seem. By 1683 England was finally entering a period of peace and relative prosperity: the financial hardships that had been felt by the royal musicians over the previous twenty years were not yet finished, but conditions were improving. Charles clearly had no intention of being dragged into another war, and courteously replied to every overture from his European allies that he could not afford the expense of battle and did not wish to recall parliament to vote him the extra funds that would be necessary. On 27 April the king demanded a report to investigate the arrears in royal payments for the period 1671-83. The list makes dreadful reading, with dozens of musicians owed sums of money ranging from £16 up to £145. Several of the musicians concerned were already dead, including Matthew Locke, Thomas Purcell and John Jenkins, but the sums owing would have been due to their widows and families. Although many of the arrears had still not been cleared two years after the report, the very fact of its existence shows that the authorities were at last starting to try to deal with the backlog.[32]

If it was not a comment on the improving financial situation, perhaps the arrival of John Gostling at court was the spur for the composition of the verse anthem 'It is a good thing to give thanks'! The instrumental writing is full of the dancing, dotted rhythms that so pleased Charles II since he had first heard them in the French court before his restoration. The symphony is written in the conventional two parts, the first a duple-time, pompous section typical of a French opera overture, and the second a lively triple-time section whose music recurs in many of the subsequent ritornelli. Almost every section from the three solo voices is concluded with an instrumental ritornello, with the midpoint marked by a repetition of the triple-time episode of the symphony. After this interlude Gostling was provided with a recitativo-like section, full of word-painting and making much use of vocal and harmonic colour, and covering an enormous vocal range, from low D on 'very deep' to notes two octaves and more above. As is so often the case in Purcell's church music, the full choir was provided with very little music – in this case just a simple Alleluia at the conclusion. Practicality would seem to have been the reason behind this, for it would not have taken long to teach the choirboys such music.

During May 1683 Purcell embarked on a new commercial venture by offering his first instrumental publication. The *Sonatas of Three Parts* were offered to subscribers for 10s, the post-publication price being 15s. The notice in the *London Gazette* for 24-28 May advised customers to subscribe to 'Mr. Playford's and Mr. Carr's shops in the Temple' and on 11 June another advertisement announced to subscribers that their copies should be collected from Purcell's house in St Ann's Lane. The publication, billed as 'a just imitation of the most fam'd Italian masters', was clearly a success, for in October another advertisement announced that copies were now on sale at three shops in London. The long and much-quoted preface (quite possibly written by the publishers) dedicated the work to the king, and the first violin part also contained an embellished portrait of the composer at the age of twenty-four. At around the same time as the *Sonatas* were published, Playford presented eight more of Purcell's works in the fourth book of *Choice Ayres and Songs*, including the devotional song 'Sleep, Adam, sleep' and the secular songs 'From silent shades' (better known by its sub-title of 'Bess of Bedlam'), 'Let each gallant heart' (a lovely song on a ground), 'Rashly I swore I would disown', 'She who my poor heart possesses', 'When Strephon found his passion vain' and a song written for the earlier stage production of *King Richard the Second*.

Two other songs by Purcell have also been dated to 1683. His response to Thomas Stanley's mournful poem, 'Draw near, you lovers that complain', where an unsettled spirit sadly calls from its grave, is a

Advertisements.

☞ These are to give Notice to all Gentlemen that have subscribed to the Proposals Published by Mr. Henry Purcel for the Printing his Sonata's of three Parts for two Violins and Base to the Harpsecord or Organ, That the said Books are now compleatly finished, and shall be delivered to them upon the 11th of June next: And if any who have not yet Subscribed, shall before that time Subscribe, according to the said Proposals, (which is Ten Shillings the whole sett) which are at Mr. William Hall's house in Norfolk-street, or at Mr. Playford's and Mr Carr's Shops in the Temple; for the said Books will not after that time be Sold under 15 s. the Sett.

marvellous example of the composer's unrivalled skill in setting English text, full of wistful harmony and elegantly shaped vocal phrases for the solo soprano. The appearance of a bass singer, almost as a ghost, in the epitaph 'Here lies to Love and Fate an equal sacrifice', is quite magical. 'Amidst the shades', found in a manuscript also dating from 1683, is another fine song, full of a wealth of detail and pictorialization. Damon is so miserable in his unreciprocated love for Aminda that the birds, sorry for his plight, decide to try to cheer him up with their singing. The birds 'tremble' with a fluttering, downward scale, and their murmuring builds from near-silence, rising as their confidence grows. But their efforts are in vain: nothing can Damon's 'sad soul inspire', and his heart is so much 'by grief oppress'd' that a desolate sigh 'breaks from his breast' and frightens the 'harmless birds, And damps the cheerful choir'. The melisma on 'cheerful' which closes the song could not be more poignant.

On 28 July 1683 the Bishop of London presided at St James's at the marriage of Prince George of Denmark to King Charles's niece, Lady Anne (later Queen Anne). On 19 July Luttrell had recorded that 'in the afternoon, Prince George, brother to the king of Denmark, arrived at Whitehall, and was kindly received by their majesties and their royal highnesses, being come to make his address to the Lady Ann, daughter to his royal highness'. We are not sure at what part of the celebrations Purcell's ode 'From hardy climes and dangerous toils of war' was performed, but the ode was perhaps his finest to date, full of good ritornelli and expressive vocal writing. The symphony was especially notable, inventive and unpredictable in its restrained nobility. In the midst of the anonymous text which welcomes the prince to 'our benigner Isle' Purcell utilized a formula that never failed in any of his odes: that of a solo over a ground bass which is then transformed into a string ritornello. On this occasion the solo voice is a tenor, who weaves a lyrical melody, 'The sparrow and the gentle Dove', which is then capped by a string ritornello of quite melting beauty.

During the summer of 1683 the final details of the previous autumn's bungled Rye House plot had become publicly known and provided the anonymous author of that autumn's royal ode a peg on which to hang his poetry. London celebrated with a special day of thanksgiving on 9 September, and a few weeks later Purcell's ode 'Fly, bold rebellion' was performed. It is not sure whether the performance celebrated the king's return from Winchester (25 September) or Newmarket (20 October), but as the previous year's plot had been hatched to take place as the king returned from Newmarket, the October date might be more likely. Amidst the already-established selection of choruses, trios and solos, interspersed with Purcell's delightfully scored string ritornelli, one movement stands out. Purcell had a great affinity with the alto voice, and in the odes provided it with many of his best movements: it was for this voice that he set 'Be welcome then, great Sir'. Over a three-bar walking ground bass the soloist winds an entrancing melody which develops into an exquisite string ritornello.

There was no let up in Purcell's compositional output. An organization called 'The Musical Society' commissioned him to set a libretto by Christopher Fishburn for their first celebration of St Cecilia's Day on 22 November. The event must have proved popular, for the society had to move to larger premises for their next celebration – although, in the event, they did not call on Purcell again until 1692. The freshness of 'Welcome to all the pleasures', and its highly original string ritornelli, ensured its popularity, and the ode was duly published the next year by John Playford under the title of 'A Musical Entertainment perform'd on November XXII, 1683, It being the Festival of St Cecilia, a great patroness of music'. One movement proved especially successful: the alto solo 'Here the Deities approve the God of Music and of Love' (written over an imaginative ground bass and moving into a most elegant string ritornello) was published separately in 1689 under the title of 'A New Ground' in *The Second Part of Music's Hand-maid*. Fishburn's text gave the composer an opportunity for gentle word-setting at 'Beauty, thou scene of Love', and Purcell obliged with a movement given first to a solo tenor (with a delicious, perhaps slightly malicious, discord at the mention of the lute) which is then taken up by the string ensemble. The quiet ending must have been especially striking to the audience, as 'Iô Cecilia' fades away leaving just the bass instruments and singers to conclude the ode.

Another of Purcell's four odes written to celebrate St Cecilia's Day may well have been written for the same occasion, although 'Laudate Ceciliam' seems to have made far less impact. This is Purcell's smallest ode, both in overall scale and in the forces required for performance. It is also Purcell's only ode written in Latin and, in its use of 'old-fashioned' white notation (minims and larger-denomination note-values) was probably making an intellectual point. Just three voices, alto, tenor and bass, are required, together with two violins and continuo. The style of writing is more akin to that of the verse anthems, and the most noteworthy music occurs in the centre of the ode with a touching duet for alto and tenor, 'Dicite Virgini': the phrase 'O beata Cecilia' ('O blessed Cecilia') is set with especial affection.

The winter of 1683/84 was one of the coldest in living memory, and the Thames completely froze. By January, according to Evelyn, the ice 'had become so thick as to bear not only streets of booths, in which they roasted meat, and had divers shops of wares quite across as in a town, but coaches, carts and horses passed over'.[33] He reported that 'sleds, sliding with skates, a bull-baiting, horse and coach races, puppet plays and interludes, cooks, tippling and other lewd places' made the river look like a 'bacchanalian triumph' while 'it was a severe judgement on the land, the trees not only splitting as if lightning-struck, but men and cattle perishing in divers places, and the very seas so locked up with ice that no vessels could stir out or come in'.[34] Playford used the weather as an excuse to explain the late arrival of

During the winter of 1683/84 the Thames froze.
A contemporary woodcut shows all the activities
and amusements described by Evelyn in his Diary:
a street of booths, roasting oxen, 'sleds, sliding with
skates, bull-baiting and horse and coach races.'
Another engraving resurrects a prophecy by 'Erra
Pater' 'some ages past.'

his fifth book of *New Songs and Ayres*, as 'the last dreadful frost put an embargo upon the press for more than ten weeks'. A further seven of Purcell's songs appeared in this volume, including 'A thousand sev'ral ways I tried' (which had probably been written in 1681), 'Beware, poor shepherds', 'He himself courts his own ruin', 'In Cloris all soft charms agree', a beautiful setting of 'Through mournful shades and solitary groves', 'Let us, kind Lesbia' and 'When gay Philander left the plain'.

The cold that delayed Playford's printers may also have hastened the death of John Hingeston, the royal keeper of instruments: with his demise, Purcell came into another appointment. He had been Hingeston's assistant for ten years and, as his master had grown older, had probably been taking on many of his responsibilities. On 17 December a warrant was issued from the Lord Chamberlain's department to the Gentlemen Ushers 'to swear and admit Henry Purcell as keeper, mender, maker, repairer and tuner of the regals, organs, virginals, flutes and recorders, and all other kinds of wind instruments, in the place of John Hingeston, deceased'[35] and on 16 February 1684 a rather more detailed job description was provided in the warrant which went for the king's signature. From this we can see that the post, albeit a supervisory one, may have been quite time-consuming. Purcell was granted the place of 'keeper, maker, repairer and mender and tuner to all and every his Majesty's musicall wind instruments; that is to say all regalls, virginalls, organs, flutes, recorders and all other kind of wind instruments whatsoever', and was authorized the money necessary for the 'workinge, labouringe, makeing and mending any of the instruments aforesaid... And also lycence and authority to the said Henry Purcell or his assigns to take up within ye realme of England all metalls, wyer, waynscote [boarding or wooden panelling] and other wood and things as shalbe necessary to be imployed about the premisses, agreeing, paying, and allowing reasonable rates and prices for the same. And also in his Majesty's name and upon reasonable and lawfull prices, wages and hire, to take up such workmen, artificers, labourers, worke and store houses, land and water carriages and all other needeful things as the said Henry Purcell or his assignes shall thinke convenient to be used on ye premisses. And also power and authority to the said Henry Purcell or his assignes to take up all tymber, strings and feathers, necessary and convenient for the premisses, agreeing, paying and allowing reasonable rates and prices for the same, in as full and ample manner as the said John

Hingston…formerly had.'[36] The appointment carried a salary of £60 per year[37] but Purcell would have been wise to be a little wary of the finances, for Hingeston was owed, at the time of his death, £124 for various expenses he had incurred as long ago as 1679.[38]

The large-scale verse anthem with strings 'I will give thanks unto thee O Lord' (contained in one of three large volumes now held in the British Library) dates from around 1683 or 1684. Five soloists are required and the symphony (repeated in full at the mid-point) is another fine composition, full of intense harmonies and dropping chromaticism, melancholy yet curiously uplifting in the sadness which pervades so much of Purcell's music. We know that his younger brother Daniel was still a senior chorister at the Chapel Royal in April 1683[39] but it is only supposition that he was the chorister for whom the solo 'I will worship tow'rds thy holy temple' was written. The centrepiece of the anthem is another vocal tour-de-force for John Gostling. Setting 'For though the Lord be high, yet hath he respect unto the lowly', Purcell exploited his colleague's voice over nearly two and a half octaves, probing the highest and lowest extremes of his range. There can be little wonder that this particular anthem is now so rarely performed, but how effective is Purcell's writing when there is a singer able to cope with not only stratospheric and subterranean vocal ranges but also Purcell's subtle textual nuances.

Another of Purcell's best verse anthems with strings, 'My heart is fixed, O God', also dates from around this period. Unusually, he does not start with an instrumental symphony, but instead launches straight into a lively triple-time movement with the three solo voices. The reason for the displaced symphony becomes apparent as the voices command 'Awake up my glory; awake lute and harp': only at this stage do the instrumentalists obediently make their first sounds. Even then, the listeners are kept waiting but, when it finally arrives, Purcell's instrumental writing is stylishly melodic and wonderfully harmonized. King Charles and his royal violinists must have adored such joyful, elegantly dancing music. The build up of the anthem is brilliantly handled. Over the three voices and the continuo at 'Set up thyself, O God' Purcell superimposes the two violins, creating a luxurious six-part texture; the inexorable harmonic progressions at 'and thy glory above all the earth' are anchored by strong continuo foundations before another marvellous string ritornello leads into the Alleluias. Here too Purcell is at his most compelling: melodically innovative, harmonically individual, and building musical tension in a way that none of his contemporaries ever managed.

Purcell's new appointment as royal instrument keeper would have brought him into frequent contact with leading instrument makers, and when the organ builders Bernard Smith and Renatus Harris were both invited to tender to build a new organ for the Temple Church, Purcell found himself invited by Smith to help to try to secure the contract. It was decided that the two rival firms should both set up their instruments in the church, and a committee was formed to try to judge which organ was better. By the summer of 1684 both instruments were in place. The two firms enlisted the best keyboard players available to demonstrate their wares: Harris took on Giovanni Battista Draghi (described by Evelyn as 'that excellent and stupendous Artist')[40] and Smith countered with the strong combination of Purcell and Blow. Public recitals were given by both firms and, according to Tudway, 'they thus continued vying with one another near a twelvemonth'.[41] The problems seem to have been compounded by the rivalry between the Benchers of the Middle Temple and those of the Inner Temple: as one might expect when so many lawyers were involved, the decision process took an inordinately long time. By June 1685 the Middle Temple Benchers had decided that the 'tedious competicion' had run long enough: Smith's organ was best suited 'both for sweetnes and fulnes of Sound (besides the extraordinary Stopps, quarter Notes, and other rarities)' and Harris's effort was 'discernably too low and too weake'.[42] The Inner Temple members disagreed and required that impartial judges should be appointed. The final choice of that 'impartial' judge was an amazing one: George Jeffreys was a man of little learning and a dreadful temper who had nonetheless risen swiftly up the judicial ranks, becoming Lord Chief Justice of the King's Bench and a member of the Privy Council at the age of only thirty-eight. In the case of the Temple Church organ there is no actual record of ill-conduct by Jeffreys, but Dr Burney tells of a report from 'old Roseingrave' that foul play took place on the night before an important part of the contest when supporters of Harris damaged the bellows of Smith's instrument, after which both sides 'proceeded to the most mischievous and unwarrantable acts of hostilities'.[43] It was only in 1688 that Jeffreys finally made his decision, awarding Smith the contract: the Temple paid the maker £1,000, a cost which was split evenly between the two sets of Benchers. Harris's instrument ended up partly in St Andrew's, Holborn, and partly in Christ Church, Dublin.

Dating from around the time of the start of this acrimonious contest (though its subject matter was probably coincidental) is the verse anthem 'Why do the heathen so furiously rage together'. The anthem clearly proved popular, for it survives in at least six manuscript sources besides Purcell's autograph. Psalm 2 (a source to which Handel's librettist turned some forty years later for four movements of 'Messiah') provided a text which begins in a splendidly bellicose fashion. After the opening string symphony a solo bass interrupts with the blustering question, 'Why do the heathen so furiously rage together?', his irritation given added emphasis by the repetition of 'why?'. Two more voices join in as 'the kings of the earth stand up' against the Lord, and lively running figures depict the breaking of bonds and casting away of cords. God's answer to this challenge of his authority is to 'laugh them to scorn', illustrated by the bass's jagged scotch snaps. A longer, more thoughtful section was maybe intended for Purcell's friend John Gostling, whose illustration (over two octaves) of the 'uttermost parts of the earth' would have brought a smile to the royal face.

King Charles appeared determined to relish his last years. He made it clear that he had no intention of recalling parliament, although his own Triennial Act had specified that there should be a meeting at least every three years. The army was kept permanently outside the gates of London to remind the Whigs of the king's power and James was left more or less isolated in Scotland, where he nonetheless governed with much resource. Hyde was sent to Ireland to strengthen the crown's authority by whatever means necessary, and Godolphin, now head of the Treasury, was regulating government expenditure with considerable efficiency. Bruce remarked that 'We had no generals to march themselves at the head of superfluous armies, nor had we one penny raised on land tax',[44] and Charles felt secure enough to release Danby after nearly five years' imprisonment. Judge Jeffreys was instructed to be more lenient with Catholics imprisoned as a result of popish plots. Increasingly Charles 'was not much disposed to be drawn from his divertisements' and went frequently to Winchester, where he impatiently viewed the progress in the building of his new palace. He avoided London as much as he could, although he travelled each Sunday to Hampton Court for a meeting of the Council: instead he went walking on the Downs or visited the Isle of Wight.

As part of his relaxation, Charles commissioned a yacht which he named 'Fubbs', the nickname he gave to his mistress, the Duchess of

Portsmouth. James Hawkins, always a good embroiderer of a story, recounts that on the first voyage John Gostling was invited on board, but did not much enjoy a severe storm in which the boat was caught. On his return to London, so Hawkins says, Gostling selected some verses from the Psalms which were particularly apposite to his experience, and Purcell set them to music. Whether the circumstances are entirely true is debatable, but 'They that go down to the sea in ships' does appear to have been composed around 1684 or 1685, for in Purcell's 'Royal' autograph manuscript[45] the writing breaks off less than a quarter of the way through the work, after which come two blank pages. In his index Purcell lists two anthems to come after this one, but they too were never copied. Instead there follows the coronation anthem for King James, suggesting that the death of Charles II interrupted Purcell's fair copying of the anthem. 'They that go down' was almost certainly written for Gostling, trawling the depths of the sea at the very bottom of his range and rising up 'to heav'n' before being carried 'down again to the deep'.

For Charles's official return to Whitehall in September 1684 after his summer recess the poet Thomas Flatman wrote an ode 'From those serene and rapturous joys' which Purcell set to music. Flatman's ode makes elegantly veiled references to the king's diplomatic 'Summer's progress' and Purcell's reflective setting mirrored the mood of a king enjoying the autumn of his life. The tranquil opening verse, extolling the virtues of the quiet country life now much enjoyed by Charles, was set for solo countertenor (probably William Turner), and then transformed and extended into a string ritornello full of Purcell's inimitable harmonic and melodic twists; the soloist is joined in his welcome by the full ensemble in an elegantly swinging triple time. Two sopranos prettily tell of the king's peaceful conquest of his subjects; 'Welcome as soft refreshing showers' again tested the extremes of Gostling's range. Once more it is a ground bass which produces the most remarkable movement of the ode, 'Welcome, more welcome does he come'. The ground is unusual for Purcell in that it is not continuous, having rests at both the beginning and end. This allows him the option of either covering this hole with the voice or, as he does on a few occasions, inserting a most effective pause. Combined with the ravishing string ritornello that follows the tenor solo, here is yet another example, all the more effective in being quietly understated, of the unique genius of Purcell.

During the autumn of 1684 Purcell seems to have moved house. The churchwardens' accounts for the parish of St Margaret's Westminster show that the composer paid 10s 6d of his yearly rate of 14s for his property in Great St Ann's Lane, suggesting that he moved to his new house, in Bowling Alley East, before the remaining 3s 6d was due to be paid for the fourth quarter of the year. In the margin of the account book is simply written the single word 'Gone'. The rate for the new house remained at 14s, suggesting that it was not a vastly superior dwelling to the previous one, though it would clearly have been advantageous to live a little nearer Westminster Abbey and the Chapel Royal.

The job of Master of the Choristers at the Chapel Royal was not always an easy one: two lines noted in the Lord Chamberlain's accounts for 1 November 1684 for an account payable to 'Dr John Blow, master of the twelve children of the Chapel for his bill' points to an event which must have been distressing to all the members of the Chapel Royal. On one line is the entry 'For a nurse for one of the Children £3. 12s.' and on the next line the bald statement 'For burying Edward Frost £7. 5s. 8d.'.[46]

Two other fine anthems were also completed by this time. 'Praise the Lord, O my soul, and all that is within me' is a large-scale work, full of glorious string writing, surrounded by solo sections in six parts. The falling bass line after the first eight bars of triple-time symphony is especially daring in its harmony. The soloists at first answer each other antiphonally, the upper voices calling to the lower trio, and then join in sumptuous harmony. For the middle section Purcell turns to more introspective writing, and reduces the vocal texture and also provides another of his splendid bass solos for Gostling (it was at around this time that Evelyn described Gostling's voice in his diary as 'stupendous').[47] The exalted position of the heavens is contrasted with the lowly state of the earth, and the east is separated from the west by a suitably spacious interval. The antiphonal trios return, but this time the strings are added, creating a ten-part texture of three choirs who exhort us to 'speak good of the Lord … in all places of his dominion'.

One of Purcell's most famous anthems, the so-called 'Bell Anthem', seems to have acquired its title early on in its career, for an early eighteenth-century copy in the British Library (which is also the source for the second violin and viola parts, missing from the autograph) labels it 'Rejoice in the Lord … with a Symphony imitating Bells (it was originally call'd the Bell Anthem)'. Tudway's score of

1716 simply calls it 'the Bell Anthem'. In the radiant opening prelude (not given the more usual label of 'Symphony') the pealing of bells is everywhere, not only in the bass part, where Purcell's ten-beat ground is repeated five times, but also in the intertwining upper parts, where the juxtaposition of joyous scales with Purcell's wistful harmonies gives the music a bittersweet quality. Three solo voices break in with the eight bars of triple-time they reiterate throughout the anthem, and their new theme is quickly taken up and extended by the strings, the more lyrical middle section of Purcell's symphony contrasting with the dancing opening. At the mid-point the choir joyfully break in, their rejoicing interspersed with the solo trio's exhortation 'and again'. The instruments take the instruction literally, and we are treated to a complete repetition of the symphony. The solo bass brings a more staid tone with his instruction to prayer and supplication, 'Be careful for nothing', and the triple time is replaced by a more thoughtful passage of homophony for 'and the peace of God which passeth all understanding'. The strings develop the idea, but they are interrupted by the return of the soloists' triple section: eight bars of this, repeats of both the instrumental ritornello and the chorus (complete with the soloists' cries of 'and again') bring to a close one of Purcell's most enduringly popular anthems.

The winter of 1684-85 was to be King Charles's last. He was having trouble with his legs, and was unable to take his regular 3-mile walk, but was treating his condition with home-made drugs. The king talked excitedly of the new palace at Winchester, saying that 'I shall be happy this week as to have my house covered with lead'.[48] Purcell is thought to have composed 'O Lord, grant the King a long life' at around the time of Charles's last illness. The work is interesting, for it shows the way in which Purcell's larger-scale works with orchestra were developing: he employs a smaller quantity of text, and repeats phrases and sentences more often than in earlier anthems, dividing the music up into more clearly-defined sections of greater contrast. Musically the most interesting section is the minor key movement, 'O prepare thy loving mercy', where we find the imploring writing that characterizes many of Purcell's great later works: there are phrases which look forward to the 'Te Deum and Jubilate' of 1694.

Evelyn noted that behaviour at court was as loose as ever. 'I can never forget the inexpressible luxury, and profaneness, gaming, and all dissoluteness, and as it were total forgetfulness of God (it being Sunday evening) the King sitting and toying with his concubines

OPPOSITE: *Detail from Morden and Lea's map of London, about 1700, showing four of the streets where Purcell is known to have lived (marked by arrows) – all within a few minutes walk of Westminster Abbey (called here 'St Peter's Abbey').*

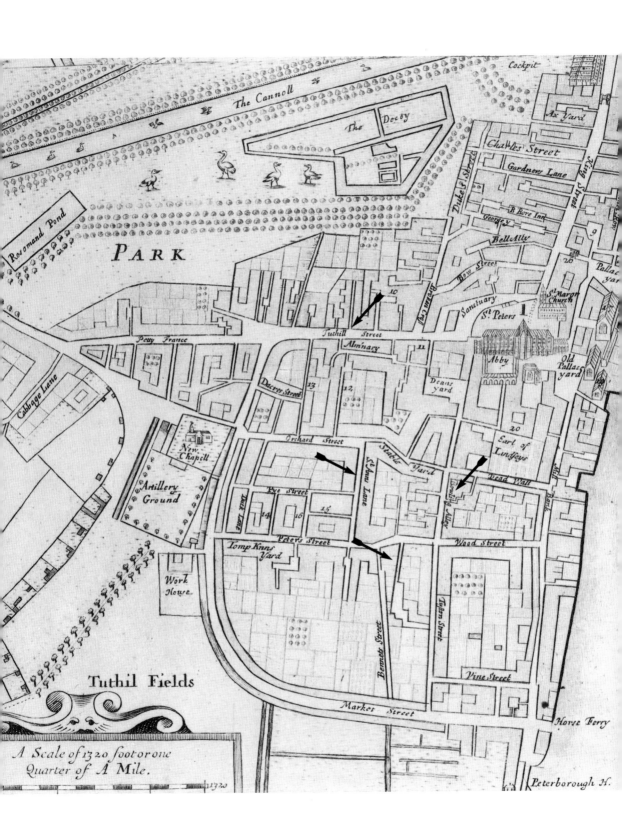

Cockpit

The Cannoll

The Decoy

Ax Yard

Charles Street

Gardners Lane

King Street

B Bore Inn

Georg y

Bell Alley

9

20

Duke Street

Bow Street

Pallac
yard

Rosomond Pond

PARK

Sanctuary

St Margts
Church

Bridg Street

St Peters

10

Petty France

Tuthill Street

Almnary

Abby

Old Pallac
yard

11

Deans
yard

Cabbage Lane

Dacres Street

13

12

20

New
Chapell

Orchard Street

Stable
Yard

Earl of
Lindseys

Dead Wall

Mill Bank

Artillery
Ground

Pye Street

St Ann Lane

Bowling Alley

14

16

15

Dirk Lane

Peters Street

Wood Street

Tomp Kins
Yard

Bennett Street

Tufton Street

Work
House

Vine Street

Tuthil Fields

Market Street

Horse Ferry

A Scale of 1320 foot or one
Quarter of A Mile.

1320

Peterborough H.

Portsmouth, Cleaveland, and Mazarene, &c, a French boy singing love songs in that glorious gallery, whilst about 20 of the great courtiers and other dissolute persons were at basset round a large table, a bank of at least £2,000 in gold before them, upon which 2 gentlemen who were with me made reflexions with astonishment'.[49]

As he was getting up on the morning of Monday 2 February 1685, after an unusually restless night, Charles had a heart attack. Over the next two days he showed signs of recovery, though his doctors attempted cures which now seem barbaric. On the Thursday it became clear that the recovery was to be brief and, in almost his last act, Charles received the last rites of the Roman Catholic church. Only on his death-bed could he admit to his conversion. Just before midday on the Friday he died.

It was the end of an era in many ways. For all his faults, Charles had been a good monarch. Purcell's tribute was the moving lament 'If pray'rs and tears', subtitled 'Sighs for our late sovereign King Charles the Second' and written in much the same graphic style as had been his ode on the death of Matthew Locke. John Evelyn summed up King Charles with his usual elegance: 'A prince of many Virtues, & many greate imperfections, Debonaire, easy of accesse, not bloudy or cruel: his Countenance fierce, his voice greate, proper of person, every motion became him, a lover of the sea, & skillfull in shipping, not affecting other studys, yet he had a laboratory and knew of many Empyrical Medicines, & the easier Mechanical Mathematics: Loved Planting, building, and brought in a politer way of living, which passed to Luxuries & intollerable expense…the History of his Reigne will certainly be the most wonderfull for the variety of matter & accidents above any extant of many former ages: The death of his father, his banishment, his miraculous restauration, conjurations against him; Parliaments, Warrs, Plagues, Fires, Comets…he was ever kind to me & very gracious upon all occasions, & therefore I cannot without ingratitude [but] deplore his losse'.[50]

CHAPTER IV

Changing Fortunes: Purcell and King James, 1685-1688

The coronation of King James II on 23 April 1685 was an opulent affair, and one which was recorded in detail by Francis Sandford.[1] A fifer led the colourful procession, followed by four drummers and the drum-major, eight trumpeters and the royal kettle-drummer: various court employees, marching four abreast, were followed by the eight 'Children of the Choir of Westminster', the twelve boys of the Chapel Royal, sixteen adults of the Westminster choir and the full thirty-two Gentlemen of the Chapel Royal: eight countertenors, eight tenors and sixteen basses. Seven of the Westminster men were also members of the Chapel Royal choir and so supplied deputies who were 'other persons skilled in music'. Behind the choirs came more court and Abbey employees, the full complement of dignitaries of the City of London and the entire English nobility. The magnificent service in the Abbey was accompanied by a large instrumental ensemble, including the Vingt-quatre Violons (for once at their full strength; Sandford's engravings show around twenty string players), and an organ specially set in the Abbey by Purcell in his official capacity as keeper of the instruments, for which the secret service footed the bill for £34 12s: 'To Henry Purcell for so much money by him disbursed & craved for providing and setting up an organ in the Abby Church of Westminster for the Solemnity of the Coronacion and for the removing the same'.[2]

The service was similar to that for Charles II, though now Mary of Modena also had to be crowned queen. Nine anthems were sung, beginning with Purcell's newly-composed setting of 'I was glad when they said unto me' which was sung at the entrance of the king and queen. Sandford reports that 'By this time [i.e. after the peers had

The coronation of James II, in which Purcell played a major role. There were nine anthems, some for five-part and even eight-part choirs; the musicians were placed on both sides of Westminster Abbey and the choir-master in the gallery upper left is clearly finding it stressful to keep them all under control. The illustration is from Sandford's lavish History of the Coronation of James II, *1687*.

W. Sherwin sculp.

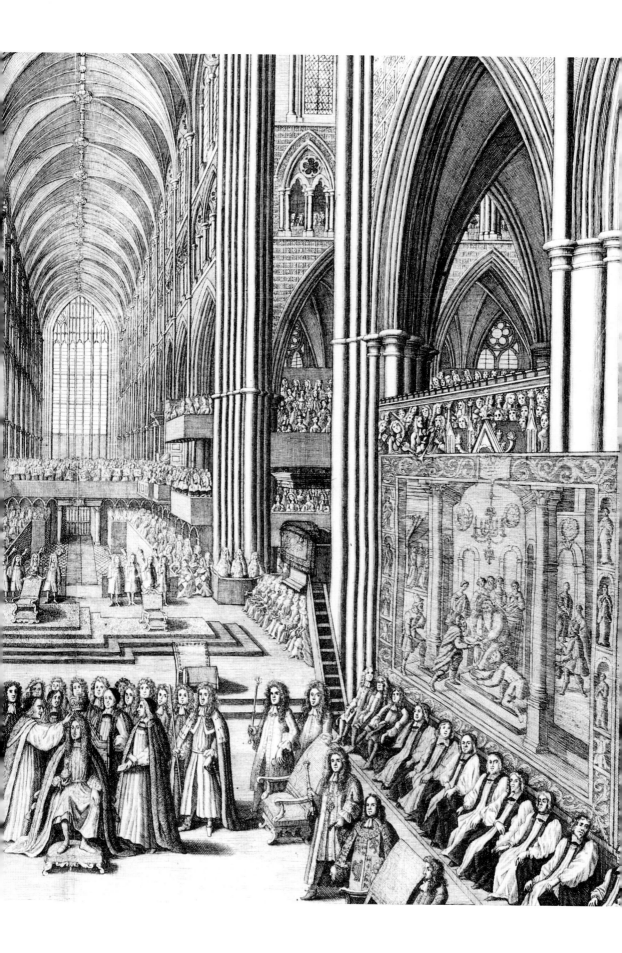

Two more illustrations from Sandford's History: *the Children of the Chapel Royal, with whom Purcell had received his formative musical training, and* (opposite) *the trumpeters and kettle-drummer.*

taken their seats] the King and Queen being entered the Church, were received by the Dean and Prebendaries, who, with the Choir of Westminster, proceeding a little before Their Majesties, sung the full Anthem following', and adds in his margin that the anthem was 'Composed by Mr. Hen. Purcel, a Gentleman of the Chapel Royal'. James Hawkins, the eighteenth-century compiler of the Ely Manuscript now held in the Cambridge University Library, mistakenly ascribed the anthem to John Blow, and it is only fairly recently that its authorship has been restored to Purcell. The anthem was scored for five part choir, including two treble lines. The opening is suitably celebratory, using rich five-part harmony and joyful dotted figurations. At 'O pray for the peace of Jerusalem' the mood alters to one of supplication, the trebles provided with an especially appealing line, before the lighter, triple-time metre returns with the hope that peace and plenteousness will bless the royal palaces. The Gloria begins exultantly, but Purcell saves his compositional tour-de-force for 'world without end': the imitative point (a four-note descending scale) is first treated conventionally, then in inversion (rising), then in inverted augmentation in the bass line (rising at half speed), and finally, as the trebles and altos contest the theme at the original speed in real and inverted form, the tenors take over the single inverted augmentation, and simultaneously the basses triumphantly halve even this speed to present Purcell's theme in double augmentation. The majority of the listeners packed into the Abbey would probably not have realized what compositional skill they were hearing.

The scholars of Westminster School sang the 'Vivats' from the gallery as the queen entered, and Blow's anthem 'Let thy hand be

strengthened' was performed by all the choirs as 'their majesties reposed themselves in their chairs of state'. William Turner's setting of 'Veni, creator' was followed by Henry Lawes' setting of 'Zadok the priest'; Blow's anthem 'Behold, O Lord our defender' was performed before the investing, and afterwards Turner's 'Deus in virtute', followed by William Child's 'Te Deum' and Blow's 'God sometimes spake in visions'. Finally the queen was crowned, and Purcell's specially-composed setting of 'My heart is inditing of a good matter' was 'performed by the whole consort of voices and instruments'. It must have made a splendid climax to a fine pageant.

Purcell's anthem was conceived on the largest scale, using four-part strings, eight-part choir and eight soloists. The sound must have been radiant in a crowded Westminster Abbey, for Purcell's textures, the lower end dominated by three bass chorus parts, the trebles, altos and tenors taking the middle and higher ground and the upper strings giving a sheen to the ensemble, were magnificent. The symphony was grand, its opening section majestically spacious and the triple section dancing through adventurous sequences, exploring sonorities as well as lilting harmonies, and leading straight into the first chorus. Purcell brought in the voices gradually, building up the texture gradually to its full eight parts. Amidst its pomp and ceremony the anthem also included more intimate sections of solo verse writing: we may assume that the treble soloists were the Chapel Royal's two senior choristers, Charles Allison and the young Jeremiah Clarke. The pathos of the verse section 'Hearken, O daughter', especially 'Forget also thine own people', is striking and leads to a sumptuous harmonic moment as all eight voices combine at the cadence leading to the new triple section.

The block chords of 'Praise the Lord, O Jerusalem' would have echoed throughout Westminster Abbey, waking even the most tired dignitary (the service would by now have lasted several hours), for here is Purcell at his grandest, writing in twelve parts. The final bars of the Alleluia too must have sounded stunning, with block chords spread over three octaves.

James's initial statements, made to the council and then printed, suggested that he had little desire for a radical change of direction from the policies of Charles's last years: 'I shall make it my endeavour to preserve this government both in church and state as it is by law established. I know the principles of the Church of England are for monarchy ... therefore I shall take care to defend and support it'. Loyal addresses rolled in from all over the country, and the lingering doubts of many Tories on the prospect of a Catholic king were removed. James retained most of Charles's court officers in their places, and was surprisingly magnanimous in forgiving those who had supported exclusion, provided that they now admitted the error of their ways. He believed that those who held profitable offices under the crown were obliged by both duty and self-interest to serve the king well, and so long as they did so, his duty was to uphold their actions and preserve them in their employment. Rochester was the main promotion, and was now made chief minister.

James was far more businesslike than Charles had been, especially in financial matters. He kept a careful check on his revenue and expenditure, receiving a weekly account from the Exchequer: he cut down on household expenses and did what he could to fight waste and corruption in the administration. He immediately began to settle the debts which Charles had run up: during his short reign James repaid nearly a million pounds. He paid his servants promptly. Where Charles had been amused by drunkenness and loose living, James strongly disapproved. Away from his passion for hunting, James's great pleasure was his army, and he thoroughly enjoyed putting his soldiers through their paces, especially in mock battles. The more noise there was, the better he liked it. In his private life, when he had converted to Catholicism he had tried to hide his strong sexuality, no longer openly pursuing women; when he became king he sent away his mistress, Catherine Sedley, but she soon returned and a scandal erupted in 1686 when James created her Countess of Dorchester.

On paper, James's reign should have been more stable than that of Charles. The people of England, the Civil War still in their memories,

were docile and peaceable, Scotland and Ireland were quiet, and the sea largely isolated England from the dynastic power politics of the Continent. But, despite his willingness to work hard, James lacked intelligence and, rather more significantly, did not possess the instinct to decide what was and was not politically possible. He also had no appreciable sense of humour. He was ill-advised, especially by Sunderland who, ambitious and unencumbered by his own principles, committed himself to (and tried to anticipate) the wishes of his king. James made his principal aim the advancement of Catholicism. In a country where only one per cent of the population was estimated to be Catholic, and where the Catholics had, rightly or wrongly, been blamed for almost everything that had gone wrong during the reign of Charles, this was a recipe for disaster. James rarely listened to the advice of either parliament or the Privy Council: instead he relied on the counsel of servants such as Sunderland. They told him only what they believed he wanted to hear.

As a Catholic head of a Protestant church, James's position was anomalous and it might have seemed logical for him to divest himself of his authority over the Anglicans or to submit to the Pope. James

The banquet in Westminster Hall after the coronation was accompanied by a string band. Sandford's engraving is one of the very few illustrations of such an ensemble in action.

had no intention of doing either, although in September 1685 he decided to establish diplomatic relations with Rome. His chosen ambassador, the Earl of Castlemaine, was a typically poor selection: Castlemaine was a man of much religious enthusiasm, little common sense and no diplomatic experience. Barillon remarked, rather acidly, that it was strange to choose a man whose principal claim to fame was that his wife had been one of Charles II's mistresses. But, in reopening formal contact with the Vatican, James was by no means prepared to submit fully to the Pope. For instance, he immediately insisted that he, not Rome, should have the power to appoint all bishops; indeed, the story of James's relations with Rome over the next four years proved to be 'one of ignorance, arrogance and irrelevant self-gratification'.[3]

Fairly quickly James had to deal with two separate uprisings which had both started from Holland. Early in May the rebel Earl of Argyll set sail with three ships loaded with arms and landed in Scotland. His attempted uprising was quickly defeated and he was executed. Four weeks later the Duke of Monmouth sailed from Holland with four ships, again laden with arms, and landed (on 11 June) at Lyme on the south coast. There had been considerable support for him there during the exclusion crisis. While King William waited anxiously in Holland (a usurper on the English throne would almost certainly prevent his own and Mary's accession) Feversham, James's commander-in-chief, played a waiting game, attempting to prevent recruits joining Monmouth's pick-up army. On 5 July at Sedgemoor Monmouth launched a night-attack on Feversham's forces but bungled the attempt. Once they had got over their surprise, Feversham's forces, better trained and better armed, defeated the opposition. Monmouth was captured on the morning of the 8th and, despite desperate pleas, was executed as a traitor a week later. A bloody revenge on Monmouth's followers resulted: as an example to those who might think of similar uprisings, Colonel Kirke and his soldiers slaughtered over a hundred people in Taunton, and the notorious Judge Jeffreys was sent out to the 'Bloody Assizes' where, even by his own horrific standards, his verbal violence was worse than usual, and his stretching of the laws of treason more warped than ever. He is thought to have sentenced at least three hundred people to be hanged and around eight hundred to be sold into slavery to the West Indies. For his exemplary service to the crown Jeffreys was rewarded with the office of Lord Chancellor. As news of the slaughter filtered through to Holland, the Dutch were horrified.

For the royal musicians, Purcell included, the begining of a new royal regime must have caused some uncertainty. James had made it clear that most previous appointments would be continued but, with the large amounts of administration that the new king had to oversee, the formal warrants and certificates were slow in coming. On 25 March Nicholas Staggins was confirmed 'in the place and quality of master of the musick in ordinary to his Majesty King James II'[4] and nothing more was then heard for two months. The next appointment was made on 16 May when the Gentlemen Ushers issued a certificate appointing 'Gervice Price, Esq., is sworn and admitted as serjeant of all trumpeters, drummers and fifes in England and other dominions';[5] over the next month, sixteen other trumpeters were appointed. The fact that the four sets of four trumpeters were appointed before other royal musicians shows their importance in the royal household: their ceremonial function at home and abroad was a vital piece of royal pageantry. Perhaps Price also worked rather harder to get his trumpeters officially installed than did Staggins. It was not until 31 August that the Lord Chamberlain (now the Earl of Aylesbury, replacing the deceased Earl of Arlington) notified the Gentlemen Ushers of warrants for thirty-four 'musicians for his Majesty's private musick in ordinary, with fee and salary', including string and wind players, John Abell and William Turner as countertenors, Thomas Heywood as a tenor, Gostling and Bowman as 'Bases', Henry Brockwell as 'Keeper of the Instruments', John Blow as composer and Henry Purcell as 'Harpsicall'.[6] The actual certificates of employment emerged over the next months; Purcell's was dated 9 October. Instructions to the Treasury to pay the players were sent on 21 October; Staggins was to be paid £200 per annum, and the other musicians £40.[7] James's desire for better administration had its benefits, and instructions were passed to the Chamberlain 'for the better regulating the Charges Wee shall hereafter allow to our Officers and Servants above staires to defray their Rideing Wages and Lodgeings when they attend us' with a daily allowance of three shillings being set for Gentlemen of the Chapel and musicians (though after the first week at Hampton Court or Windsor only half the allowance would be payable).[8]

Some writers have erroneously suggested that, under James, Purcell lost various of the court positions he had held during the reign of Charles II, quoting as their evidence the lack of the same detailed payment records as Charles's treasurers had kept. Despite the establishment of a separate Catholic chapel, *Angliae Notitiae, or the present state*

of England records in 1687 that three organists were still employed to serve in the Chapel Royal, and that Purcell was one of them. We also know that services were still held in the Chapel, and John Blow, the Master of the Choristers, continued to receive payments to maintain his choristers (now ten in number); choristers whose voices had broken still received the customary payments on their retirement. Individual payment records would have been kept by Thomas Blagrave, Clerk of the Cheque at the Chapel Royal, and would not have made their way into the full treasurer's accounts: these relatively minor records remain still to be discovered or more probably have been lost, possibly in the fire of 1698 which completely destroyed the Whitehall chapel. Purcell also maintained his position as tuner of the

LEFT: *The Queen's Chapel, St James's, in 1688. Inigo Jones was originally commissioned to build the Chapel when it was hoped that the heir to the throne, the future Charles I, would marry the Infanta of Spain. This never happened, but subsequent queens – Henrietta Maria and Catherine of Braganza – were also Catholic. When James II, himself a Catholic, became king, he built himself a new Chapel in Whitehall.*

RIGHT: *James's queen, Mary of Modena, by Sir Peter Lely. James had two daughters by his first wife, Anne Hyde: they became Queen Mary and Queen Anne. Mary of Modena was the mother of James, the Old Pretender.*

royal instruments, although for some while this job was carried out on a freelance basis; under James's new, more efficient administration payments for this work may have been transferred to the Lord Steward's department. In the re-shuffled Private Music Purcell was, as has already been noted, now officially a harpsichordist, rather than a composer (that job had fallen to John Blow), but it was quickly seen that he was going to contribute compositions for use at court.

King James certainly caused a major shift in Purcell's compositional output. With Charles the Chapel Royal had been an important focus, and Purcell had written large amounts of music for it. Faced with a king for whom the Anglican church was an increasing nuisance, Purcell's emphasis altered. During 1685 and 1686 it seems that he did not write a single anthem for the Chapel Royal: indeed, he only composed a total of nine anthems during the reign of James. Instead, his religious music turned towards developing the devotional song. In the early 1680s these works had usually been scored for a consort of voices. In 1683 he had briefly experimented with a more personal, introspective style with a solo devotional song, 'Sleep, Adam sleep', and it was to this model that he turned. The new, solo devotional songs were similar to some of the Italianate secular songs, including extended passages of semi-recitative which are sometimes separated by sections of arioso. Perhaps because the texts are always heartfelt in their religious fervour, often graphic and frequently mournful – textual elements which offered Purcell inspiration for fine writing – many of the devotional songs show Purcell's solo vocal writing at its best. Dating these intimate, chamber works with more than a *terminus ante quem* is difficult, for there is no record of the first performance of most: many appeared in the publication *Harmonia Sacra; or Divine Hymns and Dialogues*, published by Henry Playford in 1688.

'Awake and with attention hear', which dates from 1685, is by far the longest of Purcell's devotional songs, taking well over ten minutes to perform. It requires a considerable degree of stamina and only a singer of some strength would have been able to do it full justice; no other work quite like it survives. Purcell seems afterwards to have altered his concept of the form. The poem is a descriptive, classical work by Abraham Cowley (1618-67) which is full of bloodthirsty sentiments. Cowley was the leading English poet of his time, a notable character (briefly imprisoned on suspicion of being a spy) and was responsible for introducing the irregular Pindaric ode form which was later taken up by Dryden and others. Purcell's music alternates between sections of semi-recitative and arioso: everywhere word-painting abounds. The opening is dramatic: the 'drowsy world' is commanded to listen as the 'loud prophet' brings his message. The two poles are to 'suppress their stormy noise' – even the raging sea is miraculously calmed. A 'dreadful host of judgements' rises inexorably up the chromatic scale to 'scourge the rebel world', marching around in a winding melisma; the sword of God wreaks its dreadful revenge, copious amounts of blood are spilled and eventually nothing is left but bones. In the first section of arioso it is calmly announced that a sacrifice will be prepared by God, not of animals, but of mankind. In a momentous section, we hear that mankind will violently fall, and

*By or after John Closterman: a portrait of Purcell almost certainly painted
in the last year of his life (an engraving of it – reversed – is dated 1695:*
see p. 228)

Whitehall in 1674, when Purcell was fourteen. We are looking from St James's Park in the direction of the Thames. On the left is the Banqueting House, the only building in the picture that still stands. To its right is the Holbein Gate built by Henry VIII in 1532. (We are looking at it sideways – it leads from Whitehall proper on the left to 'the Street' running through to Westminster Abbey.) The outdoor staircase belongs to the Tiltyard Gallery. There is a covered passage to the right; further back the large turreted and battlemented building is the old Tudor tennis court, now refitted as lodgings for the Duke of Monmouth. To the right of that is the Cockpit theatre, its interior redesigned before the Civil War by Inigo Jones, its exterior adorned with figures of animals on high pedestals. General Monck lived here until his death in 1670 and it was demolished in 1675.

even 'Nature and Time shall both be slain'; the 'wide-stretched scroll of heaven' will burn and the sun will 'headlong into the sea descend'. A dolorous minor section tells that the few people who remain will be poisoned by the debris. The 'destroying angel' rhythmically struts his territory in a short section of arioso, surveying his chosen ground before an even more desolate scene of destruction is outlined, with serpents writhing in the streets, wolves howling, and the 'wing'd ill omens of the air' living in the 'gilt chambers' of mankind; even the leopard 'does not stay'. Unburied ghosts 'sadly moan' and satyrs cackle horribly at their groaning discomfort. To complete the destruction, evil spirits 'dance and revel in the mask of night'. Mankind's folly has ensured that the world has been turned topsy-turvy. Purcell's genius for setting words was rarely given such black material!

At court, although Blow was named as court composer, it was to Purcell that James turned for his first royal ode, set to an anonymous text, 'Why are all the Muses mute?'. It was probably performed on 14 October 1685 at Whitehall, soon after the court had returned from Windsor. According to the diarist Narcissus Luttrell, the occasion was marked by 'publick demonstrations of joy, as ringing of bells, store of bonefires, &c', and there was more to celebrate, as Monmouth's rebellion (which is mentioned) had recently been suppressed. The opening of the ode is unique as, at first glance, there appears to be no overture: Purcell's pictorialization of the text 'Why are all the muses mute? Why sleep the viol and the lute? Why hangs untun'd the idle lyre?' leads him to begin, magically, with a lone solo tenor. The singer manages to wake the chorus ('Awake! 'tis Caesar does inspire And animates the vocal quire'); the orchestra are harder to rouse but, when it finally arrives, their symphony is of the highest order. After this rather unconventional start the ode settles into the more established pattern of solos, duets, trios, choruses and Purcell's deliciously scored string ritornelli. For the countertenor William Turner Purcell provided one of his finest ground bass arias, 'Britain, thou now art great'. He used his well-tried formula – a ground bass, an alto solo and then a string ritornello – and once again proved the system's never-failing success with yet another unforgettable movement. The bass singer for the performance must have had an astonishing voice (we can guess that it had to be John Gostling), for his splendidly warlike 'Accursed rebellion reared his head' covers a range of over two octaves, with Caesar 'from on high' dropping to subterranean levels for the depiction of Hell. The mid-point of the ode is

OPPOSITE: *James II (portrait by Sir Godfrey Kneller) succeeded his brother in 1685. Purcell and the other court musicians were more secure financially (James was a better administrator than Charles) but patronage was less abundant. In particular, the services of the Chapel Royal were less needed because James imported foreign musicians for his Catholic chapel. Purcell composed only nine anthems during the whole of his reign.*

marked by a delightfully poised ritornello minuet, with Purcell's string writing at its most courtly and elegant, and the Monmouth rebellion is despatched by a tenor solo and chorus. Europe's fate is weighed in the balance by two basses; neither Britain nor Purcell's writing is found wanting. The ode ends perfectly: the lyrical high tenor solo 'O how blest is the Isle' develops into a ravishing string ritornello, full of Purcell's harmony at its most glorious. But there is even better to come. The composer appears at his greatest in the final chorus with a valediction worthy of Dido herself. The ending drops through the chromatic scale in devastating fashion: there is no more poignant ending in all Purcell's odes.

Purcell may well have been working on another ode at the same time: the similarity of the scoring of 'Raise, raise the voice' with 'Laudate Ceciliam' (dated 1683) has given some commentators grounds for believing the two odes may have been performed, or at least were intended to be performed, in the same concert. But 1683 also saw the first performance of the St Cecilia's Day ode 'Welcome to all the pleasures', and it would seem unlikely that Purcell would have written three odes for the same day in the same year. The 'Ritornello Minuet' was published in the second part of *Musick's Hand-Maid* in 1689, arranged for harpsichord, but the ode clearly dates from well before that time, and 1685 has been suggested as a likely year. The centrepiece of 'Raise, raise the voice' is a jaunty setting of 'Mark how readily each pliant string', where Purcell's insistently cheerful four-bar ground forms the foundations for a splendidly characterful soprano solo. The 'pliant string' prepares itself to a jazzy rhythm, the offering 'of some gentle sound' slinkily rises up the chromatic scale and, invited by the words 'Then altogether', first the two violins join the texture 'in harmonious lays', and then the whole chamber ensemble – with a wonderful line for the tenors. The best is yet to come, for the two violins' closing ritornello caps the movement with exotic instrumental writing. Here is music of considerable originality, apparently breaking all the rules of harmony and counterpoint and still somehow ending in the right key!

Another devotional song, 'Hosanna to the highest', gives us little clue as to its time of composition but it is scored, like 'Awake and with attention', for solo bass, so it may come from this same period of reorientation and experimentation with new forms. Only one score survives, and this is a manuscript now in Lichfield Cathedral Library which dates from well after Purcell's lifetime (1750). Here, amongst all the church music, is one of the finest examples of a Purcellian ground bass: four bars long, its simplicity and stark modality is hypnotic in fifteen slow-moving repetitions. Over this harmonic anchor a solo bass voice weaves its melodic spell, with Purcell treating the text not in an extrovert manner, but with controlled, quiet ecstasy: to match a text which tells not of an earthly marriage, but one greater, conceived in heaven, everywhere we find marvellous word-painting and expressive harmony. For over four minutes a solo bass takes centre stage and so the entry of a second voice, the unearthly sound of a high tenor, at 'be ravish'd, earth', is breathtaking. Earth and heaven are linked as the piece climaxes at 'heav'n never show'd so sweet a bridegroom, Nor earth so fair a bride'. Purcell often beguiles the listener, but here he provides an example of his genius at its most startlingly original.

Tom D'Urfey, a playwright and minor poet, who wrote the words for some of Purcell's songs and an Ode for Trinity College, Dublin. Purcell wrote the music for six of D'Urfey's plays.

Purcell's compositions increasingly appeared in printed editions, and part of the gap caused by writing less music for the church was filled by composing secular vocal music. During 1685, Joseph Hindmarsh printed three of Purcell's settings of Tom D'Urfey's verse, 'Farewell, ye rocks', 'Sit down, my dear Sylvia' and some music from *Sir Barnaby Whigg*, and John Playford printed twelve of Purcell's scurrilous (or just plain rude) catches in *Catch that catch can*. Taking rather more serious music, John and Henry Playford had, at the end of 1684, issued the first two books of *The Theatre of Music*, including fourteen of Purcell's songs. They included the lutesong-like 'Farewell, all joys' and the lilting 'In vain we dissemble', 'Love is now become a trade' (probably intended to be sung in a rough, street-trader's accent), a lovely setting of 'My heart, whenever you appear', 'Ye happy swains, whose nymphs are kind' and, in the second volume, 'Cupid, the slyest rogue alive', a touching setting of 'If grief has any pow'r to kill', 'Phyllis, talk no more of passion', 'They say you're angry' (a version of Abraham Cowley's poem 'The Rich Rival'), one catch, the 'Serenading Song', 'Soft notes and gently rais'd accent' (which includes an instrumental symphony for two flutes), 'When, lovely Phyllis, thou art kind' and the 'Pastoral Coronation Song' 'While Thyrsis, wrapt in downy sleep'. This last song, a well-crafted miniature much in the tradition of Dowland, and with a text full of pastoral allusions and royal imagery, was probably written to celebrate the coronation of King James. In that same collection, Purcell's setting of Tom D'Urfey's 'Musing on cares' shows the scurrilous wit that made D'Urfey so popular in the late seventeenth century and a lighter side to the composer's writing. Purcell's strophic setting recounts the pastoral scene witnessed in 'a sad cypress grove' when a young – and clearly naive – shepherd asked the conventional trilogy of gods 'how he might be saved'. Virtue recommended a pious and well-behaved course, Fame suggested defending king and country, but Love outvoted the other two in advising the shepherd to 'get a mistress fair and young' and make hay 'constantly and long'. As a lively triple-time replaces the slower metre of the first two verses the shepherd goes straight to the cottage of Sylvia and tells her (in Purcell's coyly-set 'soft expressions') what he had been instructed to do to achieve 'the way to heavenly joys'. She, who 'with piety was stored' didn't waste a moment, and 'took him at his word'.

James was continuing to make himself thoroughly unpopular. In the first weeks of his reign he had ordered the Anglican bishops to forbid the clergy to preach seditious sermons. The command appears to have been carried out very half-heartedly and some clergy were preaching openly hostile sermons. In May 1686, matters came to head when the rector of St Giles-in-the-Fields in London preached a sermon which James found offensively anti-Catholic. He demanded that the rector be sacked; the command was refused. On 8 July 1686, having clearly failed to persuade the bishops to execute the disciplinary powers that he (as head of the Church of England) had vested in them, James issued a warrant to establish an ecclesiastical commission, able to visit and discipline ecclesiastical persons and institutions, including the universities. This was another ill-judged move. The king began to persuade himself that if the Anglicans (as he saw it) were abandoning him, his alternative was to offer a general toleration and seek support amongst the Dissenters. The Tory gentry remained opposed to toleration for Catholics and the Anglican clergy were insulting his religion, so James countered by criticizing the Church of England not only for opposing his wishes, but also for persecuting Dissenters.

James could have achieved his aims simply by not enforcing the laws penalizing Catholic and Dissenting worship: instead he determined to have the penal and Test Acts formally removed. The Tory government that had been elected in 1685 would clearly not do so; the king's only move was therefore to call a general election. The shires and boroughs were strongly Tory, and would certainly return another Tory House of Commons. James needed therefore to replace the current office-holders with Dissenters and Catholics. Under the Test and Corporation Acts, these groups were excluded from such offices.

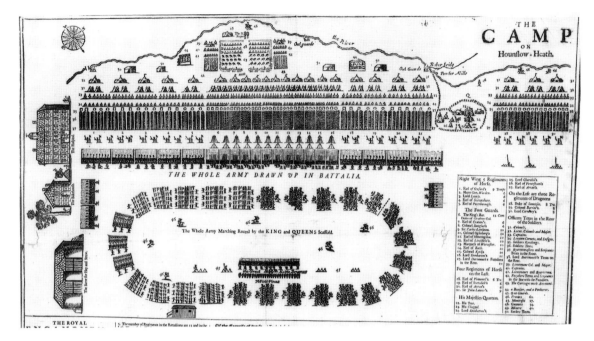

James decided that he would have to use the royal prerogative of dispensing and suspending powers. In November 1686 he prorogued parliament and started his recruitment. Seventy Catholic army officers were pardoned for having accepted commissions without taking the Test. Twelve judges assured him that he was entitled to do this, but were divided on whether the seventy officers would be immune from taking the Test again in the future. James decided that he would have to establish the fact in law by bring a test case. To ensure his victory he dismissed six judges who might have ruled against him: the ruling went the king's way, but he was storing up further trouble for the future.

It was for an increasingly disliked monarch that Purcell set the welcome ode 'Ye tuneful Muses', probably to celebrate the birthday of King James on 14 October, although some scholars have suggested that the work may also have celebrated the return of the court from Windsor to Whitehall two weeks earlier. The diarist Narcissus Luttrell recorded that 'The 14th, being his majesties birth day, was observed with great solemnity; in the morning his majesties four troops of guards were drawn up in Hide park, all new clothed very finely; and the day concluded with ringing of bells, bonefires and a ball at Court'.[9] The anonymous author provided Purcell with a text containing plenty of references to music and musical instruments – material which rarely failed to inspire the composer – and Purcell obliged with some splendid music. The overture was a good one, and the tenor solo and chorus 'Be lively then and gay' utilized the popular song tune

James's popularity waned steadily throughout his reign. By June 1686 dissatisfaction had reached such a pitch that troops were quartered on Hounslow Heath in readiness for a revolution.

'Hey boys, up go we' as a bass to the solo, as an instrumental counter-point to the chorus, and then as a bass to the dancing instrumental ritornello which concludes the section. The bass singer for 'In his just praise' must have had a range of over two octaves which Purcell exploited to the full, and the composer's humour continued into the next section where the chorus's exhortation 'Tune all your strings' leads to a furious scrubbing on the violins' open strings. The jewel of the ode was 'With him he brings the partner of his throne', sung by the countertenor (and composer) William Turner. Over a four-bar ground bass the queen's beauty is praised, with characterful writing for 'There beauty in its whole artillery tries' before the ground modulates up a fifth and Purcell provides a fine string ritornello.

Away from court in 1686 Purcell's music appeared in two publications. A second, much enlarged edition of *The Pleasant Musical Companion* (dated 1686 but which may well have got through the printing presses and into John Playford's hands in October 1685) contained catches, songs and glees for two and three voices, and the third book of *The Theatre of Music*, printed for Henry Playford, contained five songs: 'A grasshopper and a fly', 'Come, dear companions of th'Arcadian fields', 'I saw fair Cloris all alone', 'Sylvia, 'tis true you're fair' and 'Whilst Cynthia sung': this last song is a good miniature in which Purcell's two strophic verses show his individual melodic lines and imaginative word-painting. In *The Delightful Companion or Choice New Lessons for the Recorder or Flute* Purcell is credited with having written the tune 'Lilliburlero', but it is much more likely that he simply supplied a bass line and harmonization. We know that during the summer once again sadness descended on the Purcell household as Purcell buried another young son, Thomas, in Westminster Abbey on 3 August. In seventeenth-century England such tragedies were a regular, accepted feature of life.

For a prolific composer who had always worked with such frantic energy, Purcell's compositional workload during 1686 appears, on paper, to be unusually slight. Most probably he was at work on at least some of the devotional songs which were to go into *Harmonia Sacra; or Divine Hymns and Dialogues*, published by Henry Playford in 1688. We have no knowledge of the order in which these works may have been written, but two of the songs set a pair of poems by William Fuller, Bishop of Lincoln. 'Thou wakeful shepherd' is titled 'A Morning Hymn' and 'Now that the sun hath veiled his light' is 'An Evening Hymn'.

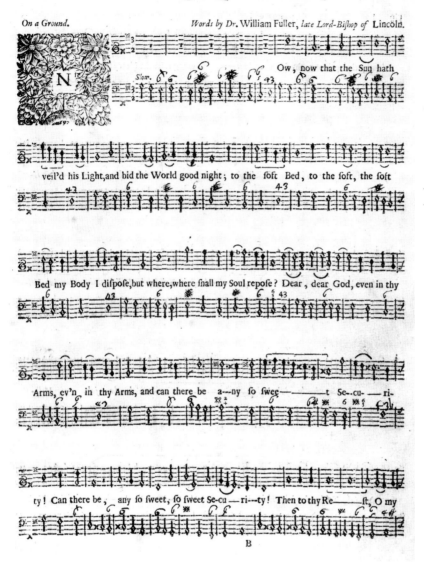

An EVENING HYMN.

On a Ground.   Words by Dr. William Fuller, late Lord-Bishop of Lincoln.

Ow, now that the Sun hath veil'd his Light, and bid the World good night; to the soft Bed, to the soft, the soft Bed my Body I dispose, but where, where shall my Soul repose? Dear, dear God, even in thy Arms, ev'n in thy Arms, and can there be a---ny so swee------t Se-cu---ri-ty! Can there be, any so sweet, so sweet Se-cu---ri---ty! Then to thy Re------st, O my

B

'An Evening Hymn' was published in 1688 in the collection called Harmonia Sacra, or Divine Hymns and Dialogues. *It is a fine example of Purcell's inventive treatment of a text and skilful use of a ground bass. Note how he (not the poet) repeats the word 'soft' in line 2 in a series of expressive phrases. The handwritten continuo figures in this copy date from Purcell's time.*

Comparison of Fuller's text of the 'Morning Hymn' (as published in Nahum Tate's collection *Miscellanea sacra: or poems on Divine & Moral Subjects)* with Purcell's version shows that the composer made numerous changes while setting the poem: indeed, nearly half of the words in Purcell's setting are not by Fuller, but by the composer-turned-poet. The result is a poignant text that is more contemplative and, in the end, less positive than Fuller's. The singer wakes, by God's goodness, to see another day, and offers up his humble 'best morning sacrifice': Purcell provides a glorious melisma at 'And sing thy praise'. After such brief confidence, regret quickly returns as the singer remembers 'the time I have mis-spent in sinful merriment' (Fuller writes 'in senseless scenes of merriment'): the innocent are pictured at the lowest end of the voice, and 'With joy I'd sing away my breath' is set to a short burst of lilting arioso, but the breath is, quite literally, stopped to usher in the final desolate question, 'Yet who can die so to receive his death?'. The 'Evening Hymn' is one of Purcell's greatest miniatures, set to one of his most eloquent ground basses: over this hypnotic anchor the singer weaves a magical melody, calmly resigned not only to end the day in peace, but also ready to accept the blessings of heaven. At 'to the soft bed my body I dispose' Purcell caresses 'soft' in a series of repetitions, and the ground optimistically modulates at 'and can there be any so sweet security' before calmly falling back at 'then to thy rest, O my soul'. The extended final series of Alleluias is personal, far removed from the extrovert settings we so often associate with that word.

Payments to musicians were still dreadfully in arrears, and on 21 September 1686 a request was made to James: the sums owed were alarming. 'Whereas it appears that £2,484. 16s. 3d remains due to the respective musicians to his late Majesty whose names follow, for the arrears of their liveries incurred during his late Majesty's reign — after making such retrenchment throughout as was intended by his late Majesty and is commanded by his present Majesty to be observed in cases of arrears of this nature, these are to desire your Lordship, out of the money which is or shall be imprested to you at the receipt of the Exchequer of the new impositions on tobacco and sugar, to pay all the sums due to the said musicians'.[10] Another note from the Lord Chamberlain to the Treasurer of the Chamber, dated 9 November 1686, requests £19 11s 6d for Nicholas Staggins for 'faire writing of a composition for his Majesty's coronation day': even for that important day, payments were still way behind.

When a new organ was installed in the church of St Katharine Cree in 1686, expert opinion was needed both to ensure that Bernard 'Father' Smith had completed the instrument to the necessary standards, and also to appoint an organist. The vestry minutes state that 'it is ordered that Mr. Joseph Cox do procure Mr. Purcell, Mr. Barkwell and Mr. Moses, masters in music, and Mr. White, organmaster, or such other competent judges in music as may be prevailed with to be at our church on Thursday next, the 30th of this instant September, at two of the clock in the afternoon to give their judgements upon the organ.' [11] On the day, Purcell was joined on the panel by John Blow, John Mosse (a member of the Private Musick) and a Mr Fforcell. 'Mr Purcell was desired to play and did play upon the organ, and after he had done playing they all reported to the Vestry that in their judgements the organ was a good organ, and was performed and completed according to contract.' After this, the four contestants for the place of organist each played in front of the judges 'and several … parishioners of this parish'; Moses Snow was chosen and 'gratefully accepted of the said place'; the post was worth £20 per annum. The whole procedure had been taken very seriously, for the expenses and fees for the four judges came to the not inconsiderable sum of £8 13s; it seems that the panel stayed at the Crown Tavern, and both Blow and Purcell were reimbursed 5s for their coach hire.

A month later, Purcell was chasing a debt which was proving extremely hard to collect. A former pupil had failed to pay for his lessons, and Purcell decided to write to the Dean of Exeter. The letter is probably the best example of Purcell's beautifully rounded, clear handwriting:

'Westminster, Nov the 2d. 1686
Sir

I have wrote several times to Mr Webber concerning what was due to me on Hodg's account and recd no answer, which has occasion'd this presumption in giving you the trouble of a few Lines relating to the matter; It is ever since the begining of June last that the Money has been due: the sum is £27, viz. £20 for half a years teaching & boarding the other a Bill of £7 for nessecarys wch I laid out for him, the Bill Mr Webber has; Compassion moves me to acquaint you of a great many debts Mr Hodg contracted whilst in London and to some who are so poor 'twere an act of Charity as well as Justice to pay 'em. I hope you will be so kind to take it into your consideration and also pardon this boldness from

Sir
Your most obliged
humble ser^t
Henry Purcell' [12]

OPPOSITE: *One of the rare personal letters of Purcell to have survived was addressed to the Dean of Exeter asking his help in the recovery of a debt. The text is given on p.141.*

We have no record of any reply, nor whether Purcell received his £27. But this was a sizeable bill, more than worth chasing.

On Christmas Day 1686, James further offended his musicians when he formally opened a new Roman Catholic chapel at Whitehall in the north-west corner of the Privy Garden. The offence was not so much that this was a chapel at which the Roman rites were observed, but that the music was provided by musicians who were largely imported from abroad – and highly paid for their services. It was now these new musicians who accompanied the king and queen on trips away from the court: the instrumentalists and singers from the former Chapel Royal lost out not only on prestigious performances but, highly significant to their take-home pay, on the daily allowance that was paid whenever they were away from London. These sums – at least 3s per day and often paid for several weeks at a time – made a considerable difference to the fairly meagre annual salary for a royal musician of £40. It is slightly uncertain what went on in the Anglican establishment during James's reign: the 'Cheque Book' still records new musicians being sworn in, and Princess Anne (as will be read below) appears to have attended services at which music was meant to be performed. James also brought in new regulations concerning the maintenance and clothing for the boys of the Chapel Royal, apparently discarding the summer liveries and changing the allocations of clothing and money made when a boy's voice broke and he left the Chapel.

The new Roman establishment was formally recorded on 26 April 1687 when a warrant was passed from James to the Officers of the Household stating

Wee have lately built a Royall Chappell in Our Pallace at Whitehall & have thought fitt to Order an Establishment for Our said Chappell in manner following:

2 Sacristans at £50 each	£100
2 Vergers at £50 each	£100
6 Preachers at £60 each	£360
4 Chaplaines at £80 each	£320
Assistant	£50
Organist	£100
Assistant	£20

7 Chappell boyes for dyett, washing, fireing, Servants Wages
£230

Westmr: Novr. ye 2d. 1686

S./

I have wrote severall times to Mr Webber concerning
what was due to me on Hodg's account and recd no
answer, which has occasiond this presumption in
giving you the trouble of a few Lines relating to the
matter; It is ever since ye begining of June last that
the Money has been due: the Sum is 27, Viz 20
for half a Years teaching & boarding the other a
Bill of 7 for nessecaryes wch I laid out for him,
the Bill Mr Webber has; Compassion Moves
me to acquaint you of a great many debts Mr
Hodg contracted whilst in London and to some who
are so poor twere an act of Charity as well as
Justice to pay 'em I hope you will be so kind to
take it into Your consideration and also pardon
this boldness from

Sr
Yor most obliged
humble Servt

Henry Purcell

Together with ancillary staff and general running expenses the cost of this new establishment came to a total of £2,042.

The musical disposition of the new chapel was recorded on 5 July 1687:

We have thought fitt to make the following Establishment for the Musick of Our Royall Chappell vizt

Seignr Fede Master	£200
Seignr Grand	£100
Seignr Sansoni	£100
Mr Abell	£60
Mr Pordage	£60
Mr Anatean	£60
	£580

Ten 'Gregorians' are also listed, with salaries totalling £490, and another nine instrumentalists, total salaries £430. The new musical establishment was thus costing the crown £1,500 per annum.[13]

During 1687 the sixteenth edition of *Angliae Notitiae, or the Present State of England* was published. This fascinating document, which had first appeared in 1669, gives a fairly detailed and, presumably, official list of the employees of the royal household (though it is not always totally accurate). The fifteenth edition had been compiled three years earlier, during the last full year of Charles's reign, and so comparison of the two editions is especially interesting. The personnel of the 'King's Chappel' (presumably the Anglican Chapel Royal of old) appears to be unchanged, with three organists: 'Dr William Child, Dr John Blow (who is also Master of the Children of the Chapel Royal) and Mr Henry Purcel' who are 'all eminent for their Great Compositions and skill in musick … The rest of the Gentlemen of the Chappel are great Masters also in the Science of Musick, and most Exquisite Performers, as: Mr William Turner, Mr James Hart, Mr Goslin, Mr Abel, Mr Thomas Heywood, Mr Alphonso Marsh, Mr Stephen Crispins, Mr Leonard Woodson.' Only these eight singers are named. There had always previously been at least twenty Gentlemen of the Chapel Royal (in 1682 there had been twenty-nine) and we have to presume that these were the senior singers, and that the others were simply not thought important enough to be named here. The musicians in ordinary (who played at court) had suffered the worst. Between 1684 and 1687 their numbers had been slimmed from sixty-two to 'about forty'. Here, if ever one was needed, was proof of the low importance of music for King James. The royal trumpets (who held an important ceremonial role) were unchanged: a sergeant commanded sixteen trumpets in ordinary, who were divided up into four troops of four trumpets. Each troop was allocated a kettle-drummer, two drummers and two hautbois.[14]

James's Queen Mary too was not especially interested in music. In the list of 'Persons belonging to Her Majesties Chappel' nearly £4,000 was being spent annually, but the only payment to a musician was an organist at £100: the six 'Boys of the Chappel' (at £20 each per annum) were serving boys. The Benedictine monks (costing £1,500 per annum) presumably supplied plainchant music.

But whilst James was prepared to spend large sums of money at the Catholic chapel, keeping up even the tuning of the instruments at the Anglican establishment was proving much harder. In King Charles's time the post of instrument tuner had been treated as an important one. Now the payments to Purcell for this work were in arrears, and a report in the Calendar of Treasury Books noted that 'The organ is so out of repair that to cleanse, tune and put in good order will cost £40 and then to keep it so will cost £20 per an. at the least'. Purcell had also apparently been working on a freelance basis, having not been confirmed officially in the post, and was now requesting an annual salary of £56. He also took the opportunity to press for payment of a bill already submitted for recent tuning and repair services for £20 10s.[15]

For Purcell, 1687 was a busy year composing and supervising the publishing of new works. According to Cummings, his touching 'Pastoral Elegy' with words by Tate, 'Gentle Shepherds, you that know', was written in memory of John Playford, nephew of Henry Playford and youngest son of 'Honest John' Playford, the music publisher. It seem more likely however that Purcell's tribute was to John Playford the elder (Henry's father), who died around November 1683. The Elegy is a fine piece of music, especially its opening: the 'tuneful breath' is deliciously discordant, 'harmony' richly harmonized, and the chromatically-falling 'lament' particularly touching. The ground bass that is introduced at 'Theron, the good' repeats itself over and over again like a tolling bell, over which fountains weep, mountains graphically rend themselves, dales dolefully groan and vales echo. After another section of semi-recitative bells again return, this time in the same descending scale that Purcell had used to such effect in the symphony to his famous 'Bell Anthem'.

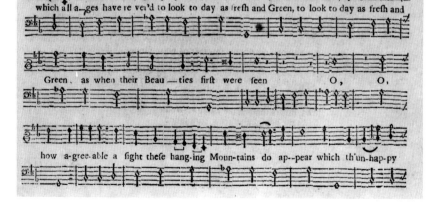

Purcell's song 'O Solitude' from Comes Amoris, or the Companion of Love *is a technical tour de force as well as a glorious composition: there are twenty-eight repetitions of the four-bar ground bass.*

In the same year John Carr printed the first book of *Comes Amoris; or the Companion of Love,* included in which were five of Purcell's works. The preface to the buyer was a musical one, headed a 'catch by way of epistle to the reader', and was set by Purcell, beginning 'To all lovers of music, performers and scrapers'. Of infinitely more musical worth was the setting of 'O solitude, my sweetest choice': here is one of the great jewels amongst his solo songs. The author, Katherine Philips, one of the most popular poets of Purcell's youth, spent most of her life in seclusion in Denbighshire, and retirement was a favourite theme. 'O solitude' was a skilful abridgment of a close translation by Philips of a poem by Antoine-Girard de Saint-Amant (1594-1661) who came to England before 1643. Over twenty-eight hypnotic repetitions of a four-bar, melancholy ground bass, the singer weaves an exquisite vocal line, full of musical illustrations of a fine text. Purcell's skill in achieving harmonic and melodic variety over an anchor which is apparently so strongly in C minor is quite wondrous. Henry Playford evidently thought highly of this song, for he printed it almost simultaneously in his fourth book of *The Theatre of Music.* Also in the first book of *Comes Amoris* came a setting of a D'Urfey poem, 'When first Amintas sued for a kiss', and settings of two Cowley poems, 'Fill the bowl with rosy wine' and 'Oft am I by the woman told'.

In total, Playford's fourth book of *The Theatre of Music* contained ten Purcell works, although four of them were repeat versions of songs contained in *Comes Amoris.* 'Ah, how pleasant 'tis to love' is charming in its simple, lutesong setting. 'Cease, anxious world' (a poem by Sir George Etherege) may well have been written as early as 1684 and presents the continuo players as the grinding world in a four-bar ground before the song ends – rather unusually for Purcell – in carefree mood. Also included were 'When first my shepherdess and I', 'Hence, fond deceiver', 'How sweet is the air' and 'In some kind dream'. John Playford reprinted *The Second Book of the Pleasant Musical Companion* and John Carr included three works by Purcell in the first book of *Vinculum Societatis,* a catch and two songs – 'Let formal lovers still pursue' and 'Spite of the god-head'. John Playford included two of Purcell's tunes in *Apollo's Banquet:* a jaunty instrumental version of 'When first Amintas sued for a kiss', now entitled 'Mr Purcell's Jig', and 'A New Scotch tune', which found its way into a whole series of Scottish folk-songs, even being set, nearly a century later, for two violins, two voices and continuo by Haydn.[16]

Purcell also returned in 1687 to composing church anthems. 'Behold, I bring you glad tidings' is a highly evocative anthem with strings with a text (three verses from Chapter II of St Luke's Gospel) which suggests that it was written for Christmas in the Chapel Royal. Surprisingly, it is Purcell's only anthem composed specifically for the Feast of Christmas, and the spread of manuscripts around the cathedrals of Britain indicates that it was quite a popular work. The rising string arpeggios of the symphony create a suitably mystical mood and later provide a sumptuous accompaniment to the opening bass solo. Another work with a prominent bass solo, 'Praise the Lord, O my soul; O Lord my God' also ascribed, by its copyist, to 1687, though Zimmerman proposes that a version in St Michael's College, Tenbury may be an earlier version.

'Sing unto God, O ye Kingdoms of the earth' also dates from 1687, and Purcell once again turned to the voice of John Gostling. The first hearing in the Chapel Royal must have turned a few heads, for Purcell was clearly determined to use every available note of this bass's vocal range. Purcell responded to 'Lo, he doth send out his voice, yea and that a mighty voice' by taking the singer from above the musical stave to well below it in a series of imposing phrases. As so often, though, it is the slow section which is most musically effective: the melismas of 'O God' majestically expand, as the key turns from minor to major, on the word 'wonderful'.

Gostling's voice featured strongly in another anthem (this time without strings) from 1687, 'Thy way, O God, is holy', which has been preserved in an unusually large number of sets of cathedral partbooks. Apart from a short concluding Alleluia, the anthem is scored for two soloists, a high tenor and a bass, and contains sections of marvellously dramatic music. The opening two bars of 'Thou art the God that doth wonders' are theatrically repeated, transposed a third upwards, before the tenor joyfully celebrates, at the top of his vocal register, the God who has 'mightily deliver'd thy people'. The bass rumbles away to represent the troubled depths of the sea, and the clouds pour out their contents: scales tumble from both singers as the air thunders and arrows fly. Calm is briefly restored but leads into another vocal storm as 'the voice of thy thunder was heard round about', lightning flashes in the voices and the earth moves and shakes.

Also composed no later that 1687 was 'Thy word is a lantern unto my feet'. This verse anthem appears in many manuscripts copied during the twenty years after Purcell's death, suggesting that it was an especially popular piece around the British cathedrals. The majority of the work is for an alto/tenor/bass trio, and the chorus only sing two short sections of material that an average choir could learn rapidly. This is one Purcell anthem – by no means his best – that has remained solidly in the cathedral repertoire.

Whilst Purcell was writing and presumably performing at the Chapel Royal, some of the royal musicians were either in rebellious mood or extremely disorganized, as a command sent on 21 October 1687 from the Lord Chamberlain to Dr Staggins, Master of his Majesty's Musick, explains: 'Whereas you have neglected to give Order to ye Violins to attend at ye Chappell at Whitehall where Her Royal Highnesse ye Princess Ann of Denmarke is present. These are therefore to give notice to them that they give theire attendance there upon Sunday next & soe continue to doe soe as formerly they did.'[17]

In the country as a whole rather more serious royal commands were also being openly disobeyed. As ever, they were brought about by King James's rigidity and his knack of listening to bad advice. The Church greeted James's Declaration of Indulgence for Dissenters with much suspicion and coolness, and the king made up his mind to reform the clergy. The universities played a vital part in training the clergy and in forming the religious views of the sons of the nobility and gentry. By law, only those who took the oaths of allegiance and supremacy could matriculate, take degrees and hold college fellow-ships, which effectively excluded Catholics and Dissenters. Believing that free discussion between Catholics and Anglicans would result in many being convinced by the truth of Catholic arguments, James first of all simply dispensed Catholic dons or undergraduates from taking the oaths or attending prayers. In October 1686 he put in a Catholic dean at Christ Church, Oxford and, three months later, ordered the fellows of Sidney Sussex College, Cambridge to appoint Joshua Bassett, a Catholic, as their Master (despite the fact that their statutes, as an Elizabethan foundation, forbade this). In March 1687 the President of the richest Oxford college, Magdalen, died, and James commanded that Anthony Farmer, a Catholic, be appointed in his place. He was a poor choice; he was not qualified for the job (the statutes laid down that he must have been a fellow there or at New College, which he had not) and even the ecclesiastical commissioners described him as 'a very bad man'. The fellows appointed John Hough as president and quickly admitted him before a royal order arrived commanding them not to do so. The ecclesiastical commission declared the election void but accepted that Farmer was ineligible, so James demanded that the Bishop of Oxford, Samuel Parker, be appointed. The fellows disagreed and even defied James to his face when he visited Oxford in September. James was livid and exploded: 'I am your king. I will be obeyed ... let them that refuse it look to it; they shall feel the weight of their sovereign's displeasure.'[18] The fellows remained obstinate, and the commission had Parker installed as president; Catholics were admitted in the places of most of the original fellows, who were deprived of their fellowships and declared unfit to hold any benefice in the church. Politically, depriving subjects of their property – the tenure of benefices and fellowships was seen as a freehold – was a serious mistake. Even some of the king's advisors said so, but James was too angry to back down. By such vindictiveness he completed his alienation of the Anglicans.

At court, James had driven away most of the Protestant nobility, and extremist Catholics now dominated. He was depriving himself of vital information. The French envoy Bonrepaus remarked that 'The English Court is very badly informed of what is happening abroad and is even ignorant of most of what happens in London and the provinces.'[19] James would clutch at any evidence, however flimsy, which supported his views and dismiss any, however substantial, which contradicted them. Only Sunderland, amongst those whom he trusted, was acute enough to see that what was happening would lead to disaster, but he was trapped by the very means he had used to clamber to power. The Catholics whom he had put into power were now more influential than he, and he could no longer control them.

Relations between King James and William and Mary were going from bad to worse. Previously they had mainly disagreed on relations with Louis in France and the refusal of the Dutch to clamp down on anti-James factions resident in Holland. Now James tried to enlist William's help in supporting the repeal of the penal laws and Test Acts. William replied saying that he disliked religious persecution but thought that the Test Acts were an important protection for the Protestant religion: he would allow Catholics freedom of worship but not admit them to public office. William also feared that his own and Mary's claims to the throne were being threatened; rumours were circulating that James might be persuaded to disinherit Mary in favour of a Catholic, and William (much exaggerating the strength of English republicanism) also feared that the king's measures might lead to a rebellion and the establishment of a republic.

William of Orange was a constant, looming presence during the whole of James's reign. James knew that if the country rejected him it would turn to William – a Protestant, a grandson of Charles I and married to James's Protestant daughter Mary.

During mid-September 1687 Purcell's baby son Henry, who had been baptised on 9 June, died. What with a growing national crisis in the monarchy and another personal sadness, Purcell could have been forgiven if his 1687 birthday ode for the king, 'Sound the trumpet, beat the drum', was not one of his greatest. The celebrations in London were rather more muted than usual, there being 'no bonefires, being so particularly commanded', and the scoring, just for strings and a consort of voices, was fairly small-scale. But what emerged was a revised style of ode, with fewer string ritornelli ending movements: instead, the tendency was to move straight into another contrasting vocal section. The overture was a splendid one, and the alto duet 'Let Caesar and Urania come' is transformed into a fine string ritornello. The bass, John Bowman, must have been another singer with a huge range, for 'While Caesar, like the morning star' ventures from high E down to bottom D. Equally notable is the chaconne which Purcell included at the mid-point of the ode: this is as good an example of the form as he ever wrote, using a multitude of compositional devices and including a striking minor section. Purcell too must have been pleased with the movement for he re-used it, four years later, in *King Arthur*.

On 7 November Henry Playford advertised his *Harmonia Sacra; or Divine Hymns and Dialogues* which contained twelve devotional hymns by Purcell. Purcell had also taken on, it would seem from Playford's introduction, the role of music editor for the collection: 'As for the musical part, it was composed by the most skilful masters of this age; and though some of them are now dead, yet their composures have been reviewed by Mr. Henry Purcell, whose tender regard for the reputation of those great men made him careful that nothing should be published, which, through the negligence of the transcribers, might reflect upon their memory'. Five of Purcell's contributions have already been mentioned elsewhere; the remaining seven songs brought music of astonishing quality. They also showed how Purcell, when free to choose his own texts, reacted to inspired poetry.

In every phrase of the 'Penitential Hymn' 'Great God and just' word-painting is to the fore, both in the angular vocal line and also in the harmony: man's miserable state is constantly illustrated at both ends of the vocal range. The author was the Cambridge-educated preacher Jeremy Taylor: this example of his colourful literary style was full of remorseful sentiments and not sparing on vivid description. Purcell's imagination must have revelled in such a text, and his setting is one of the most extreme in the collection. 'How have I strayed' is one of five settings Purcell made of devotional poems by William Fuller: here the mood is thoughtful and introspective, as is the restful 'Close thine eyes and sleep secure'. In another of Fuller's texts Purcell was on splendid form with a doom-laden, fallen Christian in 'In the black dismal dungeon of despair', subtly colouring the text and producing an impassioned setting. Though in Nathaniel Ingelo's 'We sing to him, whose wisdom form'd the ear' Purcell again demonstrated his responsiveness to the text, this is one of the less noteworthy songs in the collection.

The same could not be said of Purcell's inspired, poignantly restrained setting of Francis Quarles's poem 'The earth trembled' (subtitled 'On our Saviour's passion') which paints a scene of worldly destruction at the crucifixion. Everywhere pictorialization abounds: heaven closes its eyes with a large downward interval and the clouds drop tears. The dead rise, graves 'gape to be his tomb', heaven sends down 'elegious thunder', the very foundations of the world are loosened and the veil of the temple is torn in two. But, all this violence now described, desolate sadness returns 'to teach our hearts what our sad hearts should do', the central word 'heart' given especial emphasis. The key change and pathos of 'Can senseless things do this' are almost unbearable, and tears return, first in an emotional outburst 'drill forth my tears', before they slowly trickle down, one by one.

'How long, great God' (subtitled 'The Aspiration') is an equally wonderful setting, this time of a work by the poet and philosopher John Norris (1657-1711). Norris, though captured in life's torments, sees visionary salvation in words of almost Shakespearean colour and imagination, and Purcell responds with one of his finest solo miniatures. The opening is sublime, the voice beginning on a startling discord as he asks God how long he must 'Immured in this dark prison lie'. Glimmers of harmonic optimism emerge with the 'gates and avenues of sense', and continue with the 'faint gleams of thee' which, in a wonderful vocal line, 'salute my sight, Like doubtful moonshine in a cloudy night'. The 'magic sphere' is tantalizingly harmonized, and the coldness of the clime is warmed as 'my sense Perceives ev'n here thy influence'. The mood strengthens further as the prisoner feels 'thy strong magnetic charms', and the vocal line colours his panting and trembling 'like the am'rous steel': the 'erroneous needle' of Norris's compass falls, and then, as suddenly, 'turns and points again to thee'. The section climaxes as he longs 'to see this excellence', and the 'impatient soul' struggles to free itself. In a lilting triple time, Love is asked to set the prisoner free: full of optimism, the captive would 'fly, and love on all the way'.

At the end of 1687, much to the surprise of even James's supporters, and much to the suspicion of his enemies, it was announced that Queen Mary was pregnant; she had previously failed on numerous occasions to produce a successor to the throne and had last miscarried in May 1686. Purcell was commissioned to write an anthem, 'Blessed are they that fear the Lord', and whatever his feelings may have been towards the king, he obliged with an especially good work. At the end of the autograph manuscript comes a note, most probably in the hand of John Gostling: 'Composed for the Thanksgiving appointed to be in London & 12 miles round Jan 15. 1687 [the old-style year numbering actually means 1688] & on the 29th. following over England for the Queen's being with Child'. All churches within the area celebrated the 'solemn and particular office' on 15 January, and the rest of the

153

country did so a fortnight later. The text, from Psalm 128, was carefully chosen not only to mention the breeding of children, but also to allude to the benefits that would ensue from continuity of the House of Stuart. Purcell's first section of the symphony is wistful, with the chromatic harmony, full of suspensions, tensioned and anchored by the bass violins' opening sustained pedal which descends, after five bars, to the instruments' richest depths. The verse sections are set for four voices – two trebles, high tenor and bass – who are cast as different characters: the solo bass takes the role of the husband, striving in the fields ('For thou shalt eat the labour of thy hands'), the high tenor takes on a commentating role ('And happy shalt thou be'), and the two trebles, in thirds over a dominant pedal, repeat the phrase 'O well is thee'. The fore-square section for solo bass 'The Lord thy God from out of Sion' is interrupted by a poignant repetition by the trebles of their phrase 'O well is thee'. The tenor sings of the peace that Israel's children's children will see (and that England hopes to see from the same continued succession) and leads into the most remarkable section of the anthem. The two trebles repeat their touching 'O well is thee'; the idea is taken up as well by the two lower voices, giving rise to sumptuous harmony.

Four other anthems also emerged during 1688. 'The Lord is King, the earth may be glad' was a splendid anthem with strings featuring a solo bass. William Flackton's manuscript copy[20] carries the inscription 'This copied from a MS in the Revd. Mr Jon. Gostling's possession & of Mr. Purcell's handwriting'. Whether or not Gostling was the soloist at the first performance, Purcell provided music that allowed the singer rumbustious passages telling of tempestuous weather and also highly expressive moments such as 'The hills melted away'. 'Blessed is he that considereth the poor' probably dates from 1688 and is a much simpler affair, set only for three solo voices. The chorus that is found in certain manuscripts was almost certainly not written by Purcell. For the celebrations (usually held on 12 December) of Founders Day at Charterhouse, the famous school on the edge of the City of London, Purcell was commissioned to write an anthem. 'Blessed is the man that feareth the Lord' may well have been an arrangement of an earlier work, for the William Kennedy Gostling manuscript states that it was 'sung by Mr Barincloe and Mr Bowman. This is a duet, but an extra part for the tenor is inserted into the book.' Intriguingly the preacher at Charterhouse in 1688 was John Patrick, nine of whose texts Purcell had set as devotional songs.

The most famous church work dating from 1688 was 'O sing unto the Lord' (the dating again comes from the Gostling manuscript). The style and scale of this verse anthem seem to suggest that it was written for a special occasion: it shows Purcell's church writing at his most Italianate, with vigorous antiphony between voices and instruments, and between the prominent solo bass and the chorus. The opening is grand, and before the imitative section that almost always makes up the second half of the symphony in the anthems Purcell unusually adds an expressive section (marked 'Drag' in some manuscripts). Again, behind the overtly celebratory writing is the melancholy quality which is a feature of so much of Purcell's music. After the symphony a solo bass ceremoniously opens the proceedings, followed by two lilting choral Alleluias, before we are treated to the first of a series of imaginative instrumental ritornelli. The four-part verse 'Sing unto the Lord and praise his name' leads straight into the mysteriously-coloured 'Declare his honour', which blossoms into a full chorus. The duet for treble and high tenor 'The Lord is great', set over a ground bass, is capped by another inventive string ritornello. The central section of the anthem is the quartet 'O worship the Lord in the beauty of holiness', radiant in its restrained wonderment, after which antiphony between the solo bass, choir and strings returns at 'Tell it out among the heathen'. Purcell treats the final section of alleluias gently.

Between 1681 and 1688 Purcell seems to have composed no music for the theatre except a health to King James, 'How great are the blessings' which was performed for a Tate adaptation of *Eastward Ho!* in 1685 and, the same year, a catch for a Ravenscroft comedy, *The English Lawyer*. Curtis Price[21] has suggested that this gap resulted from Purcell's unfortunately timed move from the Dorset Garden Company to the King's Company in Drury Lane, which went under at the end of the 1681/82 season and was obliged to merge a few months later with its former rivals. The new United Company, encouraged by Charles II's love of things French, favoured the music of Louis Grabu, and during the reign of James (with his favouritism of foreign musicians), English composers fared little better. Only in April 1688 did Purcell's big break come in the theatre when he was asked to compose the songs for D'Urfey's comedy *A Fool's Preferment*: he provided eight songs (performed by the versatile actor William Mountfort) which showed his genius for the dramatic. Price suggests that, had it not been for the Glorious Revolution later that year, which all but stopped the production of new theatre works, this play alone

A
Fool's Preferment,
OR, THE
Three DUKES of Dunstable.
A COMEDY.

As it was Acted at the Queens Theatre in *Dorset-Garden,* by Their MAJESTIES Servants.

Written by Mr. D'urfey.

Together, with all the SONGS and NOTES to 'em, Excellently Compos'd by Mr. HENRY PURCELL. 1688.

Licensed,
May 21. 1688. R. P.

Eupolis atq; Cratinus, Aristophanesque Poetæ,
Atq; alii, quorum Comædia prisca virorum est;
Si quis erat dignus describi, quod Malus, aut Fur,
Quod Mæchus foret, aut Sicarius, aut alioqui
Famosus; multa cum libertate notabunt.
Hinc Omnis pendet Lucillius. ———   Horat. Saty. 4.

Printed for *Jos. Knight,* and *Fra. Saunders* at the *Blue Anchor* in the *Lower Walk* of the *New Exchange* in the *Strand,* 1688.

Under James II court patronage of the Chapel Royal's musical resources declined, and Purcell started to write again for the theatre. In April 1688 he provided eight songs for D'Urfey's comedy A Fool's Preferment.

RIGHT: *The first volume of Henry Playford's* Banquet of Musick *featured a lively woodcut of a singer, violinist and virginals player on its titlepage and contained six works by Purcell. One of them was 'Anacreon's Defeat', in which the Greek poet is defeated not by arms but by love.*

would have established Purcell as the principal composer for the United Company.

Purcell's reputation as London's leading writer of songs was further enhanced with the publication of the first two volumes of Henry Playford's *The Banquet of Musick.* The first volume was licensed on 19 November 1687 and contained six works by Purcell: two catches, the 'Dialogue between Strephon and Dorinda', 'Has yet your breast no pity learned?' and two works on texts by Cowley, the song 'Here's to thee, Dick' and a cantata for two solo voices, two recorders and continuo, 'How pleasant is this flow'ry plain'. The sixth work was one of only two secular solo songs Purcell wrote for bass: 'This poet sings the Trojan wars'. In all the other non-theatrical songs a bass singer always performs in combination with at least one other voice.

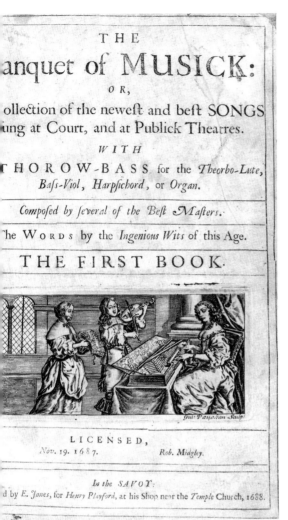

To a twentieth-century listener who may lack the detailed classical knowledge that was the norm for an educated seventeenth-century listener, many of the textual subtleties that fill Purcell's songs can be missed. Some texts are thoroughly ordinary, invoking pastoral names unthinkingly and reorganizing stock material to no apparent purpose, but others skilfully call on classical names and allusions, often recalling specific poems by Anacreon, Theocritus, Catullus, Propertius and Horace. As Richard Luckett has written 'They are not remarkable for imagery or vocabulary, which is why they respond well to setting. But they do explore all kinds of complexities and ironies of amatory experience, albeit by means of small variations on a limited number of themes. And they repeatedly conjure up that small but significant body of Greek and, on a much greater scale, Latin poetry which educated men of the age were likely to have known by heart.'[22]

'This poet sings the Trojan wars' (subtitled 'Anacreon's Defeat'), though unusual in its scoring for solo bass, is a good example of this: an educated listener of Purcell's day would have known that Anacreon was a Greek poet in the early sixth century BC and that he wrote lyric poetry noted for its gaiety, wit and avoidance of serious subjects. His poems were much translated and imitated in mid- and late-seventeenth-century England, particularly in the wake of versions by Abraham Cowley. This defeat of Anacreon, we discover as the song progresses, was not a military one. Neither 'fleets at sea' nor 'ranks and files of infantry' have vanquished the poet; only in the last bars, as the tempo and style radically change, do we hear that it is those 'encamp'd in killing eyes' that have caused his downfall (i.e. the looks – and worse – of ladies). The sexual overtones of the last line, 'Each dart his mistress shoots, he dies', require no explanation!

The second volume of *The Banquet of Musick* followed in May 1688, and contained a further four songs: two gentle, lutesong-like numbers, 'Ah, how pleasant 'tis to love' and 'Love's power in my heart', and two rather more wry songs, 'Phyllis, I can ne'er forgive it' and 'Sylvia, now your scorn give over'. On 24 May the second book of *Vinculum Societatis* was published, but the works definitely attributable to Purcell are only a catch, and repeat printings of 'Ah, how pleasant 'tis to love' and 'Sylvia, now your scorn'.

The second book of *Comes Amoris* contained four of Purcell's catches. Nearly sixty of these have survived, but writers have sometimes attached rather greater musical importance to them than they deserve. Certainly Purcell's catches (mostly set for three voices who enter in turn, as in a 'round') show his contrapuntal ingenuity, and the words were sometimes so obscene that early twentieth-century editors bowdlerized them to bring them within then current standards of decency. Others have read into these humorous diversions all sorts of character traits (including the totally spurious story that 'My wife has a tongue as good as e'er twanged' referred to the equally fictitious story that Purcell's wife locked him out of the house on a late, drunken return from the tavern, whereon he caught a cold and died) but the lewd humour that the catches usually demonstrate is no different from the level that professional musicians have always shown through the ages: one only needs to spend a little time with a modern-day English orchestra or a top-notch choir to see that good humour, often unrepeatable, is as much part and parcel of the job (and a merciful balance to the need to maintain a public image) as it seems to have been in Purcell's day. But it has to be said that anyone who can write a catch, as did Purcell, where two voices combine, one singing 'He pulled out his' and the other 'nine inches', must have been extremely good company in the local tavern after a trying Evensong or a particularly tedious day of court rigmarole.

On 20 March 1688 James issued an order re-arranging the disposition of the Catholic Chapel Royal: the running costs and salaries of the new establishment, which included two sacristans, two vergers, eight choristers (and their clothes, chaplain, a 'Master to teach them Latin etc', a housekeeper and the rental of their house), six preachers, four 'French Fathers' and an 'Assistant of their Order', a porter, seamstress, washer, eight singers (under 'Seignor Fede'), Giovanni Baptista Draghi as organist, 'A Servant to blow the Organ', seven 'Gregorians' (with 'Seignor Albrici to supply at the Organ') and twelve instrumentalists together with their administrative expenses, came to nearly £4,000 per annum. The listing is especially detailed, even naming the eight choristers as William Lane, William Jolly, William Clarke, Thomas Woolmar, James Langhorne, Charles Gaultier, James Le Febure and Richard Cole.[23] A payment of 3 April 1688 records £137 13s being paid 'To Rene [=Renatus] Harris for fitting and preparing an Organ for the Chappell in Whitehall'.[24] Many of the musicians mentioned had been amongst the forty-one 'persons, gentlemen, musicians and other officers of his Majesty's Chapel' who had been paid a total of £623 8s for their attendance at Windsor Castle the previous summer. Seventeen musicians also received 3s per day (and their master, Dr Staggins, 5s) for their attendance. Purcell was not amongst their number, nor that of the ten 'gentlemen of her Majesty's Chapel' who received payment.[25]

Despite King James's administrative efficiency, royal employees still had to battle on occasions to receive prompt payment for their services. On 5 March 1688 the king sent a warrant to the Officers of the Household as Henry Purcell had found it necessary to make official representations through the Dean of the Chapel Royal (also the Bishop of Durham): 'Whereas it hath bin represented to Us by the Bishop of Duresme that Eighty one pounds is due to Henry Purcell for Repaireing the Organ, and furnishing of Harpsicords to Xmas last: And that it is Necessary for that service to allow the Sum of Fifty six pounds p. ann. These are to require you that the same be passed, allowed & paid accordingly'.[26] That command seems to have got somewhere, for the quarterly payments for October–December 1688 show a payment of £14 to 'Henry Purcell for repairing ye Organs and furnishing Harpsicords at £56. p.a.'.[27]

Purcell's financial need would have been greater than usual, for his wife Frances was again pregnant. On 30 May she gave birth to a daughter, also named Frances, who survived into adulthood. On 10 June Queen Mary followed suit and gave birth, unexpectedly early (she had been playing cards until late the evening before), to Prince James Edward, later to be known as the 'Old Pretender'. The public rejoicing that James might have expected this birth to generate did not materialize: he had just made his greatest error of political judgment to date.

Faced by a bewildering array of totally conflicting advice at court, after much hesitation James finally decided not to recall parliament until he could be sure that it would be one that would repeal the Test Acts. He had convinced himself that public dislike of his policy was due simply to a misunderstanding of his intentions; to correct this he decided that all Anglican clergy should read his Declaration of Toleration in church. By doing so he was effectively commanding the clergy to endorse it. In Holland, William watched with a mixture of amusement and amazement as, predictably, the majority of clergy refused to read the Declaration. On 17 May Archbishop Sancroft and six of his colleagues drew up a petition which pointed out that the dispensing power on which the Declaration rested had been declared illegal in parliament, notably in 1663 and 1673. James was furious, protesting that 'This is a standard of rebellion'. Even the Dissenters agreed with the bishops and, after more dithering and ill-advice, feeling that he must reassert his authority, James chose the worst possible course of action. He would proceed against the bishops in law, but reserve the right to show mercy after they were convicted. The bishops refused to give sureties for good behaviour and were sent to the Tower, blessing the cheering crowds as they went to prison.

The birth of James's son would have been an excellent pretext to pardon the bishops. Instead, he changed the charge from 'scandalous libel' to the more serious 'seditious libel' and remained confident of a conviction even after the judges of the King's Bench granted bail to the bishops. On 29 June the trial began in front of four judges. Despite repeated purges, some of the judiciary had shown misgivings about the legalities of the tasks they were being asked to perform, especially on the ecclesiastical commission. Two of this panel clearly

Sala Reggia

favoured the bishops, one was unusually moderate and only one, the Catholic Allibone, was hostile. The audience in the public gallery was splendidly biased, hissing Sunderland so loudly when he gave evidence (having just compounded his unpopularity by becoming a Catholic) that he could hardly be heard. The two moderate judges, Holloway and Powell, roundly condemned the dispensing power, stating that 'If this once be allowed of, there will need no Parliament; all the legislature will be in the King.' After a night's deliberation, the jury, following such a strong lead from the bench, found the bishops not guilty.

The news spread round the city. For the birth of the new prince the reaction had been thoroughly muted. Now London had something to celebrate. Soldiers encamped on Hounslow Heath gave a great shout, bonfires were lit, church bells rang and an effigy of the Pope was burned outside St James's Palace. We do not officially know Purcell's reaction to the event but, some months later and secure with a new

James's queen opportunely produced a son and heir on 10 June 1688 – but the news failed to win the king the popularity he needed. The baby was christened James, and it was through him that the Stuart claim was to be kept alive for another fifty years.

monarch on the throne, he set a catch on 'the seven who supported our cause', 'True Englishmen drink a good health'. Whilst London celebrated and the king licked his wounds, seven men – including Whigs, Tories, a bishop and the former Lord Treasurer – invited William to invade, assuring him that 'Nineteen parts of twenty of the people…are desirous of a change.'[28] The navy and army, they said, would not resist. William needed no other invitation.

Still James refused to back down. The two judges who had supported the bishops were dismissed from the bench. James ordered the ecclesiastical commissioners to summon the clergy who had refused to read the Declaration. This meant the vast majority, and no-one took the order seriously: nothing was done. Those who had lit celebratory bonfires were taken to court: grand juries found them not guilty, even after judges sent them back to reconsider their verdicts. Though there was no likelihood of outright rebellion in England, now it seemed certain that the people were unlikely to help James if he was attacked. At court too James must have made himself thoroughly unpopular with the musicians, demanding that they play for the queen's maids as required: 'I do hereby order that a number of his Majesty's musicians shall attend the Queen's Majesty's maids of honour to play whensoever they shall be sent to, at the homes of dancing, at such homes and such a number of them as they shall desire. And hereof the master of the musick and the musicians are to take notice that they observe this order'.[29]

During the summer James was surprisingly lax in preparing for an invasion which, to everyone but him, seemed almost inevitable. Only in late September did panic grip him and as he mobilized his forces he began to see that only with the support of the Anglican bishops might he have any chance of resisting William's invasion. After more uncertainty he reinstated the fellows of Magdalen College, Oxford, dissolved the ecclesiastical commission, restored the charter for the City of London and began to remove the Catholics he had placed in the seats of Tory JPs and deputy lieutenants. But he did not – claiming he could not whilst the threat of invasion was so strong – meet the most essential demand of all, that for a free parliament. William's fleet set sail on 20 October, but was beaten back to port by terrible storms. The delay was only for a week and, when the wind changed to the east, the Dutch fleet sailed down the Channel. The English fleet, needing to sail west, were trapped in Dartmouth by the same winds and got out too late to do anything. William, deciding to land well

Intreede van Zyn Koninglyke Hoogheid, Willem de Derde, binnen Londen, den 28 Ianuary. 1689.

away from London, disembarked at Torbay on 5 November. From the start, the prognosis for James was not good, and his flow of accurate information about William's progress was even worse. Gradually over the next few weeks King James's support trickled away, eventually turning into a flood of defections. Finally, on 9 December he told his wife and young son to flee to France. William of Orange reached London on 18 December; James fled to France on 23 December 1688, landing there, after a miserable crossing, on Christmas morning. By the end of December William controlled the civil and military governments of England. He summoned a convocation of parliament which, with little choice in the matter, declared that, by deserting his people and breaking the laws, James had abdicated.

At the invitation of parliament, William of Orange landed in England in November 1688, negotiating a constitutional settlement in return for the crown. Meanwhile James fled to France and William entered London to universal acclaim.

163

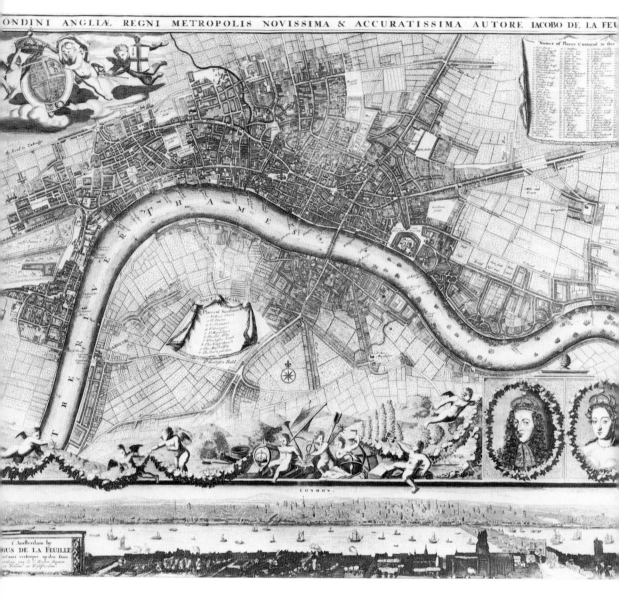

London in 1690 had grown since Purcell's childhood and the ravages of the Fire had been repaired. Comparing the panorama underneath this map with the one on p. 12–13, the most noticeable difference is the absence of St Paul's. The old cathedral had gone; Wren's new cathedral was only just begun.

CHAPTER V

Maturity cut short:
Purcell under William and Mary,
1688-1695

O n 13 February 1689 the crown was offered jointly to William
and Mary. Luttrell recorded that 'The Lords and Commons
assembled at Westminster, came both houses to the Banqueting
House at Whitehall, and there presented the Prince and Princess of
Orange with the instrument agreed on for declaring them King and
Queen.'[1] Halifax read the Declaration of Right, the Prince promised
that he and Mary would govern entirely by the laws of England and be
guided by the advice of both Houses, and William and Mary were
declared king and queen of England, Scotland, France and Ireland.
Trumpets sounded, the crowds cheered loudly and the rest of the day
was 'spent in the ringing of bells, bonfires at night and other expressions of joy, though a great many looked very sadly upon it'.[2] The
Jewel House archive records 'Delivered unto Sergt Trumpeter for the
proclaimeing of ye Prince and Princess of Orange King & Queene &
as soon as the service is over to bee returned vizt One Large Mace 342
[ounces in weight]'.[3]

The coronation was scheduled for 11 April 1689, and the usual
rush of preparations took place. The General Wardrobe was commanded to produce scarlet mantles for the thirty-nine musicians who
were to attend, and scarlet cloth was ordered for the Children of the
Chapel Royal. On 5 April an official list of the musicians of the
Private Music who were to take part was printed: gone were almost
every one of the fancy foreigners so beloved by James, replaced by
familiar names, Purcell's included. Luttrell's description of the actual
coronation service is surprisingly brief: 'The coronation of their
majesties was performed at Westminster, much in the manner the
former was.'[4] The king and queen left Whitehall at seven o'clock in

The movement that brought William and Mary to the throne – the Glorious Revolution of 1688 – was a turning point in English constitutional history. The monarchy was obliged to surrender most of its effective power to parliament. Left: *the Bill of Rights being read to William before he is finally offered the crown.* Below: *the parliament of 1689, a Dutch engraving that is not wholly faithful to the real setting. William is on the left, the Speaker on the right.*

William and Mary, crowned and sceptred, receiving the homage of their subjects.

the morning, went by barge to Westminster and met the nobility in the House of Lords. Three hours later the whole procession moved across blue carpets into Westminster Abbey. Archbishop Sancroft claimed illness, and Compton took his place. Mary, as Queen Regnant, wore a crown of stupendous value (specially made, along with a crown for the king), two sceptres and an orb. The manufacturing cost came to £7,260, but the jewel stones, part of the crown treasures, were valued at £126,000 and contained 2,725 diamonds, 71 rubies, 59 sapphires, 40 emeralds and 1,591 large pearls.[5] The ceremony differed from previous ones in that William and Mary swore that they would govern according to 'the statutes in Parliament agreed upon and the laws and customs of the same'; they also promised to uphold the Protestant reformed religion. There was, however, some offence caused by using a cohort of Dutch guards, and William, who thoroughly disliked ceremonial, appeared relieved when it was all over.

We are not sure of the actual musical arrangements for the service, but one event was recorded in considerable detail. As organist of

Westminster Abbey, Purcell had control of the organ loft, from which an excellent view of the proceedings could be gained. At previous coronations a wooden scaffold had been erected, tickets sold and a handsome profit made. Purcell and his friend Stephen Crespion, the chanter and a petty canon at the Abbey, either ignored or, quite possibly, knew nothing of a regulation passed at the Abbey on 25 March which stated that 'all such money as shall be raised for seats at the Coronation within the organ loft or churchyard shall be paid into the hands of the Treasurer and distributed as the Dean and Chapter shall think fit'.[6] A scaffold was built (and must have been a fairly large structure), tickets were sold, and some £500 taken. Within a week of the service Purcell was ordered to pay the receiver at the Abbey 'all such money as was received by him for places in the organ-loft... before Saturday next...And in default thereof his place is to be declared to be null and void. And it is further ordered that his stipend or salary due at our Lady Day last be detained in the hands of the Treasurer until further order.' Ironically that salary was already overdue by a month. Purcell dutifully paid the money to the authorities, saw it shared out amongst dozens of people by a complicated system, and made £35 for his pains.

The queen's birthday fell on 30 April and, even as the coronation was being held, Purcell must have been at work on the first of six birthday odes he wrote for Queen Mary. No date is given for 'Now does the glorious day appear' in the manuscript in the British Library (R.M. 20.h.8), but as odes exist for all the other years of Mary's reign 1689 seems likely. Thomas Shadwell supplied the text, which Purcell altered extensively, even cutting the last fifteen lines. The scoring was restricted to strings (though a third violin was added to give a five-part string texture) and a consort of voices. The overture is a fine one, and there are several excellent vocal movements, with the tenor solo 'Thus does our fertile isle' set to one of the shortest ground basses – on just two notes – that Purcell wrote. But the highlight of the work, a movement which stands out as one of Purcell's greatest, is the alto solo, set over a wistfully sighing four-bar dropping ground, 'By beauteous softness mixed with majesty'. One of Purcell's most ravishing solos, the voice's final phrase is overlapped with an exquisite five-part string ritornello of quite melting beauty.

Such commissions for royalty were a relative rarity during the reign of William and Mary, for it was during their reign that the court finally lost its importance as the centre of musical life in London. For

The Duke of York's Theatre in Dorset Garden opened in 1671 with a play by Dryden. It stood between Fleet Street and the Thames, with its main facade (shown here) on the river, so that the audience could arrive by boat. In the centre are the arms of the patron, the Duke of York.

Charles II, music at the Chapel Royal and the court had been vital. William, an ungracious, dour character who suffered from asthma, hated London. When Mary arrived in England in February 1689 she had been horrified by the deterioration in his health: the filthy London air caused William terrible coughing fits. He would escape to Hampton Court whenever possible, much to the irritation of the courtiers who had to spend hours commuting there. When Halifax, complaining that 'The King's inaccessibleness and living soe at Hampton Court altogether, and at soe active a time ruined all the business' suggested that William should spend at least an occasional night in town, the king answered that 'it was not to be done except he

The Dorset Garden theatre was the largest and best equipped theatre built in London up to that time. Reputedly designed by Christopher Wren, it had an elaborate proscenium arch with carving by Grinling Gibbons, and machinery capable of spectacular effects. The scene here, from Elkanah Settle's Empress of Morocco, *1673, represents Hell.* King Arthur *was performed here in 1691. The theatre was demolished in 1709.*

desired to see him dead'.[8] William also suffered terribly from home-sickness. This was not the sort of monarch for whom the arts were of great significance, although he did fill Kensington Palace (which he finally accepted as a London home) with some of the greatest paintings from the royal art collections: his palace was decorated with works by Titian, Raphael, Holbein and Van Dyck. Mary proved to be an avid collector of Chinese porcelain and exotic furniture. She also brought from Holland her troop of little dogs, Mopshonden, never before seen in England: soon it was the height of fashion to own one of these dogs, which were named Dutch mastiffs or pugs. Mary was also was one of the first people to have a pet goldfish. She was a keen reader, especially interested in history and poetry.

Royal patronage in music was diminishing. The court musical establishment was, however, retained, and during July 1689 dozens of warrants were issued to admit performing musicians to the traditional

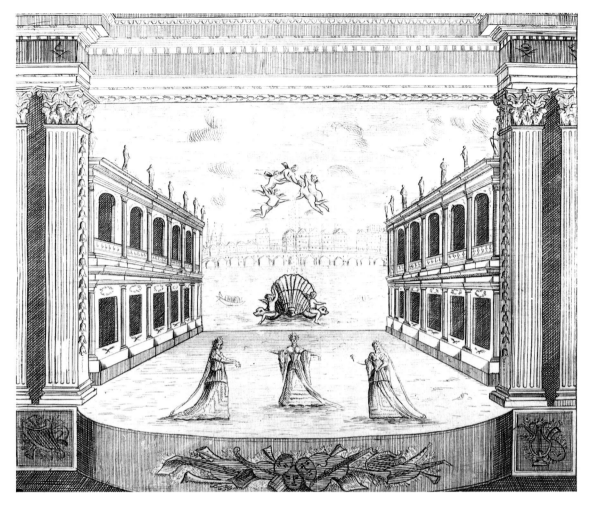

posts: on 22 July the Lord Chamberlain sent to the Gentlemen Ushers 'Warrants to swear and admit John Bannister, Robert Carr, Robert Strong, Henry Heale, Charles Powell and Henry Purcell, composer, as musicians for the private musick'.[9] From amongst the papers of Charles, 6th Earl of Dorset, who was Lord Chamberlain from 1689 to 1697, we find a complete list of the 'Musitians for the private Musick' which includes exactly forty, three of whom, Purcell, Blow and Alexander Damazene, are named as composers. Despite this official list, enthusiasm for music at court was on the wane, and the interests of performing musicians, and Purcell in particular, were turning towards public concerts and the world of theatre.

The two principal public theatres in use in London during most of Purcell's career had been in existence since the early 1670s. The Theatre Royal in Drury Lane had been built in 1674 at a cost of around £4,000, replacing an older theatre which had burned down

The Theatre Royal, Drury Lane, had been rebuilt in 1674, again to a design traditionally associated with Wren. It was smaller and less lavishly decorated than the Dorset Garden theatre. This illustration shows the prologue to an opera called Arianna, *performed there the year it opened.*

before at a cost of some £9,000. Drury Lane was 110 feet deep and 60 feet wide whereas Dorset Garden was thirty feet longer (excluding the famous portico over which the distinguished actor Thomas Betterton had a flat) and slightly less wide; the extra depth enabled the theatre to accommodate the scenic stages and the latest machinery which were its speciality. For audience comfort, the Dorset Garden theatre was the more lavishly fitted, even boasting benches covered with cloth. Drury Lane was more spartan, and concentrated on less flamboyant, more literary plays. In both theatres the pit was the main seating area. At Dorset Garden there were two tiers of boxes, each holding twenty people, and a gallery above. At Drury Lane the middle gallery does not seem to have been divided, although some alterations were made in 1696 to provide boxes on the edge of the stage. We do not know the exact capacities of the theatres but a full house would have meant serious crowding on the benches and perhaps as many as a thousand people attending in terribly cramped conditions: six hundred would have been uncomfortable. Such sell-outs were relatively rare, and calculations from the accounts suggest that an average house, with box office takings of £50–£60, was around four hundred. Just as in today's commercial West End, a production needed a long run with good average houses to generate a profit.

The design of the Restoration stage was quite different from that of its Jacobean predecessor: the fore-stage, like the earlier apron stage, was the main acting area, but the audience sat in front of it, and not round it. As the emphasis on spectacle grew, so the area behind the proscenium arch became more important. The stage machinist could conjure up incredible spectacles, changing scenes by drawing apart flats (moving on grooves in the floor) to reveal new sets behind. Devices, mechanically more and more ingenious, were invented to enable objects and people to rise from the depths, moons to wax and wane, backdrops to change, goddesses to fly across the sky and a host of other delights. Not only were songs within plays an important part of the action, but incidental music was vital to cover scene changes. Purcell already held posts at court, the Chapel Royal and Westminster Abbey, was supervisor of the royal instruments and a busy freelance composer whose compositions were appearing in print with great regularity. Over the next six years he was to add the strain of becoming the most successful theatrical composer in London.

Purcell's second ode in 1689 was a commission from an unusual source. The score of 'Celestial music did the gods inspire' is titled 'A song that was perform'd at Mr. Maidwell's, a schoolmaster on ye 5th of August 1689 ye words by one of his scholars'. That anonymous scholar certainly had a respectable grounding in the classics, and when his or her work is set alongside that of some of the efforts with which Purcell was confronted at court, compares surprisingly well. The overture was lifted directly from the 1685 coronation anthem 'My heart is inditing': Purcell rarely re-cycled his own work, so this suggests some degree of haste. Two movements were especially good. 'Her charming strains' was scored over a four-bar ground for countertenor and the 'otherworldly' sound of two recorders, but it is 'When Orpheus sang, all Nature did rejoice' that stands out. Over a hypnotic chordal accompaniment the countertenor weaves a florid line to illustrate Orpheus and his lyre delighting nature and subduing lions, tigers and even 'cruel Pluto'.

That commission for Mr Maidwell's schoolchildren was unusual, but has caused scholars little confusion and led to no controversy. The same could not be said for Purcell's only true opera, *Dido and Aeneas*. Argument has always surrounded its date of first performance: scholars have puzzled over *Dido* apparently being written for 'Josias Priest's School for Young Ladies in Chelsea'. W. Barclay Squire (writing in 1918) was the first to upset the long-held theory that *Dido* had been written in 1678, proposing instead 1689. Much more recently, musicological tongues and pens have been sent flying by the controversial suggestion of a composition date of 1683–84.[10] That argument has since been seriously questioned by several writers, most recently by Curtis Price, who points out that all the proposals for dating *Dido* have been based on a source copied around 1750;[11] this source disagrees in several aspects with the surviving 1689 libretto. Much of the argument for 1683–84 has been based on interpretation of the supposed allegorical content of the libretto and, more worryingly, on stylistic analysis of the music – a risky business with Purcell. Price illustrates his reservations about musical analysis by re-using the same musical arguments as were employed to 'prove' 1684 to give the (deliberately absurd) date of *after* 1689![12] As he concludes, all that is certain is that the first known performance of *Dido* took place at Priest's school some time before December 1689, when Nahum Tate's libretto was published.

It is not perhaps as surprising as it would first appear that a performance of such a work took place at a girls' boarding school. The school's owner, Josias Priest, later set the dances for several of Purcell's semi-operas: he was clearly a theatre enthusiast and an admirer of Purcell's music. That Purcell later worked with him on the professional stage suggests that Priest was an unusually skilled choreographer. All the solo roles except that of Aeneas could have been sung by girls (or professionals could have taken certain central roles); getting in outsiders as soloists, tenors and basses for the chorus and any necessary extra instrumentalists would presumably have posed no more problems than it has ever done for a school production (or been any more unusual than it is nowadays at an independent school). All it would have taken to entice the professional performers of London was a fee! Richard Luckett has suggested that operatic performances were probably an annual event at this particular school. To ensure that all Priest's girls could take part in the production, there was plenty of opportunity for dance in *Dido*, as a glance at the 1689 libretto shows: including the prologue, there were no less than seventeen separate dance sequences.

Purcell closely modelled the form of *Dido and Aeneas* on that of a work composed by his friend and colleague John Blow. *Venus and Adonis* had been written during the early 1680s to entertain King Charles and, according to a printed libretto of 17 April 1684, was also performed at Josias Priest's school. Like that opera, *Dido* was written in three acts with an allegorical prologue in the French style, and took as its story the ill-fated relationship between an imperious woman and a less committed man. Both operas culminate in the death of one of the protagonists, both use a marvellous series of dances to articulate the drama (showing the strong influence of the Stuart court masque), and both integrate the chorus fully into the drama. But in its development of these aspects, its carefully controlled key structure, its startling recitatives and arias (influenced by the latest developments in Italian opera), Purcell's only full opera stands proudly as one of the great monuments of English music.

The instrumental writing is superb, with a marvellous slow opening to the overture and a host of varied and characterful dance music which includes the fine 'Triumphing Dance', the splendidly characterful 'Echo Dance of Furies' and 'The Witches' Dance'. The tuneful, brilliantly-crafted chorus work ranges from the manic 'Destruction's our delight' and the echo song 'In our deep vaulted cell' to the rollicking 'Come away, fellow sailors' and the desolate final 'With drooping wings'. For the soloists, Purcell's masterful semi-recitatives and the accompagnato of the Sorceress's startling 'Wayward sisters' provide perfect dramatic substance, and the arias brilliantly illustrate the wide expanse of differing emotions. Dido's first aria 'Ah! Belinda' mournfully laments over its ground bass, Belinda's 'Pursue thy conquest, love' spiritedly exhorts Cupid's dart to do its business, the two witches gleefully endeavour to wreak meteorological havoc, the 'Second Woman' (a much more important role than her rather ordinary title would suggest) sings the gently undulating 'Oft she visits this lone mountain' and the drama culminates in Dido's famous, desolate lament 'When I am laid in earth'. Such a poignant movement could have come from no other quill than Purcell's.

That Purcell was continuing in his job (at £56 per annum) as supervisor of the royal instruments is confirmed by regular quarterly payments shown between April 1689 and September 1692 for instrument repairs. The payment at the end of September 1689 would have been particularly welcome as another Purcell son, this time named Edward, was baptised at Westminster Abbey on 6 September. Of more light-hearted interest is another entry in the same record which shows that little has changed: 'Drums, Trumpeters and Kettle Drums, Sundays only: 6 loaves; 6 gal. beer; 2 quarts claret on the days of their Majesties eating public'.[13]

The formal establishment of the Chapel Royal emerged slowly through the bureaucratic mechanism. On 5 October 1689 certificates of admission were granted to fifteen Gentlemen of the Chapel Royal: the names include 'Henry Pursell' and John Blow, who continued as Gentleman and Master of the Children. Earlier in the month four members had been admitted (including William Child, presumably as one of the three organists, and Stephen Crespion, also appointed 'Confessor to their Majesties' Household' as he had been to Charles II). By the end of November a further four Gentlemen had been admitted: the Chapel Royal strength was a respectable twenty-three.[14]

But by now, Purcell's writing for the church was almost over. The verse anthem 'Praise the Lord O Jerusalem' seems to be the only one that he wrote in 1689. The text is one for the Sunday before Advent (though Purcell had used it at the coronation of James II in 1685 as the last section of 'My heart is inditing'), and the writing suggests that this anthem was composed for a special occasion. The symphony is especially spacious, beginning with a series of four mysterious block chords before a winding series of imitative entries leads into a lyrical triple-time section of great beauty. The first vocal entry is sung not by the full choral forces but by a quintet of solo singers whose five-part texture allows rich harmonies. 'For kings shall be thy nursing fathers, and queens thy nursing mothers' contains delicious suspensions. At 'Be thou exalted Lord', constructed over a rising arpeggio, the mood brightens and gradually enlarges to include the full choir: a series of Alleluias, each more spacious than the previous one, leads to a closing seven bars of expansive duple-time Alleluias.

The uncertainty surrounding the last year of King James's reign was felt in the world of music publishing and, as a result, Purcell's name only appears in three publications of 1689. The third book of *The Banquet of Music* had actually been licensed in December 1688 but in any case only contained two of Purcell's works, a catch and the duet 'Were I to choose the greatest bliss'. The third book of *Comes Amoris* contained the charming songs 'Scarce had the rising sun appear'd', 'See how the fading glories of the year' and two duets – 'Let Hector, Achilles, and each brave commander' and 'Nestor, who did to thrice man's age attain'. In May 1689 *The Second Part of Musick's Hand-maid* was published by Henry Playford, containing keyboard music by Purcell: amongst the seven smaller pieces by Purcell came Lilliburlero (again) and three song transcriptions. More significant was the keyboard suite in C major (Z665), and a 'New Ground': this was a keyboard version of 'Here the deities' (from the 1683 ode 'Welcome to all the pleasures'), made far more busy than its gentle original with a syncopated part for the right hand.

The autumn of 1689 found Purcell's music back in the theatre with a single song, 'Thy genius, lo!', written for the Genius in a rather gruesome tragedy *The Massacre of Paris,* by the brilliant but unpredictable playwright Nathaniel Lee. This grand set-piece was sung by the actor-singer John Bowman.

As 1689 drew to a close King William's taciturn and uncommunicative ways were making him extremely unpopular with the English. Burgemeester Witsen of Amsterdam is said to have remarked that people in the coffee-houses were saying 'We have beheaded one king and thrown out another and we know how to deal with the third'.[15] Now that the former King James was in Ireland stirring up trouble, affairs there were going from bad to worse and it became clear that William would have to go to Ireland himself. In his absence Mary would have to rule the country. With the possibility of a French invasion and a Jacobite rebellion, this would not be easy. In the event, William did not depart until June 1690.

For the annual celebration in 1690 at Merchant Taylors' Hall of 'the Assembly of the Nobility and Gentry of the City and County of York' Tom D'Urfey was commissioned to write an ode, and Purcell to set it to music. In the event, elections caused a postponement from 14 February to 27 March, but D'Urfey (never the most critical of writers) recorded that Purcell's 'Yorkshire Feast Song' was 'One of the finest Compositions he ever made, and cost £100 the performing'. The libretto was suitably historical – and allegorical – in tone for the occasion, and Purcell scored the work on a grand scale, including strings, oboes and trumpets in his orchestra. As ever, it is the more intimate movements that stand out: 'The pale and the purple rose' has a gentle off-beat accompaniment and extended ritornello. The highlight is the tenor solo 'So when the glittering Queen of Night', which Purcell sets over a ground bass, just five notes long, also utilized in the main melody. D'Urfey's text here is inspired, and Purcell's reaction to it is sublime in its calm, nocturnal poise. The theme of music finds rich, six-part counterpoint (including double augmentation in the bass line) in 'Let music join in a chorus'. Principally, however, grand ceremonial was the order of the day, and one gets the feeling that Purcell's heart was not in the mighty movements – but he was no doubt extremely grateful for the fee that this rather bizarre commission brought him.

On 16 June 1690 the managers of London's Theatre Royal in Drury Lane announced the staging of the first large-scale musical work of William and Mary's reign. *The Prophetess, or The History of Dioclesian* was to be the first new semi-opera since *Circe* (1677). That Purcell was commissioned to be the sole composer was testament enough to his reputation, but he also may have had something to prove. Dryden's *Albion and Albanius* had been scored as an opera by the imported Louis Grabu in 1685; it was regarded at the time as a failure and has been panned by the critics ever since. Purcell may have wished to show that an Englishman could do a far better job. The characterization in the libretto (probably by Thomas Betterton after Fletcher and Massinger) made life difficult for the composer, for there was no sympathetic character for whom Purcell could write the expressive music in which he excelled. He clearly wanted to write a grand score. There is some splendid instrumental music (including the famous chaconne for two recorders in Act III and the 'Soft Musick that's plaid just before the Dance of Furies' that is reminiscent of Locke's Curtain Tune in *The Tempest*), some good songs (including 'What shall I do to show how much I love her'), and some excellent

John Dryden, the greatest poet and dramatist of the late seventeenth century in England, collaborated with Purcell on a number of theatrical ventures, including King Arthur. *He came to admire Purcell greatly.*

Thomas Betterton: theatre manager, impresario, actor and an occasional author. He was probably responsible for the text of one of Purcell's major semi-operas, Dioclesian.

chorus work (especially 'Let the priest and processions the hero attend'). An extended masque closes *Dioclesian*: it has almost nothing to do with the plot that has just been acted out, but it proved to be one of Purcell's most popular stage works in the next century.

At court, William was making cuts to the musical establishment. Around May 1690 he issued a command that 'the musicians be presently reduced to 24 and an instrument keeper, and that though there is provision made only for that number by the establishment, yet care will be taken for paying the rest for the time they have served'.[16] Only the trumpeters and drummers escaped his axe. No wonder more and more musicians were seeking employment in the theatres.

When Grabu had set John Dryden's *Albion and Albanius* Dryden had praised the composer in his preface: 'When any of our Country-men excel him, I shall be glad, for the sake of old England, to be shown my error'. In April 1690 Purcell was the composer of the symphony, eight pieces of instrumental music and three songs for Dryden's *Amphitryon, or The Two Sosias*. When Purcell's music was published (in October) by Heptinstall, Dryden was able to state that the composer was as fine as any on the Continent, though he did not find it necessary to eat his words completely, adding that he thought that Purcell had been so 'since his happy and judicious Performances in the late Opera [*Dioclesian*]'. This undistinguished play was to be the start of a series of collaborations between, arguably, the best play-

178

wright of the day and, undoubtedly (and not just in Dryden's rather pompous opinion), the leading composer of the age.

For Queen Mary's twenty-eighth birthday on 30 April Purcell set D'Urfey's ode 'Arise my Muse'. The scoring was the fullest yet for a royal ode, with five-part strings (two violins, two violas and bassi) and pairs of oboes and trumpets. The grand symphony made much play between these groups of instruments and the opening solo was Italianately florid in its vocal line. The chorus call to 'sound your instruments and charm the earth' was answered in splendid fashion by the assembled orchestra. The most effective movement was 'See how the glitt'ring ruler of the day' where, over an eight-bar ground, a solo tenor calls the 'attending planets all To wanton revels'. The text of the whole ode was especially topical, referring in particular to William's present troubles in Ireland – including remarks on the sadness of 'Eusebia' (England) and much flattery of William as a conqueror who would 'teach them loyalty and sense' – and the ode ends with a stirring call to the prince, 'Leave not thy work undone'.

William III's most renowned military achievement was his victory over the forces of James II at the Battle of the Boyne in July 1690.

And on 4 June 1690 William set off for Ireland, leaving Mary in charge of England, where she surprised everyone by her cool command of public affairs. In her memoirs she admits that 'I was left with this powerful fleet upon the coast, many enemies and discontented persons in the kingdom, and not above 5 or 6,000 men to defend it, not secure of these at home; great reasons to apprehend danger from abroad; so I believe never any person was left in greater streights of all kinds'.[17] William left her with a cabinet of nine men to advise her; Mary's character sketches of these reveal her as a rather more perceptive ruler than her husband. In a sea battle with the French, the English commander, Lord Torrington, proved to be a coward, and the result was a crushing defeat for him and his Dutch allies, who suffered the worst losses. Mary effectively sacked him, and her courage and determination won her much admiration in England. Meanwhile in Ireland, on 1 July at the Battle of the Boyne, William defeated James's French and Irish forces; but at home his Dutch troops were roundly beaten by the French at Fleurus with great losses. Mary could not wait for William to return and, though her public image remained strong, her letters to William became more and more desperate for his return. When he finally did so, on 10 September, it was 'so great a joy to me that I want words to express it'.[18]

Only one of Purcell's church anthems dates from 1690, and a copy now in Oxford, probably made by Henry Knight of Wadham College, bears the inscription 'H.P Sep. 9/90'. 'My song shall be alway' was scored for solo bass (the soprano version, possibly by Playford, does not appear until 1703). Despite being composed on a large scale there is, besides the symphony (repeated at the mid-point), almost nothing for the upper strings to do: the choir are treated even more lightly. The solo bass dominates, first in tuneful arioso but then, more characterfully, in sections of recitativo. In 'O Lord the very heavens' Purcell is at his most Italianate, changing pace and mood with great subtlety and at 'O Lord God of hosts' he writes music that would be at home in the opera house: the sea rages, full of running semiquavers and bluster. As is so often the case, Purcell's concluding Alleluia is restrained and quietly understated.

Purcell had clearly established himself as the leading composer for the theatre, for the new season, which began in the London theatres in the autumn, found his music in two productions. For Elkanah Settle's *Distressed Innocence, or The Princess of Persia* which opened at the Theatre Royal in October he wrote an overture and seven pieces of incidental music, and for Thomas Southerne's highly successful comedy *Sir Anthony Love, or The Rambling Lady* a fine overture, some instrumental music, a song and a duet.

Purcell's works, new and old, continued to appear on sale in the shops. In the fourth book of *The Banquet of Music*, published towards the end of October, Playford included a catch, and three works that had already appeared in Carr's *Comes Amoris*, and the sixth edition of *Apollo's Banquet* emerged 'with new additions' including eight pieces, some of them keyboard transcriptions, by Purcell. On 2 December 1690 the licence was granted to Playford for the fifth book of *The Banquet of Music* which contained the catch 'Young Collin cleaving of a beam', the lovely duet 'Lost is my quiet forever' and the 'Dialogue between Thyrsis and Daphne' 'Why, my Daphne, why complaining'.

On 17 January 1691 King William left England again for Holland, taking with him a large entourage of attendants, including a number of the royal musicians. Scholars, including both Westrup and Zimmerman, have suggested that Purcell was among these musicians, but the available records suggest that they were mistaken. The larger proportion of the royal musical household travelled with the king, but a number of performers stayed in London to perform for the queen. The Earl of Dorset (Lord Chamberlain between 1689 and 1697) made three lists of players who took part in the trip; he seems inadvertently to have caused confusion in two of those three lists by also naming the remaining members of the musical establishment who stayed in London. Staggins and sixteen members of the royal violins were 'the part that attended his Majesty in to Holland' and nine made up 'The Remaining Part that Attended the Queen'. Lower in the list come five 'Hooboys' who were specially contracted to go on the voyage: they were not regular members of the royal establishment, and a special note is made that 'These are to be payd for their Journey into Holland, & no longer'. The confusion arises because directly beneath the oboists' names are those of John Blow and Henry Purcell, respectively named as composer and 'Harpsicall', and the names of the ten members of the 'Vocall Consort'. It is clear in all three records that the Vocal Musick stayed in London: Blow and Purcell were attached to that arm of the royal music as composers, a fact confirmed in one of Dorset's three lists.[19] They would thus have been unlikely to go on the trip, and the king (who was not an especial fan of vocal music, as he demonstrated in his cuts to the musical establishment) would hardly have taken two composers with him if the musicians for whom they were meant to compose were still at home. Final confirmation comes from the third of Dorset's lists,[20] which records the 'Musitians and others who attended His Ma[jes]tie into Holland': there follow the names of Staggins and seventeen of the violins, five hautboys, John Mosley (keeper of the instruments) and William Broune (chamber-keeper to the musick). The names of Purcell and Blow do not appear.

William was away until April; he had desperately missed Holland, and was delighted to be back in his homeland. In The Hague he host-ed a congress whose impressive guest list contained half the rulers of Europe; after some days of talking they agreed to put an army of about 220,000 soldiers into the field against the French for the season, but little was done to ensure any formal diplomatic co-operation. The result was that when Louis XIV, catching the allies off-guard, attacked Mons, the most important fortress in the southern Netherlands, 50,000 soldiers were at the assembly point south of Brussels, but there was no sign of the promised Spanish transports. Mons capitulated as William looked helplessly on, Louis returned in glory to Versailles and William returned, furious with his Spanish allies, to London. On 9 April, just before his arrival, fire broke out at Whitehall, destroying much of the Stone Gallery down to the waterside and the apartments of the Duchess of Portsmouth. In a desperate attempt to stop the fire spreading further, several other buildings were blown up.

While William was abroad, Purcell was not only still in London: he was also clearly hard at work. In early 1691 Purcell himself pub-lished all the vocal and instrumental music in *Dioclesian*, offering the edition by private subscription. The preface, penned in the most flow-ery language, was probably not written by Purcell. An 'Advertisement' at the back bears the hallmarks of an apologetic and slightly frazzled composer:

> In order to the speedier Publication of this Book, I employed two several Printers; but One of them falling into some trouble, and the Volume swelling to a Bulk beyond my expectation, have been the Occasions of this Delay. It has been objected that some of the Songs are already common; but I presume that the Subscribers, upon perusal of the Work, will easily be convinc'd that they are not the Essential Parts of it. I have according to my Promise in the Proposals, been very carefull in the Examination of every Sheet, and hope the Whole will appear as Correct as any yet Extant. My desire to make it as cheap as possibly I cou'd to the Subscribers,

prevail'd with me so far above the consideration of my own Interest, that I find, too late, the Subscription-money will scarcely amount to the Expence of compleating this Edition.

At least two of the songs had been published in 'pirate' editions: maybe the troublesome printer had been the source of the piracy. Elsewhere, Playford's second book of *Apollo's Banquet* included a number of Purcell's smaller works, many in arrangements for the violin, flute or flageolet, the third book of *Vinculum Societatis* presented a few songs and instrumental items from the theatre, and also on offer to the public went some of the music Purcell had written for *Amphitryon*.

For the queen's birthday on 30 April Purcell provided another fine birthday ode, 'Welcome, welcome, glorious morn'. This was an expansive work which required not only the customary strings but also pairs of oboes and trumpets whose presence is felt right from the extrovert start of what is a particularly good symphony. The instrumental writing throughout the ode is especially fine, including a dancing ritornello following the duet 'At thy return the joyful earth'. The tenor (or perhaps high bass) solo 'And lo! a sacred fury' is a compositional tour-de-force, with a dramatic recitativo-style opening leading into the extended section 'To lofty strains', which is set over a remarkable dotted six-bar ground bass. The last chorus, 'Sound all ye spheres', is stirring stuff, as first a solo tenor and two trumpets announce the theme, and then in augmented counterpoint the entire ensemble end the work in triumphant vein.

While Purcell was working on this ode, he was probably also at work on an even larger project, Dryden's *King Arthur*. Dryden had originally written the libretto in 1684, at the same time as he was working on *Albion and Albanius,* but with the death of King Charles his work remained unperformed. By the time Dryden came to resurrect the manuscript, the political climate was very different and, although the 1684 libretto has not been found, we can safely presume that much of the allegory that would have been intended to reflect and glorify the position of Charles in contemporary Britain would have needed to be altered. In his 1691 prologue Dryden admits that he was forced to 'alter the first design' so as 'not to offend the present Times, nor a Government which has hitherto protected me': although he was not especially keen on William, Dryden could not afford to offend him. Not only did politics force Dryden to re-write – so did his composer. In the introduction to *King Arthur*, he reveals that Purcell made him alter some lines: 'the numbers [i.e. metre] of poetry and vocal music are sometimes so contrary that in many places I have been obliged to cramp my verses, and make them rugged to the reader, that they may be harmonious to the hearer'.

The first performance of *King Arthur* took place in the Dorset Garden theatre in May or June 1691. No complete version survives from then, and modern editions have had to gather together music from some sixty sources. Many twentieth-century performances have ignored the fact that there was plenty of dialogue between the musical numbers and leaving it out renders a curious plot almost unfathomable. *King Arthur* was revived at least twice during the composer's lifetime and performed frequently during the winter of 1691–92. The probable hurry to get the music ready for the first performances, the string of revivals and the tailoring of sections for masques and gala concerts after Purcell's death may all have added to the musicological confusion. The performances were a great success: indeed, in commercial terms the opera was Purcell's most successful stage work, with the composer receiving accolades both at the time and for many years afterwards. If we consider the quality of some of the other theatre music Purcell produced between 1689 and 1695 this is slightly puzzling. Although *King Arthur* contains much excellent music, there was little scope for Purcell to introduce pathos or tragedy. Opera audiences, presumably, were not especially interested in drama whose content was too serious.

As ever, the standard of the instrumental writing was wonderfully high, with a series of marvellous symphonies and act tunes (including two movements borrowed from odes, suggesting that compositional time was indeed short). The dramatic highlight was the famous frost scene where the Cold Genius rises and sings 'What power art thou' to a highly effective, shaking string accompaniment; Comus's comic 'Your hay it is mow'd' would no doubt have brought the house down. But, these aside, the two most memorable vocal movements are, perhaps predictably, gentle ones; the Shepherd's pastoral 'How blest are shepherds' and the famous song for Venus, in praise of Britain, 'Fairest Isle'.

Though *King Arthur* must have taken a considerable amount of Purcell's time, this was not the only stage work to which he put his mind in 1691. Earlier in the season he had composed instrumental music to *The Gordian Knot Unty'd* (a production whose libretto has subsequently disappeared), producing eight movements. Time must again have been short, for several of these were arrangements of earlier works, including an air based on a movement from the ode 'What shall be done in behalf of the man', and the rondeau-minuet and another ritornello from the ode 'From Hardy Climes'. For Dryden and Howard's *The Indian Emperor, or The Conquest of Mexico* at Drury Lane sometime during 1692 Purcell set a song, 'I look'd and saw within': the melancholy repetitions of 'never' at the close look forward to 'The Plaint' from *The Fairy-Queen*, whereas the play (a sequel to the 1665 production of *The Indian Queen*) looks forward to the major musical production in 1695 based on that same story. In December 1691 Purcell contributed four songs to Southerne's comedy *The Wives' Excuse, or Cuckolds make Themselves*. In one section of the play a character complains to another, a composer, that a lyric he had earlier written has not yet been set to music: the composer counters that 'the Words are so abominably out of the way of Musick, I don't know how to humour 'em: There's no setting 'em, Or singing 'em, to please any body but himself'. Purcell might have allowed himself a wry smile.

King William had by now set an apparently regular plan. In the early part of the year he would leave England to confront Louis in Europe, and in the autumn he would return to do battle with parliament, attempting to drum up enough funds for his next campaign. In his absence Mary would reign, noting with discomfort the lack of regard in which William was increasingly held. An absentee king, who made it clear that he detested London and would much rather stay in Holland, was not likely to be a popular one. Often his court musicians would not see him for months on end, a fact which seems to be borne out by the scarcity of musical mentions in the Lord Chamberlain's records. One curiosity from 1691, recorded by Lafontaine (which has not been subsequently traced), was the order 'that the King's Chapel shall be all the year through kept both morning and evening with solemn musick like a collegiate church'.[21] The demand would have made life for the three organists at the Chapel Royal, of whom Purcell was still one, that little bit busier. Proof of that continuance of employment is given in the 1692 edition of *Angliae Notitiae*, where Purcell is not only named as one of the three organists (at £100 per annum) but is also mistakenly credited with Blow's position as Master of the Twelve Children (an error which is corrected in the next edition of 1694). Purcell was also still one of members of the Vocal Musick with a salary of £40.[22]

By January 1692 it was clear that the success of *King Arthur* was going to be followed up. *The Gentleman's Journal* of that month

Now I ſpeak of Muſic I muſt tell you that we ſhall have ſpeedily a New Opera, wherein ſomething very ſurpriſing is promiſed us; Mr. *Purcel* who joyns to the Delicacy and Beauty of the *Italian* way, the Graces and Gayety of the *French*, compoſes the Muſic, as he hath done for the *Propheteſs*, and the laſt Opera called King *Artbur*, which hath been plaid ſeveral times the laſt Month. Other Nations beſtow the name of Opera only on ſuch Plays whereof every word is ſung. But experience hath taught us that our Engliſh genius will not relliſh that perpetual Singing. I dare not accuſe the Language for being over-charged with Conſonants, which may take off the beauties of the Recitative part, tho in ſeveral other Countries I have ſeen their *Opera's* ſtill Crowded every time, tho long and almoſt all Recitative.

The Gentleman's Journal *for January 1692 contains the announcement that Purcell was at work on a new opera,* The Fairy-Queen, *and adds an interesting comment on English taste: 'Other nations bestow the name of opera only on such plays whereof every word is sung. But experience hath taught us that our English genius will not relish that perpetual singing.' A later issue of the same journal (June 1692) printed Purcell's second setting of the song 'If Music be the Food of Love'.*

(27)

A Song ſet by Mr. *Henry Purcell*, the words by Colonel *Heveningham*.

IF Mu—ſick be the food of Love, Sing on, ſing on, ſing

on, ſing on till I am fill'd, am fill'd with joy: For

then my liſt--ning Soul you move, for then my liſt—ning

F

announced: 'I must tell you that we shall have speedily a new opera, wherein something very surprising is promised us: Mr Purcell, who joins to the delicacy and beauty of the Italian way the graces and gaiety of the French, composes the music as he hath done for… King Arthur, which hath been played several times the last month'.[23] The readers were given a taste of the composer's music with the publication of the song 'Stript of their green'. During the year Motteux, clearly a fan of the composer, published a further four Purcell songs in *The Gentleman's Journal;* in June he printed the delicious song 'If music be the food of love'. This was the first of two similar versions that were printed: the other appeared the next year in the fourth book of *Comes Amoris.* Motteux's version was in G minor, that in *Comes Amoris* in A minor; the latter setting, though less well-known nowadays, is perhaps even more entrancing, with the slightly risqué list of qualities – 'your eyes, your mien, your tongue' – which ardently declare 'That you are music everywhere', giving the last two lines a panting, ecstatic quality. 'Music' is set to a ravishing melisma. Purcell's songs were still appearing in a variety of publications: in March Carr and Playford advertised in *The London Gazette* that the sixth book of *The Banquet of Musick* was ready, containing two Purcell songs, the dramatic, cantata-like 'Fly swift, ye hours' and a delightfully tuneful setting 'On the brow of Richmond Hill'.

Purcell's 1692 offering for the queen's birthday on 30 April was a setting of Sir Charles Sedley's ode 'Love's goddess sure was blind'. The fourth of Purcell's odes for Mary, this was the most intimately scored, requiring just strings and a pair of recorders. The two-section symphony was one of his finest, with a viola part in the first, wistful section that the player must have relished. The melody comes once in the violins, but three times in the viola, and is wrapped in the most glorious harmony. The triple-time second section appears, on paper, to be lighter in character, but (as with so much of Purcell's music, which needs to be played to discover its true riches) in practice still has an underlying current of melancholy, heightened at the end as the opening mood returns. Charles Sedley's opening words are given to a countertenor soloist, leading into an elegant, extended string ritornello. Other notable movements include the gently undulating duet, 'Sweetness of nature' (where Purcell pairs alto and high tenor with the pastoral sound of two recorders), the compositional tour-de-force of the duet 'Many, many such days' (set over a two-bar ground bass), the chorus 'May she to heaven late return', which is another example of Purcell's mastery of counterpoint, and the pathos-laden quartet 'As much as we below', which is full of discords, especially in the descending chromaticism of 'mourn'. Of the movement 'May her blest example chase' the music historian Sir John Hawkins tells a story which, whether true or not, gives an idea of the problems of working for royalty. Demanding musical entertainment one day, the queen sent for the soprano Mrs Hunt, the bass John Gostling and Purcell. They performed several of Purcell's songs, but the queen was clearly not satisfied with such sophisticated music, eventually requesting that Mrs Hunt sing the Scots ballad 'Cold and Raw'. Mrs Hunt complied, and accompanied herself on the lute. Purcell meantime sat at the harpsichord 'unemployed and not a little nettled at the queen's preference for a vulgar ballad to his music'. When he came to write 'Love's goddess sure' Purcell, hopefully by now amused by the episode, must have remembered the queen's request, and used the ballad tune as the bass line to 'May her blest example chase'. Harmonically it is not a particularly good line, but Purcell managed to force a melody over it: the rustic string ritornello works rather well. The ballad itself had been published in 1688 in the second book of *Comes Amoris*.

There is a story of Arabella Hunt (opposite), a much admired soprano of her day, singing Purcell songs for Queen Mary who, however, soon tired of such high art and asked her to sing a Scottish ballad called 'Cold and Raw'.

By the time of Queen Mary's birthday, Purcell had apparently moved house from Bowling Alley East. The St Margaret's parish accounts for Bowling Alley have the word 'Gone' written against Purcell's name, but next to it is written 'Ann Peters – 2 houses'. Perhaps Ann Peters was a relation of Purcell's wife. From the St Margaret's vestry books it seems that Purcell did not give up the house in Bowling Alley, but sub-let it: an entry for 28 April states that 'At Mr Purcell's in Bowling Alley, Mrs Ann David, Mrs Lucy David, Rebecca David, Letitia Davis to be summoned to appear to show cause why they should not be assessed £1 per quarter' and, a little further down the page, 'Madame Carhile at Mr Purcell's to be summoned'. If Ann Peters too was living at the address, there would have been six tenants in Purcell's house. In the St Margaret's overseers' accounts two years later we find Purcell named as the tenant of a house in Marsham Street occupied until 1692 by one Ann Law.[24] No evidence has yet been found that Purcell moved to Marsham Street immediately on leaving Bowling Alley, but it would be fairly safe to presume that he would have moved with the least possible inconvenience to his wife and young children.

While Purcell was moving house, his new opera was well into its rehearsals. The story-line was taken from Shakespeare's *A Midsummer Night's Dream* and it was called *The Fairy-Queen*. We do not know who made the adaptation: Elkanah Settle has been suggested by several historians (though without any real evidence); Curtis Price proposes Thomas Betterton. Whoever was Purcell's collaborator, critics have been rather unkind about his efforts but Shakespeare's basic story emerges without too much damage, especially if at least some of the spoken dialogue (all too often missing in twentieth-century

M.^{RS} ARABELLA HUNT Dyed December 26.th 1705.

Were there on Earth another Voice like thine, The late afflicted World some hopes might have,
Another Hand, so Blest with skill Divine,   And Harmony recall thee from the Grave.

G. Kneller S.B. Imp. et Angl. Eques Aur Pinx.   I. Smith fec. it ex. 1706.

performances) is presented. Based in a fantasy world, the story was perfect for a Stuart masque.

The production, which opened on 2 May 1692, was a costly affair. Narcissus Luttrell reported that the Theatre Royal spent £3,000 on it; the prompter, Downes, wrote that while the 'Court and Town were wonderfully satisfy'd with it... the Company got very little by it'.[25] The largest part of that £3,000 had been spent on stage machinery and costumes for the singers and dances: the production must have been a glittering affair. Purcell's music was of the highest quality, surpassing that of his two recent operas. For the scene changes and Josias Priest's dance sequences Purcell supplied a wealth of instrumental music, from the dreamy prelude to the 'First Music' (which so beautifully sets up the magic, other-worldly setting), the imposing overture and canzona to Act I, music to accompany swans coming forward, the 'Sonata while the sun rises' and the 'Dance for the Green Men' through to the 'Chacone' to which the Chinese Man and Woman danced. Many of the vocal numbers are prefaced by brilliant instrumental preludes, and throughout the quality of the songs and choruses is of the highest order. One of the most striking features of the opera is the way in which Purcell sets a song for soloist and continuo, and then transforms it into an instrumental ritornello or a chorus, turning already beguiling music into virtually new pieces by the addition of imaginative inner parts. The dancing 'Sing while we trip it', the mysterious bass solo 'Hush, no more' and the charming 'If love's a sweet passion' all show Purcell's harmonic facility at its most appealing.

The Fairy-Queen was by no means Purcell's only offering to the London stage in 1692. A month before the opera opened, Dryden's tragedy *Cleomenes, the Spartan Hero* was staged, and included the song 'No, no, poor suff'ring heart'. In January Purcell had already contributed the duet 'As soon as the chaos was made into form' for D'Urfey's new play, *The Marriage-hater Match'd*, and in June John Crowne's *Regulus* also featured a song by Purcell, 'Ah me! to many deaths decreed', which was published in the August edition of *The Gentleman's Journal*. In November Purcell wrote a song for a new play, probably by William Mountfort, *Henry the Second, King of England*. Two other productions for which Purcell wrote music, but whose dates of performance are not definitely known, have been ascribed to 1692 by historians: for Dryden's *Aureng-Zebe* he wrote the song 'I see she flies me' (published in 1694 in the fifth book of *Comes Amoris*) and for *Oedipus* he provided an instrumental prelude, three trios, a

OPPOSITE: *A page from Purcell's manuscript of* The Fairy-Queen, *a 'semi-opera' based on Shakespeare's* A Midsummer Night's Dream. *It opened at Drury Lane in June 1692.*

191

bass solo and, perhaps his single most famous theatre song, 'Music for a while'. This song was the second of three lyrics set to continuous music in Act III and was intended to charm the three Furies, thus enabling the ghost of King Laius to escape from the 'eternal bands' of hell and pronounce his daughter Euridice innocent of his murder and his son Oedipus guilty. The trio that precedes the famous song introduces the raised chromatic notes that are such a strong feature of the ostinato bass line. Besides the version in the second book of *Orpheus Britannicus* more than a dozen eighteenth-century manuscripts preserve 'Music for a while' and between them they raise many musicological contradictions. Late seventeenth- and early eighteenth-century notational conventions simply could not cope with the complexities of Purcell's chromaticism. (Purcell himself was a meticulous copyist who would show every single accidental, but his autograph does not survive.) The twentieth-century Purcell Society editors failed when confronted with the mass of contradictory source material and their efforts have been described by Curtis Price as a 'fictitious conflation'. Significantly, none of the reputable sources include the C flats at the word 'eternal' which appear in many modern editions.

In 1683 Purcell had composed 'Welcome to all the pleasures' for performance in celebration of St Cecilia's Day. Though the event had become an annual one, he had apparently not been asked to write another piece during the following nine years. For November 1692 the 'Gentlemen Lovers of Musick' turned to him to 'propagate the advancement of that divine Science'. Purcell produced his largest ode: a major, thirteen-movement work in praise of Cecilia, music and the instruments of music. Brady's poem was derived directly from Dryden's ode of 1687, which was the first to call for obbligato instruments, and also the first to suggest that Cecilia invented, rather than simply played, the organ. For his court odes Purcell was dependent on the forces available: for this celebration he was able to call on what Motteux described as 'the best voices and hands in town', and with 'Hail, bright Cecilia' Purcell excelled himself.

The composer chose to mix large, contrapuntal choruses with a sequence of airs for soloists and obbligato instruments. The canzona of the extensive symphony contains a fugue on two subjects, and is thematically linked to the fugato which closes the work in ingenious double augmentation. At the centre of the ode comes the powerful chorus 'Soul of the World' closing in 'perfect harmony'. Between this and the large-scale choruses that frame either end of the ode come an inspired selection of airs, based around an imaginative collection of compositional devices. 'Hark each Tree' is a sarabande on a ground, whilst 'Thou tun'st this World' is set as a minuet; 'In vain the am'rous Flute' is set to a passacaglia bass, and 'Wond'rous Machine' splendidly depicts a chugging organ with an inexorable ground bass. Motteux inadvertently caused confusion with the amazing tenor solo ' 'Tis Nature's voice' by writing that it was performed 'with incredible graces by Mr. Henry Purcell himself'. The traditional view has been to read that Purcell sang the movement, but a more realistic interpretation would be that those 'incredible graces' (i.e. ornaments) were written out by Purcell, rather than being left to the improvisatory skills of the soloist. Purcell's partial autograph in the Bodleian Library states that John Pate sang the movement; Evelyn described him as being 'reputed the most excellent singer, ever England had'.[26] In 'With Rapture of delight', the solo quartet that brings a moment of respite to the final chorus, the inexorably rising entries 'Of infinite Felicity' and the tension of the discord caused by the countertenor's sustained top C# is one of the most spine-tingling moments in all Purcell's large-scale music.

One of the violinists at the first performance may well have been John Goodwin, who gives another insight into the life of a musician. Two days after the success of Purcell's ode, Goodwin was on a charge: 'Whereas John Goodwyn one of his Majesties private Musick hath abused Dr. Richard of ye Treasury Chamber, with Scandalous and menaceing language, I do therefore suspend him in his place and all profitts thereto belonging untill I shall give further order. Dorset'.[27] Presumably Goodwin made amends, for nothing more about him appears in the record books until he made his will on 3 July 1693; he was buried a week later in Westminster Abbey.

For Purcell, it was undoubtedly another busy winter, although the unfortunate death of William Mountfort, actor, playwright and musician, in a street brawl, and the rather more conventional passing of the comedian Anthony Leigh brought a temporary halt to theatre life. By February, proceedings were back to normal and in each of the next four months another new play opened containing music by Purcell. In February Thomas Southerne's comedy *The Maid's Last Prayer, or Any rather than Fail* opened. In Act IV Southerne pictures a public concert of Marx Brothers-like pandemonium; this leads straight into the song 'Though you make no return to my passion' and, without any intervening dialogue, the famous duet 'No, resistance is but vain'. For the last act Purcell provided a setting of Congreve's 'Tell me no more I am deceived'. The next month Congreve's comedy *The Old Bachelor* opened: as well as providing two songs (including 'As Amoret and Thyrsis lay'), Purcell contributed nine contrasted instrumental numbers including a fine three-movement symphony. In April, for D'Urfey's curious comedy *The Richmond Heiress, or A Woman once in the Right* Purcell wrote an ambitious mad-dialogue, 'Behold the man with that gigantic might'. May 1693 saw the opening of Thomas Wright's pretty bad adaptation of Molière's *Les Femmes savantes*, titled *The Female Vertuoso*; Purcell wrote a duet for two sopranos, 'Love, thou art best'.

Despite his busy theatre schedule, Purcell also had his regular commission to fulfil for the queen's birthday. For 30 April 1693 (with King William away campaigning in Flanders) he set Nahum Tate's ode 'Celebrate this Festival', utilizing strings, a pair of oboes and recorders and the trumpeter John Shore. Purcell's trumpet writing, especially the obbligato in the bass solo 'While for a righteous cause', is testament to Shore's expertise on the instrument. The list of eleven singers preserved in the 'Royal' manuscript included Mrs Ayliff and 'the boy', who has been presumed to be Jemmy Bowen. For the overture Purcell raided 'Hail bright Cecilia', transposing the music from D major into C: the inference is that he had simply not had enough time to write a fresh piece. The intricate passage work for the two sopranos in the opening chorus suggests that both Bowen and Mrs Ayliff were accomplished singers: highly effective too is the seven-part vocal texture at 'Repeat Maria's name', the delicate scoring of 'Return, fond Muse' (written for tenor, two recorders and viola) and the quietly ecstatic setting for alto, over a ground bass, of 'Crown the altar'.

In an already busy year, Purcell also found time to return to writing music for the church. With a break of three years since his last verse anthem, 'O give thanks unto the Lord' invites comparison with earlier works. The two solo violins are provided with only the briefest of ritornelli at the close of sections and there is not even an opening symphony. The writing is often highly Italianate – in the vigorous interplay between choir and soloists and between major and minor sections, and also in the floridity of some solo sections. Predictably, however, the most original parts of the work are not exchanges between choir and soloists but the solo movements. There is a lyrical duet for alto and bass, 'Who can express', and an intricate alto solo, 'That I may see', which looks forward to the 'Te Deum' and 'Jubilate'

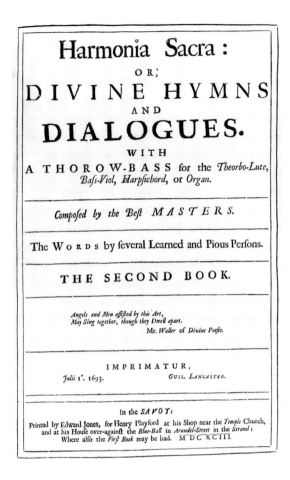

The second book of Harmonia Sacra appeared in 1693, containing five of Purcell's finest devotional songs.

of 1694, but the highlight of the anthem is the ravishing four-part verse 'Remember me, O Lord'. With its chromatically rising theme, its minor tonality and its highly charged, pleading repetitions of 'Remember me' and 'O visit me', it contains emotional writing as intense as anywhere in Purcell's output.

In the sphere of smaller-scale church music Purcell had also been busy. In early July 1693 the second volume of *Harmonia Sacra* was advertised for sale, contained in which were five of Purcell's finest devotional songs. Like the duet 'Let these amongst themselves' in the 1692 St Cecilia's Day Ode, 'Awake, ye dead' was set for two basses. Here was a far superior composition, its scoring unique in all the church music. Nahum Tate's cataclysmic 'Hymn upon the Last Day' was a work which clearly inspired Purcell. The opening shakes the dead from their slumbers; brief respite comes from the contrasting minor harmony of 'to sleep no more'. The continuo instruments violently launch 'Hark! from aloft', their thunderous repeated semiquavers competing with the vocal parts, imitating a 'noise so loud it deafs the ocean's roars', and the 'clatt'ring orbs' tumble from the top of the singers' ranges. The 'virtuous soul alone' enters in gently swinging triple-time, to be replaced by violent semiquavers as the very foundations of the earth shake. The virtuous soul 'ascends and mocks the universal wreck', whose destruction has been so vividly characterized in just three minutes of chamber music. 'Begin the song, and strike the living lyre' was the second of two religious poems by Abraham Cowley set by Purcell. Purcell clearly enjoyed setting Cowley's descriptive, classical ode 'The Resurrection', and the result is a striking composition which is full of word-painting.

'In guilty night' is unique among all Purcell's sacred music: it fits into no single category, combining elements of the devotional song with those of the cantata and the oratorio. Taking an episode from the Book of Samuel, Purcell produced an astonishing dramatic scena. According to the Bible, Saul had 'put away those that had familiar spirits, and the wizards, out of the land' but, about to go to war with his troops against the Philistines and receiving no reply to his prayers from either God or the prophets, in desperation he has to turn to one of those banished witches. His advisors tell him that one such character remains at Endor; Saul, disguised, goes to visit her. Purcell's opening sets Saul's stark desolation; the three voices enter quietly, building up the sense of tense theatricality with magical harmony to the first, chromatically dropping entries of 'Forsaken Saul' which then build to a powerful climax. Saul demands in semi-recitative that the witch 'call pow'rful arts together' to raise up a departed spirit; the woman, ignorant of her visitor's identity, desperately responds that she is fearful to do so, for 'cruel Saul' has 'kill'd and murder'd all that were wise and could on spirits call'. Saul assures her that 'No harm from Saul shall come to thee for this', and the witch agrees to his request, asking who it is her visitor wishes to call. Saul replies that it is 'Old Samuel'; the woman realizes who Saul is, and that she will now die. Her cries of 'Alas' are as powerful as any in Purcell's output. Saul again reassures her and, asked what she can see, the woman describes 'the gods ascending from below' and 'an old man mantled o'er'. Samuel's visit from the underworld has begun. He angrily demands why he has been robbed of his rest to see 'that which I hate' and Saul explains his position, desperately pleading 'Oh! for pity's sake, tell me, what shall I do'. Samuel looks into the future and grimly replies that Saul's army will be slain, his kingdom will fall and that 'tomorrow, thou and thy son shall be with me beneath'. (In the Bible, all three of Saul's sons are slain, and Saul, already injured, falls on his own sword rather than be taken by the Philistines.) The closing chorus, setting just two words, 'Oh! Farewell', is a superb ending to one of Purcell's best compositions.

Harmonia Sacra also contained two magnificent settings for solo soprano which demonstrate how Purcell had taken the dramatic, declamatory Italian style and created his own variant, brilliantly colourful yet always aware of every subtlety in the text. His opening to William Fuller's 'Divine Hymn' 'Lord, what is man?' is full of vocal details and subtle harmonic emphasis, with the opening question first asked gently, then repeated with more anxiety, the singer amazed that the son of God should become 'a poor, tormented man'. Man is 'lost' at the lower end of the singer's voice, the Son of God's glory rises optimistically through the scale, only to 'become a poor, tormented soul'. The deity is graphically 'shrunk' into a human lifespan, and 'wond'rous love' blossoms magnificently. The singer calls on the 'glorious spirits' to say 'which was more prevalent' – their joy, pictured in a fine melisma, or their astonishment represented by the dropping interval. The contrast between the 'worm' that is man and the exalted position of God is vividly captured in the music. An arioso section follows, calling for a quill 'to write the praises', and then, with Purcell inspired as ever at the mention of music, for 'a voice like yours to sing that anthem here which once you sung'. An extended section of Alleluias closes the work: the compelling variety of moods and phrases create such momentum that it is easy to forget Purcell is setting just one word.

If the setting of Fuller's work is remarkable, Purcell's treatment of Nahum Tate's 'Tell me, some pitying angel' (subtitled 'The Blessed Virgin's Expostulation') is one of the greatest examples of Purcell's genius for setting words and capturing changing emotions, and arguably one of the best solo settings in the whole English musical repertoire. The twelve-year old boy Jesus has gone to the Temple with his mother, and is now missing. Tate's text captures Mary's sense of desperation and anxiety, and is vividly enhanced by Purcell's music. The opening is immediately urgent, with Mary demanding and repeating that 'some pitying angel' should tell where her son has gone; mention of her 'sweet darling' brings an affectionate richness to both melody and harmony. Memories of Herod's slaughter of the innocent children draws an angular melisma on 'cruel', immediately countered by the gentle 'Ah, rather let his little footsteps press', leading to a winding melisma on 'through' which represents the arduous journey of Mary and Joseph in their escape from Judaea. The oxymoron of the 'milder savages' is treated to calm harmony, a contrast to the vehement, high-tessitura 'tyrant' that expresses Mary's loathing for Herod's court. The four repetitions of 'why', each one higher in pitch, show the mother's concern for her lost child; Purcell's repetition of 'was it' represents Mary's growing disbelief in reality, that everything may have been 'a waking dream' that foretold 'Thy wondrous birth'. Mary calls for Gabriel, her trumpet-like phrase 'I call' rising to a repeated top G: she demands, four times, the archangel's presence. He does not appear, and again four times Mary calls his name. Her confidence wanes as the phrase progresses, and by the fourth call, reality has struck: 'flatt'ring hopes, farewell' illustrates her utter desolation with wistfully falling harmony. Temporarily recitative is replaced by a gently swinging arioso, 'Me Judah's daughters', but the mood is quickly broken with the sudden harmonic shift and the return of recitativo at 'Now fatal change'; the acute interval for each repetition of 'mother' is capped by the sobbing, Italianate *gorgia* on the final 'distressed'. The final section of recitative is a mini-masterpiece: the extraordinary interval Purcell uses in the voice for 'dear' creates a highly effective discord, and the switch from major to minor (coupled with a rich suspension) on 'I trust' brings even greater contrast with the following 'I fear'. The melisma 'But oh' winds around voice and continuo, slowly falling to the final poignant phrase: the agonies Mary has suffered have brought confirmation that here is no ordinary child.

Alongside such specialist publications as *Harmonia Sacra*, Purcell's music continued to appear in a number of popular issues. During 1693 his compositions appeared, sometimes in transcriptions or arrangements, in volumes such as the fourth book of *Comes Amoris* (which contained, alongside various songs originally heard in theatrical productions, the song 'In vain we dissemble' and the A minor setting of 'If music be the food of love'), *Thesaurus Musicus*, *Joyful Cuckoldom* and *The First Book of Apollo's Banquet* and, advertised on 14 December, the fifth book of *Comes Amoris* (which featured the charming song 'I lov'd fair Celia' and two versions of 'What can we poor females do'). Purcell's songs also appeared in editions of *The Gentleman's Journal* for January, February, April, June, September and December: in most cases the works published were arrangements or old tunes given new words. We are not sure what financial arrangement Purcell had with Motteux, the publisher, but doubtless the composer was grateful for a little extra income. We also know that Purcell was supplementing his income by teaching. Amongst his pupils was the Etonian John Weldon: the Eton College accounts show a payment of £1 10s to 'Mr. Purcell' for 'two quarters ending at Michaelmas 1693' and, in 1694, £5 for half a year's lessons. Weldon was preparing to go up to New College Oxford and presumably was being given special tutelage by an acknowledged expert; he later referred to himself as having been a pupil of Purcell's. From 1694 we also know that Purcell was teaching the harpsichord to Katherine Howard: lessons such as these were taken daily, which is why Purcell was earning £2 3s 6d per month for his troubles.[28] The volume of keyboard pieces discovered in early 1994 may well have been a teaching manual by Purcell. With high-quality, pre-ruled paper and a fancy gilt binding this was no ordinary composing manuscript, and could well have been the property of an aristocratic pupil such as Katherine Howard. The dates of her lessons with Purcell and of the manuscript certainly match well. On Purcell's death she would have had to find another teacher, which would explain the presence of keyboard pieces at the other end of the volume by Giovanni Battista Draghi, one of the most eminent keyboard players in London.

Towards the end of 1693 Purcell also earned himself a commission to set an ode which was to celebrate the hundredth anniversary of the foundation by Queen Elizabeth of Trinity College Dublin. The actual performance of 'Great parent, hail', 'an Ode by Mr Tate who was bred up in this College', took place on 9 January 1694 after a service at Christ Church Cathedral and was 'sung by the principal Gentlemen of the Kingdom'. Tate's ode was not one of his greatest literary efforts: at times Purcell must have been hard-pressed to make any sense of the words. It is a sign of Purcell's professionalism that, despite weak material, he still produced good music. The symphony is suitably celebratory, and the opening chorus full of variety and vigour. For the alto solo 'Another century commencing' Purcell wrote lyrical music for his favourite voice, but the most outstanding movement is the bass solo 'Awful Matron' whose noble solo line is supported by inspired string writing. With perhaps the worst text in all the twenty-four odes, Purcell must simply have been grateful for the fee that this commission would have brought him.

While working on his Irish commission, Purcell's reputation as the leading theatrical composer in London ensured that he had a busy winter in 1693–94. In November Congreve's *The Double Dealer* opened at Drury Lane with a large score by Purcell which contained, alongside two songs, nine pieces of instrumental music. Prefaced by a stylish French overture, the play presented some of Purcell's most individual instrumental writing for the theatre, full of harmonic resource and bittersweet dissonance. A rather less memorable contribution was the duet 'Leave these useless arts in loving' for Shadwell's popular sex-farce *Epsom Wells* which was revived at some point during 1693. In January 1694 Purcell provided a song for Dryden's *Love Triumphant, or Nature will Prevail*, and a month later two songs for Southerne's *The Fatal Marriage, or The Innocent Adultery*. In April John Crowne's *The Married Beau, or The Curious Impertinent* opened, containing the song 'See where repenting Celia lies', a splendid two-section overture and eight other instrumental movements which, once again, demonstrate Purcell's novel harmonic language. Not only are the melodic lines highly inventive and the harmonies wonderfully fresh and individual but, as with all the greatest composers, the internal parts – the lines for the second violin and viola – are a delight.

In May 1694 the first two parts of D'Urfey's *The Comical History of Don Quixote* opened to great success. The large musical score was shared between John Eccles and Henry Purcell: Purcell's contribution to the first part included a long duet 'Sing, all ye muses', a song, an extensive trio with two violins 'With this sacred, charming wand' and the imposing bass solo 'Let the dreadful engines'. Written for the actor and singer John Bowman, this was one of the longest theatre lyrics that Purcell ever set. Its wide vocal range, especially its use of the high register, and its violent changes of mood, are proof that Bowman was an accomplished singer for whom Purcell must have much enjoyed writing. For D'Urfey's second part Purcell scored a long dialogue, 'Since times are so bad', a humorous song in Scottish vein and the famous trumpet song 'Genius of England' whose instrumental obbligato was written for Purcell's friend and trumpeting colleague John Shore (not, as has often been suggested, his father Matthias, who was well past his playing days and now in the purely administrative – and extremely well-paid – post of sergeant trumpeter).

Alongside his theatre music, Purcell was also still composing secular songs, of which a number were copied by him into a book now known as the 'Gresham' manuscript. These appear to have been copied in chronological order, presumably soon after composition. Between songs from the 1693 birthday ode and 'Sawney is a bonny lad' (dated 25 January 1694) come four songs, 'Ah, cruel nymph',

OPPOSITE *Another of Purcell's theatrical contacts was William Congreve (portrait by Godfrey Kneller), the author of some of the most brilliant comedies in the language. Purcell wrote incidental music for his play* The Double Dealer, *and keyboard versions of two movements are among the pieces in a recently discovered manuscript (below).*

'I love and I must' (whose subtitle 'Bell-Barr' has still not been convincingly explained), 'What a sad fate' and 'Not all my torments'. This last is perhaps the most ornate of all Purcell's secular songs, representing the full extent of the Italian influence. Curiously it was not included in any published collection, nor does it appear in any other manuscript. Its four lines of verse are set by Purcell in colourful style, ranging from the impassioned opening, through the manically increasing scorn with which the poet's love is greeted, to the desolate sorrows that he will take to the grave.

In April, for his regular birthday ode for Queen Mary Purcell was on sparkling form with 'Come ye Sons of Art, away'. The forces utilized appear to have been greater than normal, with an orchestra replacing the more usual single strings; the text (probably by Nahum Tate) was full of references to music and musical instruments, providing plenty of inspiration for Purcell's fertile imagination. The opening of the overture is stately, and the lively canzona which follows is full of rhythmic ingenuity amongst its three contrasting motifs. But it is in the adagio that Purcell is at his finest: the sighing motifs and poignant harmonies are full of pathos, and the use of sustained notes, which cut through the middle and bass of the texture, is notable. Rather than the expected repeat of the canzona, we are immediately led into the opening chorus, and the first of several repetitions of the main theme in various harmonizations and arrangements – a technique taken straight from the theatre. With the tune taken first by a countertenor, Purcell cleverly solves the problem of rescoring for the chorus (where the tune would have been either too low or far too high for the sopranos) by providing them with a descant, and retaining the tune in the altos, doubled by trumpet and oboe. In the famous duet 'Sound the trumpet' Purcell resisted the temptation to use the named instruments, choosing instead an insistently lively two-bar modulating ground bass over which two countertenors demonstrate their virtuosity. There would have been smiles in the orchestra at 'you make the listening Shores resound', for the two trumpeters sitting in the band would probably have been John and William Shore.

The centrepiece of the ode is an ecstatic evocation of music, 'Strike the viol'. As ever, Purcell was at his most inspired when presented with references to music. The technique he used was one that he had perfected in many previous odes, combining a ground bass with a line for solo countertenor and then turning the vocal section into an instrumental ritornello. Here he uses a modulating two-bar ground bass, with two recorders adding their gentle accompaniment, over which the soloist weaves his entrancing melody. The best is still to come, for Purcell develops an orchestral ritornello that is one of his best, alternating and combining the pair of recorders with the strings. The eloquent 'Bid the virtues' is unique, even amongst the many remarkable movements contained in the odes: a solo soprano and oboe intertwine in touching writing. The final movement, 'Thus nature rejoicing', is a rondeau, first sung as a duet by soprano and bass, and then taken up by the whole choir and orchestra. The only complete manuscript source for 'Come ye Sons of Art' is a copy, probably several versions away from Purcell's original, dating from 1765. Between this copy and some very dubious modern editions a number of curiosities have become accepted in the twentieth century as being Purcell's. The overture should be scored for one trumpet and one oboe (playing the second line); some editors have added a part for a second trumpet, completely ignoring the possible capabilities of the natural trumpet; other editors have applied eighteenth-century principles to the designation of continuo instruments, adding bassoon when recorders play, switching instruments almost every bar and creating the most appalling travesty of Purcell's original music. The eighteenth-century manuscript also contains a timpani part in the final chorus, ludicrously ornamented. Purcell very rarely wrote for timpani, and twentieth-century editors and scholars have frequently done Purcell's music a great disservice by adding timpani parts where the composer did not ever intend them to be included.

For once, King William was present at his queen's birthday celebrations, for his return to campaigning in Europe had been delayed by unfavourable winds. The war was using up large quantities of money, but parliament was being unusually co-operative: this year it had voted the king £5 million for his campaigning, and it had also passed the historic act which founded the Bank of England. One of the statutes was that the bank should at any one time lend the state £1.2 million at an interest rate of 8%. William's constant absences were a strain for Mary, for she had not only to handle the responsibilities of state, but also to put up with the constant backbiting and manipulations of politicians. She also must have heard the gossip, probably well-founded, that William's attentions were rather too frequently diverted by the handsome young Dutch courtier Arnold van Keppel: there were also equally strong rumours concerning William's relationship with one of Mary's ladies-in-waiting, Elizabeth Villiers.

Mary was never anything but totally loyal to her husband. But the long separations from him and her constant worries for his safety were wearing her down; in the spring she had been ill with a serious fever, and now, though only thirty-two, she wrote 'I believe I am becoming old and infirmities come with age.'[29] In public she let none of her concerns show, was an enthusiastic and extravagant shopper, and was as good-humoured and much-loved by her public as she had always been.

Purcell was as busy as ever. His songs continued to appear regularly in Motteux's *Gentleman's Journal*, although the financial difficulties which were eventually to put it out of business were starting to show their heads: the issue for January and February was two months behind, but when it appeared in March contained the Scottish song 'Sawney is a bonny lad'; the March and April editions contained songs from theatre productions and April also brought the charming new song 'Ask me to love no more'; the May edition printed 'Strike the viol', fresh from its performance before the queen, and July found the song 'Celia's fond', though it seems that Motteux took a pre-existing tune and forced his own words on it. For the August and September issue Purcell set the light-hearted 'Knotting Song' fresh from the pen of the notorious wit and reprobate Sir Charles Sedley, which tells of Phillis, whose enthusiastic but silent participation in London's latest craze, that of knotting fringes, was driving her lover to distraction.

Purcell also turned his hand to editing with *A Collection of Some Verses out of the Psalms of David… revised by Mr. Henry Purcell* and to writing with his only surviving theoretical work, *An Introduction to the Skill of Musick (Book III) The Art of Descant… Corrected and amended by Mr Henry Purcell*. Now into its twelfth edition, Purcell's revision, which includes sections of new material, demonstrates his clear teaching methods and sound compositional technique, and shows a logical mind at work. Though the second book of *Thesaurus Musicus*, the fifth book of *Comes amoris* and *The Songs to the New Play of Don Quixote* did not contain any newly-composed works by Purcell, he no doubt had to expend time preparing songs from recent theatrical productions for his publishers.

When the 1694/95 theatre season opened, Purcell's music was again much in demand. For Ravenscroft's obscene bedroom farce *The Canterbury Guests* he set a coarse dialogue between two feuding neighbours, and to the revival of Dryden's *Tyrannick Love* he contributed the dialogue 'Hark, my Damilcar', which neatly combines both

OPPOSITE: *William III by Sir Peter Lely. William was not interested in music, and under him the court lost its position as the centre of musical patronage. The king also preferred to live out of London. Purcell turned his attention increasingly to music for the theatre.*

*Queen Mary by W. Wissing. Some of Purcell's finest inspiration went into the
birthday odes that he wrote every year for performance on Queen Mary's
birthday. He also had the melancholy task of composing most of the music
for her funeral, an expression of genuine national grief.
His funeral march moved the listeners to tears.*

humour and drama, and the charming song 'Ah! how sweet it is to love', complete with its delicious settings of its 'pleasing pains'. The remainder of the theatre season was to find him unbelievably busy, but other non-theatrical commissions and duties also beckoned.

For the celebrations on 11 November that marked the return of King William to London from his summer's campaign in Flanders Purcell set a new anthem, 'The way of God is an undefiled way', with a text carefully chosen (from Psalm 18) for its topical allusions to a victorious king. Like Purcell's later church anthems, the music falls into a number of relatively short contrasting sections, inside which are condensed many musical devices and compositional techniques. Although much of the anthem is bellicose, with destruction and smiting of enemies, it is the duet 'They shall cry' which finds Purcell at his most appealingly mournful, with vocal lines full of angular intervals and tortured suspensions.

November also brought another major commission, and one at which it would seem Purcell was determined to show every ounce of his technical ability. For the annual celebrations of St Cecilia's Day, attended by all the most important musical figures in London, Purcell produced not an ode but a setting of the 'Te Deum' and 'Jubilate' which was performed in St Bride's church in Fleet Street. To the choir, soloists and string orchestra he also added two trumpets. The 'Te Deum' has a long text whose rather sectionalized form is reflected in Purcell's setting; and despite the thrilling grandeur of the sections for full choir and orchestra, with trumpets soaring over the assembled forces, it is the more personal, chamber movements which contain the real gems. Pictorialization abounds: two solo boys imitate cherubim and seraphim, heaven and earth are suitably represented at either end of the vocal tessitura, and the full assembly picture the majesty of God's glory. With the supplicatory text 'O Lord, save thy people' Purcell is on his best territory, providing ardent repetitions of the word 'save' and a two-octave rising phrase 'and lift them up for ever', which starts in the bass, transfers to the tenor and finally takes the countertenor soaring to the top of his register. The centrepiece of the work, which finds Purcell at his most personal, is 'Vouchsafe, O Lord'. A genuine plea from the heart, here we find the composer at his profound best, piling up sequences and dissonances and pleading for mercy in the most ravishing vocal and string writing. The serenity with which the movement ends, and the strong affirmation of the final chorus, suggests that Purcell's faith in God was firm.

In the shorter text of the 'Jubilate Deo' Purcell again shines in a pastoral movement. The duet between a solo treble and countertenor, 'Be ye sure that the Lord he is God', is especially touching in its simplicity, with Purcell's use of sequence and gentle harmony creating a movement full of pathos. But on an occasion at which every important musical figure in London would have been present, Purcell would no doubt have also wished to demonstrate his contrapuntal ingenuity. In the 'Te Deum' he showed his technical skills in movements such as 'Thou art the King of Glory', coloured by ingenious double counterpoint. In the Gloria of the 'Jubilate' he treats his theme first with close imitation and then inversion; at 'world without end' he adds a new theme which he treats with the same techniques as before, also stretching the theme out in the bass in powerful augmentation; at the final Amen all the strands come together, ending in a blaze of sound. That the work was considered a success is demonstrated by a repeat performance before William and Mary in the Chapel Royal on 9 December.

But joy was rapidly turning to sadness. Smallpox was sweeping London: in the week before St Cecilia's Day eighty-five deaths had been reported, and the autumn total was well over a thousand. John Evelyn reported that this was 'An extraordinarily sickly time especially of the smallpox, of which divers considerable persons died'. William fell ill, not of that disease, but probably of exhaustion. As Mary nursed him, she too was taken ill. At the start of December fears were aroused, for she had never had smallpox. On 21 December she woke up feeling ill and noticed that a rash had broken out on her arms. Seeing the clear symptoms of the disease and already upset by the knowledge that William was again planning to leave for the battlefields, she seems to have lost her will to live. That evening she went through all her personal papers, burning some and putting the others in order. She even wrote instructions for her funeral. The superstitious were alarmed to know that the oldest of the lions in Tower of London had suddenly sickened and died: the same had happened at the time of the death of Charles II. By Christmas Day the effects of the disease were worsening, and the doctors prescribed all the treatments they could muster: draughts, potions, bleeding and the gruesome application of red hot irons to blister her temples. All was in vain, and early on the morning of 28 December, Queen Mary died.

London was plunged into mourning, and life in the capital came to an abrupt halt while preparations were made for the funeral. In the event, a combination of the smallpox epidemic, political indecision

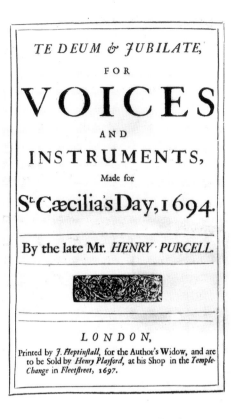

Purcell wrote his 'Te Deum' and 'Jubilate' for the annual celebration of St Cecilia's Day, 22 November 1694, to be performed at St Bride's church, Fleet Street. They were published after his death.

and a freezingly cold winter delayed the funeral: even the lying-in-state did not begin until 21 February. Finally, on 5 March 1695 a solemn procession made its way through the streets of London. Narcissus Luttrell reported that three hundred old women led the funeral cortège wearing long black gowns, each woman having a boy as her trainbearer. The ceremony 'was performed with great solemnity, and all the shops in the city were shut'. John Evelyn estimated that the whole ceremony cost £100,000 and, much moved, wrote: 'Was the Queen's funeral infinitely expensive, never so universal a mourning; all the Parliament men had cloaks given them, 400 poor women, all the streets hung, and the middle of the streets boarded and covered with black cloth: there was all the nobility, mayor, and aldermen, judges etc'. In that procession were the state trumpeters and drummers, and also, according to the official 'Order and Form' 'the Gentlemen of the Chapel and Vestry in capes and the Children of the Chapel'. Purcell, in his capacities as both the leading composer of the day and organist of Westminster Abbey, produced music for the major parts of the service.

In the centuries since Queen Mary's funeral, music historians and scholars have often misreported or simply distorted the musical events

Flatt trumpet reconstructed by Crispian Steele-Perkins. At the funeral of Queen Mary Purcell's March and Canzona were played by a consort of four of these sonorous instruments.

that took place to fit their own theories. The king's trumpeters and the royal drummers took a leading part in the procession as they escorted the coffin through the streets: they may have played traditional funeral marches or, alternatively, the trumpets may have been symbolically silent. The Lord Chamberlain's accounts report that the five side drums were muffled in '20 yards of black baize' (which cost 3s 6d per yard) and the kettle drums, mounted on their horse (or possibly carried on a man's back) took up 8 yards of cloth. It is inconceivable that these outdoor instruments, played by parade-ground soldiers, would have been used inside the Abbey. That task would have fallen to the highly-skilled household musicians. For the choral music Purcell reworked settings he had made fifteen years earlier of the Funeral Sentences, and wrote a new anthem which was, according to the former Chapel Royal chorister Thomas Tudway, who was present at the funeral, 'accompanied with flat Mournfull Trumpets'. For those four 'Flatt Trumpets' Purcell also composed a march and canzona. Though Purcell's copy of the instrumental music does not survive, Tudway carefully transcribed what he heard (or perhaps saw in manuscript). Significantly he makes no mention of any drum (kettle or side) playing during these pieces, and nor is there any contemporary account of any drummer in the Abbey during this or any other similar service.

The Flatt Trumpets (first recorded as having been played in London in 1691 after their introduction by the Moravian composer Gottfried Finger) were trumpets with a reverse slide (one that moves *behind* the player's shoulder – the opposite direction to the slide of a trombone or sackbut). They were probably played by John Shore, his uncle William, Theophilus Fitz and Edmund Flower. The primary advantage of this instrument over the more conventional, 'natural' trumpet was that the slide allowed a whole range of extra chromatic notes which, for instance, enabled the musicians to play in minor keys. For a funeral, the instrument's clear connection with the sackbut, often used to symbolize death, made it all the more suitable (whereas a trumpet was normally symbolic of triumph and celebration). Even with the period instrument revival, it was only in 1993 that four matching instruments were reconstructed (for a recording on the Hyperion label): it proved almost inconceivable that the Flatt Trumpets could have been played whilst 'on the move', as the playing technique required makes this impractical. Thus Purcell's march and canzona would seem to have been written for static performance in the Abbey (where their sound would have been far more moving): this

also fits with Tudway's description of the service. In an outdoor procession their playing would have been totally drowned against all the background noise of horses' hooves, carriage wheels, three (or four) hundred ladies, the royal trumpeters and, largest competition of all, the royal drummers. Even with muffled drums, their sound would have obliterated that of the Flatt Trumpets: thus the participation of side drums in Purcell's march and canzona is impractical. Thurston Dart (and others since) have hypothesized that a timpani part was written and played, though there is no mention in Tudway or anyone else's account; such theories are based on musical conventions of some decades later. In any case, the belief that trumpets and kettle drums generally played together in Purcell's day is one that is based on precious little musicological evidence. What Dart wrote, charming though it sounds, is implausible, for it requires four timpani – an orchestration that had no real presence for another century and a half!

The death of Queen Mary on 28 December 1694 provoked genuine national mourning. Her lying-in-state (above) was followed by an elaborate funeral in Westminster Abbey at which Purcell's music played a major role. It was one of the last great public occasions to which he would contribute.

Replica of a late seventeenth century side drum. This type of instrument was in daily use by the royal drummers.

Others have attempted to write a part with just two timpani, and the result is equally unsatisfactory. Even assuming that the instruments could be taken off their horse (or if they were carried on a man's back, unstrapped from him) and unwrapped quickly and elegantly enough, and then carried into the Abbey and set up, the music is too complicated harmonically to make this a sensible thing to do, and the royal kettle drummer is in any case unlikely to have been able to read music. There is no record of a second set of kettle drums being available, let alone set up in the Abbey: nor indeed is there any record of drums even being allowed into the Abbey before the coronation of George II in 1727. And, sadly, a much-publicized recent 'discovery' of an 'authentic' drum part proved to be a very damp musicological squib, based on erroneous information.

According to Tudway, Purcell's newly-composed 'The Queen's Funeral March' was 'sounded before her Chariot', suggesting that the four Flatt Trumpets played their stately march either as the queen's coffin was brought up the aisle of Westminster Abbey, or perhaps played once the bier was in place at the front of the congregation. Purcell's noble music was said to have moved the listeners to tears. The march is rhythmically simple, comprising five two-bar phrases, each in the same dactylic metre (long, short, short, long): it is its harmonic progression which makes it such a fine piece. Once this march had been played, twice through, the service proper would have begun and, as far as is known for certain, no further music by Purcell was heard until near the end of the service when, according to the Prayer Book, as 'they come to the grave, while the corpse is made ready to be laid into the earth, the Priest shall say, or the Priest and Clerks shall sing' the text beginning 'Man that is born of a woman'.

Purcell's setting of the Funeral Sentences found in the Book of Common Prayer contains some of his best vocal music. He had begun work on the Sentences in the early 1680s, and revised his work at least once. The majority of the setting is scored for four soloists – a treble, high tenor, tenor and bass – with the full choir concluding each of the three sections. The first Sentence, 'Man that is born of a woman', based on a verse from the Book of Job, sets a mournful tone with its stress of man's mortality. Purcell is highly responsive to his text: the four voices enter in turn, moving down the arpeggio, and the music rises through 'and hath a short time to live' but falls desolately to 'misery'. Each singer's phrase rises encouragingly through 'He cometh up' but as rapidly falls, and to lower than its starting point, at 'and is cut down', terminating with a mournful English cadence at 'like a flow'r'. Man's transience is reiterated, with an elegant setting of 'fleeth', and the chorus close the section with a repeat of the soloists' 'He fleeth as it were a shadow, And ne'er continueth in one stay'. The second Sentence, 'In the midst of life we are in death' sees some of Purcell's most individual writing, with harmonic contradictions and wandering vocal lines all symbolizing man's impermanence, summed up in the angular end of the boy treble's opening, solo phrase. The tension mounts as the singers ask to whom they may 'seek for succour, but of thee, O Lord', rising further as they acknowledge the justification for divine displeasure. At 'Yet, O Lord, most mighty', Purcell gives brief respite, imploring in his setting of 'O holy and most merciful saviour': 'Deliver us not into the bitter pains' rises through inexorable chromaticism with the most powerful melodic and harmonic language, made all the more climactic on the repeat by the might of the full choir. After such a powerful prayer, the final Sentence is a more personal plea: no secrets can be hidden from God's omnipotent eye, and the singers implore: 'Shut not thy merciful ears unto our prayers'. The opening phrases are especially poignant with their realization of human mortality, summed up in a melodic line that seems to represent man's naked vulnerability in front of God. Not all is doom: Purcell's triple-time prayer 'But, spare us, Lord most holy' gives hope before the desolate calm of 'Suffer us not at our last hour'. Purcell's last bars pray that man should not, even in the anguish of death, 'fall away from thee'. The mood of serene resignation and the dropping interval of 'to fall' suggest that this is a prayer Purcell was sure would be answered.

Tudway stated that Purcell's other composition for the service, the anthem 'Thou knowest, Lord, the secrets of our hearts', was accompanied by the Flatt Trumpets. The lines fit the instruments exactly, and the music has the same key signature as the march and canzona. The anthem is chordal almost throughout, and maintains a startling control of melodic line and harmony. There could be few prayers more passionately or more simply stated, asking that God should spare us, and that we should not, even 'at our last hour, for any pains of death' turn away from our creator. The setting was noted by many who were present at the funeral as being masterful in its restrained nobility: thirty years later, when William Croft was composing a new burial service, endeavouring 'as near as possible I could, to imitate that great Master', he included Purcell's own setting of the anthem: 'The reason why I did not compose that Verse a-new…is obvious to every Artist'.

Side drum in black mourning cover: the material not only looks funereal but deadens the sound of the instrument.

🜚 213

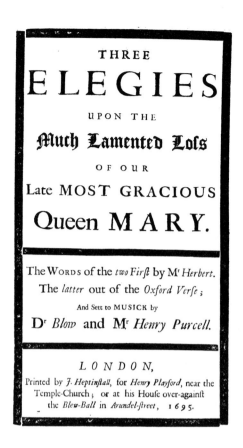

THREE

ELEGIES

UPON THE

𝔐𝔲𝔠𝔥 𝔏𝔞𝔪𝔢𝔫𝔱𝔢𝔡 𝔏𝔬𝔰𝔰

OF OUR

Late MOST GRACIOUS

Queen MARY.

The WORDS of the *two First* by Mr *Herbert.*
The *latter* out of the *Oxford Verse*;
And Sett to MUSICK by
Dr *Blow* and Mr *Henry Purcell.*

LONDON,
Printed by *J. Heptinstall,* for *Henry Playford,* near the
Temple-Church; or at his House over-against
the *Blew-Ball* in *Arundel-street,* 1695.

Purcell's two elegies on the death of Queen Mary (the third is by Blow) are among the most moving of his secular compositions.

According to Tudway, Purcell's canzona for the four Flatt Trumpets 'was sounded in the Abbey after the Anthem'. Its opening phrases were based on the same music as the march, but now skilfully developed into a four-part contrapuntal piece which showed the influence of Italian models. Purcell's development of his simple theme, his interplay between the upper and lower pairs of instruments and his harmonic ingenuity were, on such a solemn and moving occasion, the final evidence of a master at work.

Purcell's two other musical contributions mourning the loss of the queen were equally splendid. Two elegies, one in English, the other a translation into Latin, were written by a Mr Herbert (not, as is often suggested, the famous George Herbert who died in 1633). The English elegy 'No, no Lesbia' was set by Blow, and its Latin version, 'Incassum Lesbia', subtitled 'The Queen's Epicedium', was set by Purcell. Along with the duet 'O dive custos' these works were published in May 1695 by Henry Playford as 'Three Elegies upon the Much Lamented Loss of Our Late Most Gracious Queen Mary'. Purcell's startling setting of 'Incassum Lesbia' was for solo soprano: the first section is filled with grieving, wonderfully picturing a discordant lute ('lyra mea est immodulata') and the world filled with chromati-cally-rising grief ('dolorum pleno'). The triple-time aria 'En nymphas, en pastores' presents a pastoral view of the mourning, with 'admodum fletur' ('there is much shedding of tears') set to a lachrimose melisma, and 'moerore perditi' ('lost in mourning') sadly falling. The third section grows more desolate, with cries of 'heu' ('alas'), a winding roulade on 'singultu turbido' ('unrelenting sobbing') and further expressions of sadness leading to an outpouring of grief on two descending scales, 'mirum abiit' ('the marvel is gone'). Purcell's setting of the last phrase, 'stella sua fixa coelum ultra lucet' ('her star, immov-able, shines on in the heavens') is magical.

Purcell's duet setting of Henry Parker's ode 'O dive custos' is equal-ly stunning. Written in three sections, its opening is Italianate, the two voices intertwining in a series of melismas which increase in melodic and harmonic intensity to 'O superum decus in secundis'. The middle section is a triple-time aria, eloquently responsive to the text. At 'O Maria, musis flebilis occidit', heartfelt grief returns: a series of desolate appoggiaturas on 'O flete' are coloured with intense harmonies which take the music into remote keys rarely charted by composers of the age. The chromatic inflections of the final 'moriente' could have come from no other pen than Purcell's.

When the state mourning for Queen Mary was finally over, London audiences found that their theatrical performers had split into two factions. Since 1690 there had been growing dissatisfaction amongst the actors of the United Company, led by Betterton, with their management: matters worsened in 1693 – when the notorious (and totally dishonest) lawyer Christopher Rich assumed control – and came to a head during late 1694. Betterton and many of his leading col-leagues left the company and formed a rival group; in March 1694 they were granted a permit to perform in the rapidly-refurbished theatre in Lincoln's Inn Fields. With Betterton went most of the best singing actors, including Mrs Bracegirdle, John Bowman and Thomas Doggett; worse still, several of the singers decamped, including John Pate and John Reading, together with the sopranos Mrs Ayliff and Mrs Hodgson. Purcell, however, stayed with Rich. Why he did so is not known, especially when most of his leading musical colleagues had left: perhaps the small, hastily re-equipped theatre in Lincolns Inn Fields was not big enough for his next large-scale musical productions, or per-haps he knew that his music for past productions, already 'on the shelf' at Drury Lane, would be performed whether he was there or not.

Or maybe Rich, knowing the audience draw of Purcell's name as composer on a play bill, simply made the composer a financial offer he could not refuse. Purcell's new musical stars were an unlikely combination: the none-too-distinguished bass Richard Leveridge, the talented young soprano Letitia Cross, probably only fourteen years old, and the astonishing boy treble Jemmy Bowen, probably aged only thirteen. Over the next few months Purcell produced, for what seems at first glance such unlikely forces, and apparently against all the odds, some of his best vocal theatre music. Though Cross and Bowen were talented singers, their success has to be an indication that Purcell must have possessed that magnetism of personality that could draw out every ounce of potential from young musicians.

The first play produced at Drury Lane was a revival of Aphra Behn's bloody tragedy *Abdelazer, or the Moor's Revenge*, which probably opened on 1 April. Purcell's contribution was considerable. He composed ten instrumental movements, including the rondeau made famous by Benjamin Britten's 'Young Person's Guide to the Orchestra' (Op.34), and for Jemmy Bowen he wrote an extensive song, 'Lucinda is bewitching fair'. A few weeks later Bowen was back on the stage with another new Purcell composition, this time in a revival of Dryden's tragicomedy *The Spanish Fryar, or The Double Discovery*. 'Whilst I with grief did on you look' suggests Bowen's abilities to convey pathos were considerable.

During 1692 the playbook to Shadwell's *The Libertine* had been reprinted, but no record of a performance that year has ever been discovered: it seems much more likely that Purcell's music to Acts IV and V was written for a revival at Drury Lane in 1695. The score proved to be one of his most popular, and was reproduced in a large number of eighteenth-century editions. For the start of Act IV he composed a delightful string prelude and song, 'Nymphs and Shepherds, come away'. It is ironic that in the twentieth century this song has come to represent childhood innocence: in Act V of the play the revels of Shadwell's Arcadians are swiftly ended with a gruesome massacre. That act is prefaced with same solemn march that had been heard a few months earlier at the funeral of Queen Mary; once again its scoring (now doubled by strings) featured the sound of four Flatt Trumpets. Writers believing Purcell's march to have been written in 1692 have often puzzled that a piece already heard in (and written for) the theatre could have been played at an occasion as solemn as the queen's funeral; it seems much more plausible that the music was

A new Song set by Mr. *Henry Purcell*, in the Play ca'lld *Abdelazar.* Sung by the Boy.

U — cin — da is be—witch—ing fair, Lu—cin—da is be—witch—ing fair,

all o're, all————— o're in—ga————ging is her

The song 'Lucinda is bewitching fair' was written for Aphra Behn's tragedy Abdelazer. *It was sung by 'the boy', a particularly fine treble called Jemmy Bowen, for whom Purcell wrote a number of other songs.*

composed especially for the funeral, and then only afterwards reworked for the theatrical production.

One other movement from *The Libertine* has achieved fame and provides further circumstantial evidence to date Purcell's music to 1695. The second book of *Deliciae Musicae* (1695) contains the trumpet song 'To arms, heroic Prince' which it claims was performed by 'the boy' in *The Libertine*. It is unlikely that Bowen would have performed the song in 1692, when he was probably only nine or ten years old. In 1695 he was in his singing prime and ready to cope with the technical demands of Purcell's vocal writing. It would have been difficult to fit the song into the plot and none of the principal manuscripts include it: more likely Purcell, armed with a singer whose presence would draw the crowds, seized the opportunity and had Jemmy Bowen perform the song between the acts.

History has left few first-hand accounts of Purcell's character but, thanks to Bowen's participation in *The Libertine*, we get a rare insight into the composer's nature. With his own upbringing in the choir of the Chapel Royal and twenty subsequent years as a choirmaster, Purcell must have been thoroughly acquainted with a choirboy's lifestyle, respectful of his professionalism and ready to acknowledge that a top chorister in his prime can sing with an ease and natural musicality that can make adult singers despair. During the rehearsals for the play Anthony Aston recounts that one of the musicians bossily told Bowen 'to grace and run a Division [an ornament] in such a

Place'. 'O, let him alone', said Purcell; 'he will grace it more naturally than you, or I, can teach him'.[30] With that kindly, perceptive remark we get a human reason why Purcell was so admired. And if this was how he always treated his choirboys at the Chapel Royal and the Abbey, they must have adored him.

In May or June 1695 Shadwell's adaptation of Shakespeare's *Timon of Athens*, which had proved very popular in London since its first performance in 1678, was revived at Drury Lane. Near the end of the play Shadwell introduced a masque, which was revised for the 1695 performances, adding a singing role for Cupid, who is known to have been sung by a child: the score bears the name 'George' but this may well have been in a later revival, for the part was ideal for Jemmy Bowen. Purcell's score was a substantial one, and included the bubbling duet 'Hark, how the songsters', set over an insistently cheerful bass line, a charming song for the boy, 'Love in their little veins inspires' and a more florid number for the same voice, 'The cares of love'. Of the larger-scale movements, the trio 'But ah, how much are our delights' is serious in its sombre, minor key, and the chorus 'Who can resist such mighty charms' is a fine piece of work. Only two instrumental movements by Purcell for the masque survive: the overture is yet another striking example of his instrumental writing. After a stately opening come two repetitions of a lively canzona, separated by a rich slow section. The other instrumental movement, a 'Courtin Tune', is as extraordinary in his harmonic daring as any of Purcell's instrumental works, with gripping dissonances and rhythmically adventurous inner parts anchored over a particularly angular ground bass.

Rich also staged an undistinguished comedy by Thomas Scott, *The Mock Marriage,* for which Purcell contributed some songs. It is uncertain whether 'Oh, how you protest' is actually by Purcell, and doubts have been raised too about 'Twas within a furlong of Edinboro' town'. No doubts surround 'Man is for the woman made', which is one of Purcell's most amusing theatre songs, wittily imitating basic tavern harmony by getting stuck in a tonic-dominant groove for nearly half the song.

Purcell's largest single stage project in 1695 was the tragic semi-opera *The Indian Queen*. Mystery surrounds the time of its first performance, and scholars have argued for an opening night anywhere between Easter and the autumn of 1695. Part of the problem stems from the break-up of the United Company at the end of 1694.

Bass violin. Larger than a cello, the unique sound of this instrument coloured the bass line of Purcell's music in the theatres and the Chapel Royal.

During that year Betterton had been advanced £50 to 'get up ye Indian Queen',[31] and if the pattern of previous years had been followed, this doyen of British actors would have trimmed the libretto, contracted a composer and choreographer, scheduled the rehearsals and arranged for the production to be the major attraction of the spring season. Instead, by December, probably because of the dispute with the management, Betterton had not yet begun his work, and by the end of the month the company had split; an added complication would have been the death of Queen Mary. The management would have needed to engage a new arranger for the libretto, so it seems probable that Purcell did not begin work until early 1695, at which time he may not have known exactly who would be in the cast when the opera finally made it onto the stage. No help comes from the engagement as composer for the final masque of Henry's younger brother Daniel, for we do not know when he started work either, nor whether he was brought in because Henry was under too much pressure to complete the whole score, or even because Henry was ill. Indeed, all we do know for certain is that, for *The Indian Queen*, Purcell once again produced music of the highest class.

The variety contained amongst the extensive instrumental act tunes, symphonies and overtures is considerable. For Purcell's trumpeting colleague and friend John Shore there was plenty to perform, including a three-section trumpet overture to Act III (complete with an excellent canzona) that is as good as anything Purcell wrote for the instrument. There was also a repeat of the overture to 'Come ye sons of Art' to introduce Act II, here transposed down a tone. The string movements too were excellently crafted, ranging from the serious overture to Act I to the tune in Act IV that harmonizes Orazia's song 'They tell us that your mighty powers above'. For the singers there were other fine movements, including 'I attempt from love's sickness to fly' and Ismeron's famous 'You twice ten hundred deities' which was sung by the young bass Richard Leveridge: here is an aria which covers a multitude of moods from its noble opening call to the gods to croaking toads and slithery snakes, and from motionless sleep to wide-eyed waking. Though the chorus were not given a large amount of material, their celebratory 'We come to sing great Zempoalla's story' must have made a good set-piece in Act II, and the closing chorus 'All dismal sounds thus on these off'rings wait' once again illustrates Purcell's rare harmonic palette. Daniel Purcell's task in setting the final masque was difficult not only because his music had to follow that of his illustrious brother, but also because, after the tragic ending of the play, he was required to produce a happy ending for the evening's entertainment.

Confusion has also surrounded Purcell's contribution to the 1695 revival of Shakespeare's *The Tempest*: the score is traditionally believed to be by Purcell, although musicologically this would have meant his changing to a more Italianate style, and including a rash of *da capo* arias not before seen in his work. Music had first been added to Davenant and Dryden's version back in 1674 and, although no performance record survives, it is thought that the play was revived at Drury Lane in the summer or autumn of 1695. It seems improbable that the new Drury Lane company could have mounted a second, large-scale new musical production so close to *The Indian Queen*, and it is even more unlikely that Purcell would have found time to write the full score, especially in what appears to be a new compositional style. Curtis Price and Margaret Laurie have both argued convincingly that Purcell's contribution to a 1695 revival of the play, most probably in the autumn of 1695, was limited to just one new song, 'Dear pretty youth', and that others wrote the score later attributed to Purcell.

King William was slowly recovering from the shock of Mary's death, and by mid-May was ready to leave England again for the summer's campaign, appointing a council of seven men to run the country. His absence, however, meant that his court musicians had very little extra-mural activity. One exception was the celebrations for the sixth birthday of William, Duke of Gloucester, on 24 July 1695. His mother, Princess Anne, Mary's sister, produced no less than eighteen children, of whom only William even survived infancy. He was a sickly child who suffered from the congenital disease hydrocephalus, giving him a head which was out of proportion to the rest of his body. The difficulties that he encountered in walking (which his father is said cruelly to have punished by beating the little boy's legs) were brought on by the same disease, which probably resulted in the boy's death at the age of only eleven. Despite his afflictions Prince William was wildly enthusiastic about all matters military, and regularly drilled his own private regiment of twenty-two little boys, dressed in their own miniature uniforms and armed with wooden swords, in the grounds of his house in Kensington. Purcell was commissioned to set an ode to celebrate the young prince's royal birthday and, with William's love of soldiering in mind, included a prominent part for the trumpeter John Shore. For the performance of 'Who can from joy

The Conjurers Song, Sung in the Third Act of the *Indian Queen*.
Sett by Mr. *Henry Purcell*.

YOU twice ten hundred De-i-ties, to whom, to whom we dai-ly Sacrifice; Ye

Pow'rs, ye Pow'rs that dwell with Fates below, and see what Men are doom'd to doe; where

Elements in dif————cord dwell, thou God of sleep a——

——ri——fe and tell; tell great *Zempoalla*, what strange, strange Fate

A Song in the Trageby of *Bonduca*, set by Mr. *Purcell*.
Sung by Miss *Crofs*.

OH! Oh! lead me, lead me to some peace——full Gloom,

where none but sigh———ing, none but sigh——ing, sigh——ing Lovers

come; where the shrill, the shrill Trumpets never foun——

——d; never, never found, but one e——ter——nal hush, one e-ter——nal hush goes round.

refrain' Shore and Purcell were joined in Richmond House, Kew, by a select band of royal musicians and singers, some of whom are named in the autograph. For this composition Purcell was apparently pressed for time, since he repeated the overture he had written a few months previously for *Timon of Athens*, transposing it down a tone into C major. The most notable section of the ode is the gentle movement 'A prince of glorious race descended': over a four-bar descending ground bass, Purcell's elegant melody is sung first by a high tenor and then transformed into a ravishing string ritornello. The finale too is splendid; despite some silly words Purcell writes an excellent chaconne which alternates voices and instruments, including dialogue between strings, trumpet and a 'wind-band' of two oboes, tenor oboe and bassoon – this latter instrument only relatively recently introduced to England. Purcell's imaginative variety of textures, colours and rhythms is handled with all his customary skill.

While Purcell was not too heavily committed at court during the summer, he was extremely busy writing scores for the coming autumn's theatrical productions. For a composer who had always previously been so punctilious in his writing, these works, if not actually showing signs of haste, certainly indicate that Purcell was under greater pressure than ever before. In October Robert Gould's tragedy *The Rival Sisters, or The Violence of Love* opened. Purcell seems not to

Music for two other plays:
The Indian Queen *and*
Bonduca *by John Fletcher.*
The latter used the talents of another of Purcell's favourite singers, the precocious Letitia Cross.

have had time to compose a new overture, but instead inserted that written for his ode of 1692, 'Love's goddess sure was blind'. The other eight instrumental movements survive only with the two outer parts and, in view of some rough corners and the absence of the inner parts, their authorship has to be held in some doubt. The play also contained three songs, of which the most famous was the ornate, declamatory 'Celia has a thousand charms', written for Jemmy Bowen. The haste in *The Rival Sisters* may be due to his being busy on the score for John Fletcher's tragedy *Bonduca, or The British Heroine*, which opened at around the same time.

For *Bonduca* Purcell provided one of his largest theatre scores, containing seven instrumental movements and a series of vocal numbers with instrumental (rather than continuo) accompaniment. There are more prominent unifying links between the instrumental and vocal movements than in any of his other theatre scores. The arresting trumpet overture must have startled the audience with its desolate ending, foreshadowing the tragedy of the play's heroine. 'Hear us, great Rugworth' is written on an expansive scale, with strings, four soloists and four-part choir. The bass solo 'Hear, ye gods of Britain' was much admired by Burney; there are hints of Purcell working at speed, for the second half is a reworking of 'Awful Matron' from the ode 'Great parent, hail'. The duet for two priestesses, 'Sing, sing ye druids', was another remarkable movement, set over a four-bar running ground bass which was freely modulated by Purcell and extended by the addition of a chorus. The Act V song for young Bonvica (probably played by Letitia Cross) 'O lead me to some peaceful gloom' is another fine setting, desolate in its sighings and repetitions of 'never', a favoured word of Purcell's. With King William's recent victory in Namur, two of the more warlike movements, 'Britons, strike home' and 'To arms, heroic prince', were to achieve near immortality as jingoistic victory songs.

In November Thomas Southerne's tragedy *Oroonoko* opened. Purcell contributed just one movement, 'Celemene, pray tell me', a duet which represents the first sexual awakenings of a boy and a girl, sung by Letitia Cross and Jemmy Bowen. The other two songs were written by Ralph Courteville, the organist of St James's Piccadilly. Courteville also collaborated with Purcell at around the same on the music for part three of *Don Quixote* and was a good composer whom Purcell evidently trusted: Courteville was the only other composer who is known to have written songs for Jemmy Bowen before Purcell's

*Surviving English musical instruments from Purcell's time are rare.
These virginals were made by James White – 'Jacobus White fecit' – in 1656.
As much care was lavished on its appearance as on its sound. It has a particularly
appealing roundel in the centre showing a lady playing a lute.*

death. The incidental instrumental music was provided by James Paisible: Purcell was either too busy, or had health problems.

Purcell had time only to write the music for two remaining plays. For *Pausanias, the Betrayer of his Country*, probably written by Richard Norton, he wrote the wonderful song 'Sweeter than roses'. While the play itself may have been undistinguished, this song inspired Purcell to produce one of his most intense settings on the theme of love, full of the most sensual textual illustrations. The 'cool evening breeze' gently blows, the 'dear kiss' which 'trembling made me freeze' is marked with a breathtaking harmonic shift, and his setting of the next words ('then shot like fire all o'er') is as vivid a portrayal of the results as any composer could hope for. The ardent aria that follows pauses only in its triumphant proclamation of love's victory for a momentary retreat back to the ecstasy of 'that dear kiss'. Purcell also provided a charming love duet, 'My dearest, my fairest', full of suspensions in its expressions of adoration. He may not have lived to hear the first performance.

Purcell's last song was written for the third part of *The Comical History of Don Quixote*, which was rushed into production in November 1695. D'Urfey's play was not a success but, ironically, Purcell's contribution was one of his finest theatre songs. The character for whom it was written, Altisidora, is given the task of luring Don Quixote away from Dulcinea, a lady of unblemished character. By Act V all her attempts have failed, and she makes a final, extravagant attempt to seize his attentions. She announces that she will 'teize him now with a whimsical variety, as if I were possess'd with several degrees of Passion – sometimes I'll be fond, and sometimes, freakish; sometimes merry, and sometimes melancholy, – sometimes treat him with Singing and Dancing, and sometimes scold and rail as if I were ready to tear his eyes out'.[32] Her attempts climax in the mad-song 'From rosy bowers'. Printed in *Orpheus Britannicus*, the setting is headed 'The last song the Author Sett, it being in his Sickness'.

There is no record of what Purcell's 'sickness' was, and there is no factual evidence of his physical state to allow a historical pathologist anything more than an informed guess, but pulmonary tuberculosis must be a strong candidate. The disease was certainly endemic and untreatable at this time; the infection can lie dormant (though highly infectious) for up to two years, being triggered by any number of other infections, or simply just stress. If Purcell did indeed contract tuberculosis, the initial symptoms of fevers, night sweats, loss of appetite and consequent weight loss could have been mistaken in their

OPPOSITE: *Detail of an 'idyll' by Sir Peter Lely, at one time thought to represent the painter and his family but this now seems doubtful. The man, dressed informally and rather romantically, is playing a great bass viol. The open air setting, the player's soulful expression and the poetic atmosphere suggest the emotional mood of which Purcell was such a master.*

early stages for a number of complaints and ignored by a person as energetic and frantically busy as Purcell. In any case, the fatigue brought on by the disease also allows for sudden bursts of energy, often lasting around eight hours – enough to allow a day of frantic composition. It is only in the later stages, as lung tissues are damaged and pulmonary arterioles are eroded, that coughing and possible haemorrhaging may take place. Sufferers would sometimes succumb to a secondary infection such as pneumonia, respiratory failure, cardiac complications or simply general debilitation; working as hard as he had been, Purcell would have been especially vulnerable to almost any opportunistic virus or bacteria.

And so it may have been in the more acute stages of tuberculosis that Purcell penned 'From rosy bowers'. Written for Letitia Cross, the song begins in semi-recitative as the singer requests Cupid to help 'teach me in soft melodious songs to move, with tender passion, my heart's darling joy'; only the flourishes as she tells the 'little waiting cupids' to 'fly' interrupt the gentle mood. The next aria provides contrast in its regular-length phrases and airy mood of carefree jollity. Purcell's next section is horrifically autobiographical: 'Ah, 'tis all in vain. Death and despair must end the fatal pain'. The interval from 'vain' to 'Death', a diminished octave, is as extreme as Purcell could write, coloured by the desolate repetitions of 'cold' and 'falls' in the next sentence. The sense of autobiography, of a man fighting a losing battle for life, continues as tempests blow, 'my veins all shiver' and 'my pulse beats a dead march for lost repose': the off-beat funereal drum strokes are notated over a deathly, still bass line. A conventional aria restores a more normal mood, but the final movement finds Altisidora in a frenzy, gabbling and repeating words in a way that depicts complete madness.

Purcell's end apparently came with surprising haste. On 21 November 1695 his health suddenly appears to have taken a turn for the worse. If he was suffering from tuberculosis, the general level of toxicity in his lungs would have risen to a level with which his body could no longer cope. In some cases a sufferer can bleed to death as blood vessels burst in the lungs. Purcell seems to have needed to make his will in a great hurry, if we are to believe the evidence of an extremely hastily written document. The clerk's quill was unsharpened, and the untidy presentation of the document, an error in the date (corrected from the twentieth to the twenty-first) and a crossing out near the end suggest speed was of the utmost urgency.

In the Name of God Amen I Henery Purcell of the Citty of Westmr. Gentl. being dangerously Ille as to the Constitution of my Body But in good and perfect Mind and Memory (thanks bee to God) Doe by these presents publish & Declare this to bee my last Will & Testamt. And I doe hereby Give and bequeath unto my Loveing Wife Frances Purcell All my Estate both real & personall of what Nature & kind soever, to her & to her Assignes for Ever And I doe hereby Constitute & Appoint my said Loveing Wife My sole E[x]ecutrix of this my last Will & Testamt. revokeing all Former Will or Wills Witness my Hand and seale this Tewenteth First Day of Novembr. Anno. Dni. 1695 And in the seaventh yeare of the Raigne of King William the Third &c.

> Sign'd seald. published &
> Declar'd by the sd. Henry Purcell
> in the presence of
> Wm. Eeles:
> John Capelin, J.B.Peters

Purcell's signature, usually stylish, rounded and confident, was shaky and almost unreadable. He died that night. The next day was St Cecilia's Day. The usual service of celebration at St Bride's Church in the morning and the afternoon concert at Stationers' Hall must have been horribly muted.

Purcell's forlorn friends and colleagues paid him the ultimate tribute. His funeral took place, on 26 November 1695, in the same building in which he had served for sixteen years. The procession, led by his friend and neighbour Stephen Crespion, entered Westminster Abbey to the march Purcell had written for Queen Mary's funeral, played by the same Flatt Trumpeters. The Dean and all the Chapter attended in their vestments, and the choirs of both the Abbey and the Chapel Royal were present. Normally they would have appreciated a funeral for the extra fee that it would have provided: this must have been an occasion which they would much rather have not had to attend. As Purcell's coffin was buried in the north aisle of the Abbey at the foot of the organ, his own settings of the Funeral Sentences were performed by the choirs which he had directed for so many years. Every member of the congregation, and every man and child singing and playing, would have known and adored the man they were mourning. It must have been a devastatingly poignant occasion. Purcell was only thirty-six.

Oculos Exc..

I. Closterman pinx.   R. White sculp.

Henricus Purcell.

Ætat Suæ 37. 95.

EPILOGUE

Purcell's Posthumous History

Many contemporary tributes were paid to England's greatest musical figure. Lady Howard had a memorial placed on a pillar near his tomb, stating that Purcell had 'gone to that blessed place where only his harmony can be exceeded'. The *Post Boy* of 28 November wrote that 'He is much lamented, being a very great Master of Musick'; Luttrell's diary simply recorded that 'Mr Purcell, the great master of musick, was this evening buried in the Abby of Westminster'; and an anonymous author, described as 'A lover of Music', bemoaned the fact that 'Gone is the Glory of our Age'.[1] We know of more than a dozen poems which were written in memory of the composer by his friends and colleagues, of which at least five were set to music. Daniel Purcell's setting of Nahum Tate's 'A gloomy mist o'erspreads the plains' and Gottfried Finger's setting of James Talbot's 'Ode for the Consort at York Buildings upon the Death of Mr H.P.' both seem to have been lost. John Blow set John Dryden's famous ode 'Mark how the lark and linnet sing' and it was published by Playford in 1696; in the theatre, Thomas Morgan introduced a short tribute to Purcell in his score for Aphra Behn's play *The Younger Brother* when it was staged at Drury Lane at the start of 1696. Jeremiah Clarke's extensive ode 'Come, come along' also seems to have had a dramatic element, for it was performed in the theatre, rather than in the concert hall, and may well have been acted out. An innocent pastoral scene is interrupted by a messenger (played by Jemmy Bowen) bearing news of Purcell's death (recalling a similar scene in Monteverdi's *Orfeo*). The soloists and chorus embark on a series of laments which culminate in a striking funeral march: the scoring for 'Mr. Henry Purcell's Farewell' includes Flatt Trumpets and a moving representation of a slowly tolling funeral bell. Henry Hall, now organist of Hereford Cathedral

The last portrait of Purcell is that used on the frontispiece to the posthumously published Orpheus Britannicus, 1698. His age is given as thirty-seven, meaning in his thirty-seventh year. It is a copy – reversed of the oil painting on p.129.

but a former Chapel Royal chorister around the same time as Purcell, wrote a number of moving tributes: his poem entitled 'To the memory of my dear Friend Mr Henry Purcell' (not set to music) included the famous couplet 'Sometimes a hero in an age appears; But scarce a Purcell in a thousand years'. Hall's pastoral dialogue 'Yes, my Aminta, 'tis too true' may have been performed at the same occasion as Clarke's ode.

At court, the normal processes prevailed. On 30 November a warrant was passed 'to swear and admit Dr. John Blow and Mr. Bernard Smith as tuners of the regals, organs, virginals, flutes and recorders, and all other kinds of wind instruments, in ordinary to his Majesty, and in the place of Mr. Henry Purcell, deceased'.[2] At the Chapel Royal matters moved rather more slowly: that King William was not especially interested in his Chapel Royal seems apparent, for on 6 July 1702 Thomas Tudway petitioned the crown that 'Ever since the Reformation there have been three organists belonging to the Chapel Royal, to attend that duty by turns. The petitioner was bred up in that Chapel, and had a promise in '82 from King Charles II that he should have the next place which fell vacant. This occurred when Mr. Purcell died in 1696 [sic]; but his place has never been filled. Prays for it'.[3] At Westminster Abbey the wheel came full circle, and John Blow, Purcell's friend and former teacher, became, for the second time, its organist.

For Purcell's wife, Frances, there was not only the shock of losing her husband, but also the practical difficulties of how to cope financially. We do not know what, if any, money Purcell may have left Frances, but she seems to have quickly realized that the manuscripts he left could help keep her and the children. Early in 1696 she arranged for *A choice Collection of Lessons for the Harpsichord or Spinnet* to be printed and sold by Henry Playford and, presumably finding that this edition had been successful, in 1697 arranged for Heptinstall to print *A Collection of Ayres, Compos'd for the Theatre, and upon Other Occasions*; this large volume was sold by three traders including Playford. Also in 1697 the same team put on sale the *Ten Sonata's in Four Parts*; these were mostly early works, maybe written at around the same time as the Fantazias, but never before published.

In February 1698 the *Post Boy* advertised the first volume of Henry Playford's *Orpheus Britannicus... compos'd by Mr Henry Purcell*. In this extensive volume came over sixty of Purcell's 'choicest songs for one, two, and three voices... together with such symphonies for violins and flutes as were by him design'd for any of them: and a through-bass to each song; figur'd for the organ, harpsichord or theorbo-lute'. A good number of the items had been seen before but a number of works were appearing in print for the first time. Someone, perhaps Frances Purcell, had been doing extensive research in Purcell's manuscripts. Published for the first time, for instance, was the lament on the death of King Charles, 'If pray'rs and tears', an extensive setting of Abraham Cowley's poem 'I came, I saw', the solo songs 'What a sad fate' and 'Love arms himself' and the extravagant setting for solo bass 'Bacchus is a pow'r divine'. Playford followed up the first volume with a second book in 1702, amongst whose newly published songs were the touching 'Elegy upon the Death of Mr. Thomas Farmer', 'Young Thirsis' fate', 'Ah, cruel nymph', the song which was arguably Purcell's most Italianate 'The fatal hour', and 'Oh, fair Cedaria'.

It is uncertain when Purcell had written 'Oh, fair Cedaria', but it is a masterpiece. Without *Orpheus Britannicus* it might have been lost. The opening is exquisite, with a ravishing melisma on 'Oh' leading to a series of sighing 'hide those eyes'; the setting of the word 'dies' is quite erotic. The final stanza is extraordinary, containing a series of increasingly desolate pleas to 'pity me', and a magically-descending bass line to 'Unless I may your favour have, I can't one moment live'. Little wonder that Purcell's contemporaries held him in such universal awe.

Those remarkable qualities were never totally forgotten. Roger North, writing thirty years after the composer's death, called him 'the devine Purcell', stating that 'a greater musical genius England never had'. Writing around 1715, Tudway gives an interesting insight into Purcell's character: 'He had a most commendable ambition of exceeding every one of his time, and he succeeded in it without contradiction'.[4] Handel was at a performance of his own oratorio *Jephtha* around 1752 when he was complimented by his neighbour, Mr Savage: 'This movement, Sir, reminds me of some of old Purcell's music'. Handel's retort was telling: 'O got te teffel. If Purcell had lived, he would have composed better music than this'.[5] Handel certainly was aware of Purcell's music, and the exquisite opening of his ode for Queen Anne's birthday, 'Eternal source of light divine', is perhaps Handel's own indirect tribute to the great master, and bears much of his influence. Handel's contemporaries could quite easily have obtained some of Purcell's music had they wished to, for *Orpheus Britannicus* was still being reprinted in 1745; an abridged version by John Johnson was being sold even as late as 1790.

In the cathedrals, many of which possessed manuscript copies of Purcell's anthems and services, a small quantity of his sacred music has remained on service papers almost continuously since his death. The repertoire performed has often been very limited: a glance at the shelves of an average cathedral twenty years ago might have brought half a dozen pieces to light. In 1828 Vincent Novello gathered together and published the first of five volumes of *Anthems, Hymns and other Sacred Pieces composed by Henry Purcell*; like many musicians and editors of the time, Novello felt it necessary to 'correct' Purcell's harmonies, presumably finding such an unconventional style unbelievable. A few years earlier Joseph Corfe had compiled *The Beauties of Purcell* in two volumes, and quoted in his preface Dr Burney's touching tribute: 'Henry Purcell is as much the pride of an Englishman in Music, as Shakespeare in productions of the Stage – Milton in Epic Poetry – Lock in Metaphysics – or Sir Isaac Newton in Philosophy and Mathematics'.[6]

In February 1876, on the initiative of W.H.Cummings, the 'Purcell Society' was formed with the aim of 'doing justice to the memory of Henry Purcell; firstly, by the publication of his works, most of which exist only in MS, and secondly, by meeting for the study and performance of his various compositions'. The committee comprised some of the most eminent musical figures of the day, including John Stainer, Sir John Goss, J.F. Bridge, Sir Frederick Gore-Ouseley and Joseph Barnby. Like the earlier Purcell Club (1836-63), the Purcell Society found it was unable to carry out its intention to perform the music, but it did do an invaluable service by starting to publish all the works in a subscription series. In the first ten years, only two volumes appeared but, with Cummings as editor and W.B. Squire as secretary, twenty more volumes appeared between 1887 and 1923. Between 1923 and 1928, under Gerald M. Cooper, four more volumes were published. Though musical scholarship has progressed greatly since the turn of the century, the standard of the editions was high (even if the keyboard continuo realizations were quite bizarre), and today's performers and scholars have much for which to thank those pioneering editors and subscribers. During the 1930s and 40s the Purcell Society went into a decline, but a growing band of authenticists in the 1950s led to a revival of Purcell's fortunes. The enthusiasm and determination of scholars (including Thurston Dart, Michael Tippett, Ralph Vaughan Williams, Edward Dent and J.A. Westrup) led to the completion of the thirty-one volumes by

1965, under the editorship of Anthony Lewis. Since that time, other members of the Purcell Society have embarked on a complete revision of all the volumes but, with the high cost of music printing and origination and the delays that editing by committee can bring, it will not be possible to purchase, even in the tercentenary year of 1995, all of Purcell's music.

Purcell's work received a number of important performances during the earlier part of the twentieth century. Martin Shaw conducted a performance in 1900 of *Dido and Aeneas,* Gustav Holst one of *The Fairy Queen* in 1911, and Cyril Bradley Rootham conducted Dennis Arundell's staging of *King Arthur* in Cambridge in 1928. Covent Garden brought to fruition Constant Lambert's dream of staging *The Fairy-Queen* in 1948. Benjamin Britten and Peter Pears gave performances of Purcell songs in their recitals for many years, with Britten adding a modern composer's concept of Purcell in his piano accompaniments. In the 1940s Michael Tippett revived much of Purcell's music and helped bring another great champion of

Almost three hundred years after his death, late in 1993, a manuscript music book in Purcell's own hand came to light containing about twenty harpsichord pieces by Purcell, a number of them completely unknown. This Prelude is from the Suite in A minor.

Purcell's, the countertenor Alfred Deller, to prominence. Anthony Lewis too made some notable Purcell recordings. But perhaps the greatest factor in the return to Purcell's music has been the rise of period instrument performance since the 1970s, which has enabled fine music to be brought to life in a manner which 'modern' orchestral instruments have rarely managed, and the development of new vocal styles which – whether they emulate the styles of Purcell's day or not – have given new colour to marvellous music. The commercial success of the compact disc has meant that not only have the famous stage works been presented to the public in performances which are historically aware, but that whole audio-editions of Purcell's music have been made available to the listening public. One of the first projects of Christopher Hogwood's pioneering Academy of Ancient Music was to record all Purcell's theatre music: behind that enterprise was the recording producer and indefatigable period instrument enthusiast Peter Wadland. Conductors such as John Eliot Gardiner, Roger Norrington, Andrew Parrott, William Christie and Trevor Pinnock have all made wonderful contributions on record, in the opera house and on the concert stage of Purcell's works. In the late 1980s Hyperion Records embarked on issuing all twenty-four of Purcell's Odes and Welcome Songs on compact disc. The appetite shown worldwide for the series ensured an even larger enterprise, that of recording every surviving piece of sacred music. Finally, three hundred years after his death, every ode, every sacred piece, every item of theatre music, every secular solo song of Purcell's can finally be heard on record, providing musicians with the ammunition to justify the place of this unique musician amongst the truly great composers.

Much has been written about this amazing, shadowy musical figure; a character of whom we know so little, and yet one who appears, through his remarkable music, to be so vital – almost tangible. Delightfully, it is in one of the composer's own settings, that of his 1685 ode 'Why are all the Muses mute', that we find the perfect epitaph for Henry Purcell and his astonishing music:

> 'His name shall the Muses in triumph rehearse,
> As long as there's number or music in verse;
> His fame shall endure till all things decay,
> His fame and the world together shall die,
> Shall vanish together away.'

Here lyes
HENRY PVRCELL Esqr
Who left this Life.
And is gone to that Blessed Place
Where only his Harmony
can be exceeded
Obijt 21 die Novembrs
Anno Ætatis suæ 37mo
Annoqs Domini 1695

Notes on the Text

References to standard authors are given by surname only; details are to be found under those names in the Selected Reading List on p.251

Zimmerman: references are to *Henry Purcell, his Life and Times*, 1967. See Reading List.

Van der Zee: references are to *William and Mary*, 1973. See Reading List.

Other abbreviations:
CSPD: *Calendar of State Papers preserved in the Public Record Office, Domestic Series, 1547–1704*, ed. R. Lemon et al. 100 volumes. London 1856–1972.
English Historical Documents. Vol. VIII, 1660–1714 (ed. Andrew Browning). London 1953.
New Grove: New Grove Dictionary of Music. See Reading List under Sadie, Stanley.
RECM: *Records of English Court Music.* See Reading List under Ashbee, Andrew.

CHAPTER I *A Restoration Childhood, 1659-1668*

1 Palmer, p.56
2 Patrick Morrah, *Restoration England* (London, 1979) p.39
3 English Historical Documents, pp.58-59
4 Palmer, p.36
5 CSPD 18/153, no. 123, RECM V, p.281

6 H.C. de Lafontaine, The King's Music (London, 1909)
7 RECM
8 RECM I, pp.2-3
9 Lafontaine, p.121
10 RECM I, p.4
11 Pepys, 27 July 1661
12 Evelyn, 21 December 1662
13 Palmer, p.45
14 Pepys, 13 October 1660
15 Palmer, p.46
16 RECM V, p.27
17 RECM V, p.27
18 RECM I, p.19
19 RECM V, p.109
20 Westminster Abbey Precentor's Book, 1660-71, fo.3, quoted in Zimmerman, p.8
21 Pepys, 22 April 1661
22 RECM I, p.15
23 RECM I, p.15
24 RECM III p. 253
25 RECM I, pp.15–16
26 RECM I, p.22
27 RECM V, p.109
28 RECM V, pp.107-8
29 RECM I, p.19
30 RECM I, p.20
31 RECM I, p.18
32 RECM V, p.40
33 RECM V, p.40
34 RECM V, p.37
35 RECM V, p.45
36 RECM I, p.28
37 RECM I, p.32
38 RECM I, p.32
39 RECM I, p.21
40 Palmer, p.61
41 RECM I, p.40
42 RECM V, p.40
43 RECM I, p.51
44 RECM I, pp.48-9
45 RECM I, pp.49
46 RECM I, p.49
47 RECM I, p.53
48 RECM I, p.263

49 RECM I, p.xiii
50 RECM I, p.39
51 RECM I, p.31
52 RECM I, p.67
53 RECM I, p.53
54 RECM I, p.62
55 RECM I, p.53
56 RECM I, p.viii
57 RECM I, p.39
58 Pepys, 9 February 1664
59 RECM V, p.47
60 RECM V, p.48
61 Pepys, 28 February 1664
62 Pepys, 7 August 1664
63 Pepys, 27 August 1664
64 Pepys, 4 September 1664
65 RECM I, p.54
66 Anthony à Wood quoted in *New Grove*, vol. 20, p.462
67 N. Hodges, *Loimologia; or An Historical Account of the Plague in London in 1665* (London, 1720) pp.1-2
68 RECM V, p.49
69 St Margaret's Westminster Churchwardens' Accounts, vol. LXXX
70 Zimmerman, p.16
71 RECM I, p.59
72 Duke of Clarendon, *Selections from the history of the rebellion and the life by himself*, ed. G. Huehns (London, 1978) p.410
73 Palmer, p.84
74 W.G. Bell, *The Great Plague in London* (London, 1924), p.107
75 Leasor, James, *The Plague and the Fire* (London, 1962), p.127
76 ibid. p.126
77 Palmer, p.84
78 Palmer, p.88
79 RECM I, p.60

80 RECM I, pp.63-64
81 RECM I, p.66
82 RECM I, p.69
83 RECM I, p.73
84 RECM I, p.69–70
85 RECM V, p.271
86 RECM I, p.71
87 RECM I, p.72
88 Waterhouse, quoted in Palmer, p.93
89 quoted Palmer, p.94
90 Evelyn, 4 September 1666
91 Palmer, pp.94-95
92 Palmer, p.97
93 Palmer op. cit. p.97
94 W.G. Bell, *The Great Fire of London in 1666* (London, 1920) p.229
95 RECM V, p.119
96 RECM V, p.119
97 Palmer, p.99
98 Palmer, p.100
99 CSPD, 29 March 1667
100 RECM, p.I 75
101 Pepys, 20 February 1667
102 CSPD 4 August 1667
103 RECM I, p.78
104 Pepys, 15 November 1667
105 RECM I, p.81
106 *New Grove*, vol. 8, p.777

CHAPTER II *Learning the Trade, 1668-1679*

1 Westrup, p.5
2 Zimmerman, p.272
3 Zimmerman, p.27
4 RECM I, p.85
5 RECM I, p.89
6 Westrup, p.16
7 CSPD, quoted Zimmerman, pp.28-29
8 Zimmerman, pp.28-29
9 CSPD, quoted Zimmerman, p.29
10 Pepys, 21 December 1663
11 Zimmerman, pp.324-6

12 Anthony à Wood, *Notes on English Musicians* (Bodleian Library, Oxford MS. Wood D 19 (4))
13 for instance RECM V, p.125
14 RECM I, p.169
15 British Library, London. Harl. 7338, quoted Westrup, p.200
16 W. Barclay Squire, 'Purcell as Theorist', in *Quarterly Magazine of the International Musical Society,* July-Sept. 1905 p.567
17 Fitzwilliam Museum, Cambridge MS 88
18 Lafontaine, p.485
19 RECM I, p.98
20 RECM I, p.115
21 RECM I, p.98
22 RECM I, p.102
23 RECM I, p.104
24 Lafontaine, p.235
25 RECM I, p.116
26 RECM I, p.117
27 RECM I, p.117–118
28 RECM I, p.111
29 RECM I, p.118
30 RECM I, p.117
31 RECM I, p.119
32 RECM I, p.125
33 RECM I, pp.121 and 123
34 RECM I, p.131
35 RECM I, p.128
36 RECM I, p.129
37 RECM I, p.126
38 RECM I, p.131
39 RECM V, p.162
40 RECM I, p.135
41 RECM I, p.137
42 RECM I, p.138
43 RECM I, p.130
44 RECM I, p.147
45 RECM I, p.132
46 RECM I, p.137
47 RECM I, p.140
48 RECM I, p.140
49 RECM I, p.144
50 British Library, London, Add.MS 34072
51 British Library, London, Add.MS 30933
52 RECM I, pp.156-57
53 RECM I, p.141
54 Zimmerman, p.326
55 RECM I, pp.162-64
56 RECM I, pp.158-61
57 RECM I, p.279
58 RECM I, p.154
59 RECM I, p.96

60 *New Grove,* vol. 11, p.109
61 Zimmerman, pp.46-47

CHAPTER III *Rising star: Purcell at the Court of Charles II, 1679-1685*

1 RECM I, p.173
2 RECM V, p.79
3 RECM I, p.192
4 Zimmerman, pp.52-54
5 Fitzwilliam Museum, Cambridge, MS 88 (23.H.13)
6 Palmer, p.198
7 Palmer, p.210
8 Palmer, p.242
9 RECM I, p.183
10 Zimmerman, p.84
11 Palmer, p.246
12 Palmer, p.247
13 Price, p. 37
14 British Library, London, Add MS 19759
15 British Library, London, Add.MS 33234
16 Palmer, p.274
17 Falkus, p.192
18 Zimmerman, p.88
19 *New Grove,* vol. 15, p.471
20 RECM V, p.80
21 Zimmerman, p.94
22 Westrup, p.41, quoting the 'Cheque Book' for 19 December 1663
23 RECM I, p.194
24 RECM I. p.195
25 RECM I, p.203
26 RECM V, p.76
27 *New Grove,* vol. 7, p.565 quoting *The Gentleman's Magazine* 1777, p.210
28 RECM I, p.204
29 RECM I, p.200
30 RECM I, p.200
31 RECM I, p.200
32 RECM I, pp.286-7
33 Evelyn, 9 January 1684
34 Evelyn, 24 January 1684
35 RECM I, p.208
36 RECM I, p.210
37 RECM V, p.82
38 RECM I, pp.208–9
39 RECM I. p.206
40 Evelyn, 28 January 1685
41 Westrup, p.52
42 Westrup, p.52
43 Westrup, p.53
44 Palmer, p.280
45 British Library, London Royal MS 20.h.8

46 RECM I, p.212
47 Evelyn, 28 January 1685
48 Palmer, p.291
4 9 Evelyn, 6 February 1685
50 Evelyn, 6 February 1685

CHAPTER IV *Changing fortunes: Purcell and King James, 1685-1688*

1 F. Sandford, *The history of the Coronation of… James II* (London, 1687)
2 RECM V, p.273
3 Miller, p.154
4 RECM II, p.1
5 RECM II, p.1
6 RECM II, pp.2-3
7 RECM II, p.4
8 RECM II, p.4
9 Franklin B. Zimmerman *Henry Purcell.. an Analytical Catalogue of his Music* (London, 1963) p.177
10 RECM I, p.289
11 Now in the Guildhall Library, London, MS 1196/1, quoted in Zimmerman p.137
12 Reproduced in facsimile in Westrup opposite p.85
13 RECM V, pp.83-84
14 RECM V, p.285
15 Quoted in Westrup op. cit. p.57
16 British Library, London, Add.MS 35273, f 89v
17 RECM II, pp.15-16
18 Miller, p.170
19 Archives Nationales, Paris, K1351, no 4, f58 quoted in Miller ibid.
20 British Library, London, Add.MS 30931
21 Price, p.21
22 Hyperion Records, Purcell, *Complete Secular Solo Songs,* vol. 1, sleeve booklet
23 RECM V, pp.85-87
24 RECM V, p.274
25 RECM II, pp.16-17
26 RECM V, p.85
27 RECM V, p.234
28 Miller, p.187
29 RECM II, p.20

CHAPTER V *Maturity cut short: Purcell under William and Mary, 1688-1695*

1 Zimmerman, p.162
2 Reresby quoted in Van der Zee, p.277
3 RECM II, p.22
4 Zimmerman, p.165
5 Treasury papers quoted in Van der Zee, p.278
6 Zimmerman, p.169
7 Zimmerman, pp.170-71
8 Van der Zee p.284
9 RECM II, p.27
10 B. Wood and A. Pinnock in *Early Music,* August 1992, pp.372-90
11 Tenbury manuscript 1226, now in the Bodleian Library, Oxford
12 C Price, in *Early Music,* February 1994, pp.115-125
13 RECM V, p. 234
14 RECM V, pp.88-89
15 Van der Zee, p.285
16 Zimmerman, p.187
17 Van der Zee, p.323
18 ibid. p.335
19 Kent Archives Office: U.269/067/4
20 Kent Archives Office: U.269/067/2
21 RECM II, p.43
22 RECM V, pp.287-8
23 Zimmerman, p.204
24 Zimmerman, pp.210-211
25 Price, p.327
26 *New Grove,* vol. 14, p.299
27 RECM II, p.47
28 Zimmerman, pp.237-238
29 Van der Zee, p.379
30 Westrup, p.76
31 Price, p.126
32 Price, p.219

EPILOGUE
1 Zimmerman, p.334
2 RECM II, p.56
3 Zimmerman, p.329
4 Cummings, *Purcell* (London 1903) p.87
5 R J S Stevens, *Anecdotes,* MS in Pendlebury Library Cambridge
6 Preston, 1805

A Performer's Catalogue of Purcell's Works

This index lists Purcell's works in a form intended to aid performers and scholars as a general reference document and also as a useful tool in concert programming

Scholars hold divergent views on some points, especially on dating and attribution.

Abbreviations:

'Z' refers to the catalogue number given by Franklin B. Zimmerman in *Henry Purcell, 1659—1695: An Analytic Catalogue of his music* (London, 1963)
SATB = soprano, alto, tenor, bass (A usually implies countertenor)

H = high tenor (these lines can sometimes be taken by a low countertenor)
bc = basso continuo (usually string and keyboard)
brec = bass recorder
rec = recorder
ob = oboe
tpt = trumpet

timp = timpani
vn = violin
vla = viola
hpd = harpsichord

In referring to keys, capital letters refer to major keys, lower case to minor.

Pitch: this is a highly contentious area but, in the voice suggestions below, for the sacred music a high pitch (around A = 446) has been assumed, and for the remaining music a low pitch (A = 415 or even A = 392).
String continuo instruments: there is little evidence for the use of 16' instruments. Bass lines were usually played by 8' string instruments: the bass violin, larger than the cello had a low B flat.

ODES AND WELCOME SONGS

All the Odes can be performed by chorus and soloists as indicated below or by a double quartet of singers taking solos and choruses

Z	First line (Author)	Occasion	Performance	Soloists	Chorus	Instruments	Timing
340	Welcome, vicegerent of the mighty king	welcome, Charles II	1680	SATB	SATB	2vn, vla, bc	14'00
336	Swifter, Isis, swifter flow	welcome, Charles II	1681	SSAHTB	SATB	2rec, ob, 2vn, 2vla, bc	15'00
341	What, what shall be done in behalf of the man?	welcome, Duke of York	1682	SSAHTB	SATB	2rec, 2vn, vla, bc	14'40
337	The Summer's absence unconcerned we bear	welcome, Charles II	1682	SSAHTB	SATB	2vn, vla, bc	18'10
325	From hardy climes and dangerous toils of war	wedding of Prince George of Denmark	1683	SSAHTB	SATB	2vn, vla, bc	17'20
324	Fly, bold rebellion	welcome, Charles II	1683	SSAHTB	SSAATB	2vn, vla, bc	19'10
339	Welcome to all the pleasures (C Fishburn)	St Cecilia's Day	1683	SSATB	SATB	2vn, vla, bc	15'40
329	Laudate Ceciliam	St Cecilia's Day	1683	ATB	no chorus	2vn, bc	10'20
326	From those serene and rapturous joys (T Flatman)	welcome, Charles II	1684	SSATB	SATB	2vn, vla, bc	23'20
343	Why, why are all the Muses mute?	welcome, James II	1685	SSAHTBB	SSATB	2vn, vla, bc	27'50
334	Raise, raise the voice	St Cecilia's Day	c1685	STB	STB	2vn, bc	12'20
344	Ye tuneful Muses	welcome, James II	1686	SSAHTBB	SATB	2rec, 2vn, vla, bc	24'10
335	Sound the trumpet	welcome, James II	1687	AHTB	SATB	2vn, vla, bc	23'40
332	Now does the glorious day appear (T Shadwell)	birthday, Mary II	1689	SATBB	SATB	2vn, 2vla, bc	23'40
322	Celestial music did the gods inspire	for Mr Maidwell's school	1689	SAHTB	SATB	2rec, 2vn, vla, bc	17'50
333	Of old when heroes thought it base (T D'Urfey)	Yorkshire Feast	1690	AHTBB	SSATB	2rec, 2ob, 2tpt, 2vn, vla, bc	36'00
320	Arise, my Muse (T D'Urfey)	birthday, Mary II	1690	AAHTB	SATB	2rec, 2ob, 2tpt, 2vn, 2vla, bc	21'00
338	Welcome, welcome, glorious morn	birthday, Mary II	1691	SAHTBB	SATB	2ob, 2tpt, 2vn, vla, bc	27'00
331	Love's goddess sure was blind	birthday, Mary II	1692	SAHTB	SATB	2rec, 2vn, vla, bc	21'30
328	Hail, bright Cecilia (N Brady)	St Cecilia's Day	1692	SAHTBB	SSAATB	2rec, brec, 2ob, 2tpt, timp, 2vn, vla, bc	51'50

Z	First line (Author)	Occasion	Performance	Soloists	Chorus	Instruments	Timing
321	Celebrate this festival (N Tate)	birthday, Mary II	1693	SSAHTB	SSAATTBB	2ob, 2tpt, 2vn, vla, bc	32'50
327	Great parent, hail (N Tate)	centenary of Trinity College, Dublin	1694	SAHTB	SATB	2rec, 2vn, vla, bc	24'20
323	Come, ye sons of art, away (N Tate)	birthday, Mary II	1694	SAAB	SATB	2ob, 2tpt, 2vn, vla, bc	25'40
342	Who can from joy refrain? (N Tate)	birthday, Duke of Gloucester	1695	SSAHTB	SSATB	3ob, tpt, 2vn, vla, bc	20'15

ANTHEMS AND SERVICES
All anthems require SATB chorus (or larger where indicated) and bc in addition to soloists and instruments as shown

Z	Composition	First line or title	Soloists	Instruments	Timing	Comment
1	c1682-5	Awake, put on thy strength	AHB	2vn, vla	8'20	missing last chorus
2	1687	Behold, I bring you glad tidings	ATB	2vn, vla	10'50	
3	c1680	Behold now, praise the Lord	ATB	2vn, vla	5'50	
4	?pre1683	Be merciful unto me	ATB	—	7'10	
5	1688	Blessed are they that fear the Lord	SSHB	2vn, vla	9'30	
6	by Feb 1679	Blessed be the Lord my strength	HTB	—	5'00	
7	?c1688	Blessed is he that considereth the poor	HTB	—	5'30	
8	?1680	Blessed is he whose unrighteousness is forgiven	SSATTB	—	8'30	
9	?c1688	Blessed is the man that feareth the Lord	HTB	—	6'20	
10	by Feb 1679	Blow up the trumpet in Sion	SSSATBB	—	7'20	SSAATTBB choir
11	c1680-82	Bow down thine ear, O Lord	SHTB	—	7'40	
12	by Nov 1681	Give sentence with me, O God	HB	—	—	incomplete
13	c1680-82	Hear me, O Lord, and that soon	SATB	—	6'20	SSATB choir
14	pre1683	Hear my prayer, O God	HTB	—	6'20	
15	c1680-82	Hear my prayer, O Lord	—	—	2'10	first section of a larger piece (remainder ? never written)
19	1682-3	I was glad when they said unto me	HTB	2vn, vla	8'00	
—	1685	I was glad when they said unto me	—	—	4'00	SSATB choir
20	c1682-5	I will give thanks unto thee, O Lord	SSATB	2vn, vla	11'20	
21	?c1680-82	I will give thanks unto the Lord	TBB	2vn	8'20	
N67		I will love thee O Lord	B	—	6'00	
22	by Feb 1679	I will sing unto the Lord	SSAHTB	—	3'00	SSATB choir
16	c1682	In thee, O Lord, do I put my trust	ATB	2vn, vla	11'50	
17	pre1682	In the midst of life	SHTB	—	4'10	Two versions. Funeral of Queen Mary
18	c1682-5	It is a good thing to give thanks	ATB	2vn, vla	11'50	
23	by Feb 1679	Let God arise	TT	—	4'10	
24	c1682	Let mine eyes run down with tears	SSATB	—	9'10	
25	c1680-82	Lord, how long wilt thou be angry?	ATB	—	3'40	SSATB choir
26	c1677	Lord, who can tell how oft he offendeth?	TTB	—	4'10	
27	c1680-82	Man that is born of a woman	SHTB	—	2'20	Two versions. Funeral of Queen Mary
28	pre1678	My beloved spake	ATBB	2vn, vla	11'20	
29	c1682-5	My heart is fixed, O God	HTB	2vn, vla	8'30	
30	1685	My heart is inditing	SSAHTBBB	2vn, vla	16'50	SSATTBBB choir
31	prob 1690	My song shall be alway	B	2vn, vla	14'40	also later version for S solo
32	?1685-90	O consider my adversity	HTB	—	9'20	
33	1693	O give thanks unto the Lord	SATB	2vn	9'50	
34	by Feb 1679	O God, the king of glory	—	—	2'00	
35	c1680-82	O God, thou art my God	SSHTB	—	5'40	
36	c1680-82	O God, thou hast cast us out	SSATBB	—	4'00	SSAATB choir
37	c1680-82	O Lord God of hosts	SSAHTB	—	4'50	SSAATTBB choir
38	1685	O Lord, grant the king a long life	ATB	2vn	8'00	
39	by Feb 1679	O Lord our governor	SSSBB	—	10'00	
40	c1680-85?	O Lord, rebuke me not	SS	—	7'10	
41	c1680-82	O Lord, thou art my God	HTB	—	5'40	
42	c1682-85	O praise God in his holiness	ATBB	2vn, vla	8'10	
43	by Nov 1681	O praise the Lord, all ye heathen	TT	—	2'50	
44	1688	O sing unto the Lord	SSATBB	2vn, vla	13'10	
45	?c1680	Out of the deep have I called	SHB	—	6'30	
46	prob 1689	Praise the Lord, O Jerusalem	SSATB	2vn, vla	7'40	SSATB choir
47	c1682-85	Praise the Lord, O my soul, and all that is	SSHTBB	2vn, vla	10'20	
48	1687	Praise the Lord, O my soul, O Lord my God	HB	2vn	13'00	

Z	Composition	First line or title	Soloists	Instruments	Timing	Comment
49	c1682-85	Rejoice in the Lord alway	ATB	2vn, vla	8'20	
50	c1680-82	Remember not, Lord, our offences	—	—	3'30	SSATB choir
51	by Nov 1681	Save me, O God	SSATB	—	3'40	SSATB choir
52	1687	Sing unto God, O ye kingdoms	B	—	5'50	
—	?c1680-85	The Lord is king and hath put on	S	—	3'20	
53	?c1680-85	The Lord is king, be the people	SS	—	4'50	
54	1688	The Lord is king, the earth may be glad	B	—	8'20	
55	c1682-85	The Lord is my light	HTB	2vn, vla	10'40	
56	1694	The way of God is an undefiled way	AHB	—	8'20	SAAATB choir
57	1685	They that go down to the sea in ships	AB	2vn	9'10	
58B	pre 1683	Thou know'st, Lord, the secrets of our hearts	SHTB	—	3'50	Two versions. Funeral of Queen Mary
58C	1695	Thou know'st, Lord, the secrets of our hearts	—	4 flatt tpts	2'20	Funeral of Queen Mary
59	?	Thy righteousness, O God, is very high	—	—		incomplete
60	1687	Thy way, O God, is holy	HB	—	5'10	
61	?c1685-90	Thy word is a lantern unto my feet	ATB	—	4'50	
62	?	Turn thou us, O good Lord	HTB	—	5'00	
63	c1682-85	Unto thee will I cry	ATB	2vn, vla	11'00	
64	c1679-80	Who hath believed our report?	ATTB	—	8'20	
65	c1682-85	Why do the heathen so furiously rage together?	HTB	2vn, vla	10'40	
231	?	Magnificat and Nunc Dimittis in g	SSAHTB	—	3'30+1'40	
232	1694	Te Deum and Jubilate in D	SSAHTB	2tpt, 2vn, vla	14'10+8'40	SSATB choir
230	pre Oct 1682	Morning and Evening Service in B flat	SSAATTBB	—		(contains Te Deum, Jubilate, Benedicite, Cantate Domino, Deus Misereatur, Kyrie, Credo, Benedictus, Magnificat, Nunc Dimittis)

DEVOTIONAL SONGS (SACRED WORKS WITH NON-BIBLICAL TEXTS)

All these works (except Jehova quam multi sunt hostes) were probably intended for performance by solo voices with bc.

Z	Composition	First line or Title	Text/Author	Voices	Timing	Comment
198	1688	A morning hymn – see 'Thou wakeful shepherd'	W Fuller	S	2'50	
130	c1680	Ah! few and full of sorrow	G Sandys	SHTB	—	incomplete
193	1688	An evening hymn – see 'Now that the sun hath veiled his light'	W Fuller	S	4'00	
181	1688	Awake and with attention hear	A Cowley	B	12'40	
182	1693	Awake, ye dead	N Tate	BB	3'10	
131	c1680	Beati omnes qui timent Dominum	Ps 128	SSHB	4'30	
183	1693	Begin the song, and strike the living lyre	Cowley	B	8'10	
196	1693	Blessed Virgin's Expostulation – see 'Tell me some pitying angel	N Tate	S	7'30	
184	1688	Close thine eyes, and sleep secure	F Quarles	SB	4'00	
132	c1680	Early, O Lord, my fainting soul	J Patrick	SSHB	5'40	
185	?	Full of wrath his threatening breath	J Taylor	S/T	2'40	
186	1688	Great God and just	Taylor	SSB	3'50	
133	1680-82	Hear me, O Lord, the great support	Patrick	HTB	5'40	
187	?	Hosanna to the highest	anon	HB	5'20	
188	1688	How have I strayed	W Fuller	SB	4'00	
189	1688	How long, great God	J Norris	S	3'40	
134	1693	In guilty night	after Bk of Samuel	SHB	9'10	
190	1688	In the black dismal dungeon of despair	W Fuller	S	4'30	
135	c1680	Jehovah, quam multi sunt	Ps 3	TB	6'30	with SSATB choir
191	1688	Let the night perish (Job's Curse)	J Taylor	SB	4'20	
136	c1680	Lord, I can suffer thy rebukes	J Patrick	SSHB	5'30	
137	c1680	Lord, not to us but to thy name	J Patrick	HTB	0'50	
192	1693	Lord, what is man?	W Fuller	S	6'10	
193	1688	Now that the sun hath veiled (An Evening Hymn)	W Fuller	S	4'00	
138	c1680	O all ye people, clap your hands	J Patrick	SSTB	2'30	
139	?	O happy man that fears the Lord	J Patrick	SSAB	—	incomplete
140	c1680	O, I'm sick of life	Sandys	HTB	5'10	
141	c1680	O Lord our governor	J Patrick	SSHB	4'30	

Z	Composition	First line or Title	Text/Author	Voices	Timing	Comment
142	c1680	Plung'd in the confines of despair	J Patrick	HTB	4'40	
143	c1680	Since God so tender a regard	J Patrick	HTB	4'30	
195	1683	Sleep, Adam, sleep and take thy rest	anon	S	1'50	
196	1693	Tell me some pitying angel (Blessed Virgin's Expostulation)	N Tate	S	7'30	
197	1688	The earth trembled	F Quarles	S	2'10	
198	1688	Thou wakeful shepherd (A Morning Hymn)	W Fuller	S	2'50	
199	1688	We sing to him whose wisdom form'd the ear	N Ingelo	SB	1'30	
144	c1680	When on my sick bed I languish	T Flatman	HTB	4'50	
200	1688	With sick and famish'd eyes	G Herbert	S/T	5'20	
120-5	?	5 chants + Burford psalm-tune	—	SATB	—	dubious authorship
—	?	Domine, non est exaltatum	—	HT	—	incomplete
103-6	c1680	4 doxologies	—	3-4vv	—	canons
107	?	God is gone up	—	7vv	—	canon
108	?	Laudate Dominum	—	3vv	—	canon
109	1687	Miserere mei	Ps 51	4vv	—	canon

OPERA

Z	Title	Text	First recorded performance venue	Timing	Date of first recorded performance
626	*Dido and Aeneas*	N Tate	London, Josias Priest's School for Young Ladies, Chelsea	c 60'00	1689?

SEMI-OPERAS

Z	Title	Text	First performance venue	Date of first performance
627	*The Prophetess, or The History of Dioclesian*	T Betterton, after J Fletcher, P Massinger	Dorset Garden Theatre	1690
628	*King Arthur, or The British Worthy*	J Dryden	Dorset Garden Theatre	1691
629	*The Fairy - Queen*	?E Settle or T Betterton, after Shakespeare: *A Midsummer Night's Dream*	Dorset Garden Theatre	1692
630	*The Indian Queen* (final masque by D Purcell)	Dryden, R Howard	Drury Lane Theatre	1695

for *The Tempest* see 'Plays with incidental music' and 'Songs of uncertain attribution'

PLAYS WITH INCIDENTAL MUSIC AND/OR SONGS
For details of songs in plays see 'Songs for solo voice and continuo' and 'Songs for two or more voices and continuo'

Z	Title	Author	First performance date	Purcell's contribution
606	*Theodosius, or The Force of Love*	N Lee	1680	songs, ensembles, choruses
589	*Sir Barnaby Whigg, or No Wit like a Woman's*	T D'Urfey	1681	1 song with chorus
581	*The History of King Richard II (The Sicilian Usurper)*	Tate, after Shakespeare	1681	1 song
593	*The Double Marriage*	Beaumont, Fletcher	?1682-5	instr music – dubious
590	*Sophonisba, or Hannibal's Overthrow*	Lee	early 1690s	1 song
575	*Circe*	C Davenant	?1685-95?	2 songs, ensembles, choruses
571	*A Fool's Preferment, or The Three Dukes of Dunstable*	D'Urfey, after Fletcher: *Noble Gentleman*	1688	7 songs, 1 duet
604	*The Massacre of Paris*	Lee	Autumn 1689	1 song (2 settings)
572	*Amphitryon, or The Two Sosias*	Dryden	1690	2 songs, 1 duet, instr music
588	*Sir Anthony Love, or The Rambling Lady*	T Southerne	1690	2 songs, 1 duet, instr music
577	*Distressed Innocence, or The Princess of Persia*	E Settle	Oct 1690	instr music
597	*The Gordian Knot Unty'd*	?	1690/91	instr music
612	*The Wives' Excuse, or Cuckolds make Themselves*	Southern	Dec 1691	4 songs
573	*Aureng-Zebe*	Dryden	?1692	1 song
583	*Oedipus*	Dryden, Lee	?1692	2 songs, 2 trios, choruses
598	*The Indian Emperor*	Dryden, R Howard	1692	1 song
602	*The Marriage-hater Match'd*	D'Urfey	Jan 1692	1 duet
576	*Cleomenes, the Spartan Hero*	Dryden	April 1692	1 song
586	*Regulus*	J Crowne	June 1692	1 song

Z	Title	Author	First performance date	Purcell's contribution
580	*Henry the Second, King of England*	?W Mountfort, J Bancroft	Nov 1692	1 song
587	*Rule a Wife and Have a Wife*	Fletcher	?1693	1 song
579	*Epsom Wells*	Shadwell	1693	1 duet
592	*The Double Dealer*	W Congreve	1693	1 song, instr music
607	*The Old Bachelor*	Congreve	1693	1 song, 1 duet, instr music
608	*The Richmond Heiress, or A Woman Once in the Right*	D'Urfey	1693	1 duet
601	*The Maid's Last Prayer, or Any rather than Fail*	Southerne	Feb 1693	2 songs, 1 duet
596	*The Female Vertuosos*	T Wright, after Molière: *Les femmes savantes*	May 1693	1 duet
613	*Tyrannic Love, or The Royal Martyr*	Dryden	?1694	1 song, 1 duet
611	*The Virtuous Wife, or Good Luck at Last*	D'Urfey	?1694	instr music
603	*The Married Beau, or The Curious Impertinent*	Crowne	1694	1 song, instr music
582	*Love Triumphant, or Nature will Prevail*	Dryden	Jan 1694	1 song
595	*The Fatal Marriage, or The Innocent Adultery*	Southerne	Feb 1694	2 songs
591	*The Canterbury Guests, or A Bargain Broken*	E Ravenscroft	c.Oct 1694	1 quartet
610	*The Spanish Friar, or The Double Discovery*	Dryden	1694-95	1 song
600	*The Libertine*	T Shadwell	prob 1695	2 songs, ensembles, choruses
631	*The Tempest, or The Enchanted Island*	?Shadwell, after Shakespeare	c1695	1 song
570	*Abdelazer, or The Moor's Revenge*	A Behn	Apr 1695	1 song, instr music
632	*Timon of Athens*	Shadwell, after Shakespeare	May/June 1695	songs, duets, instr music, choruses
578	*The Comical History of Don Quixote, parts i & ii*	D'Urfey	May/June 1695	songs, duets, ensembles
605	*The Mock Marriage*	T Scott	?June or Oct 1695	3 songs – 2 dubious, 1 definite
574	*Bonduca, or The British Heroine*	after Beaumont, Fletcher	Oct 1695	3 songs, 2 duets, ensembles, choruses, instr music
609	*The Rival Sisters, or The Violence of Love*	R Gould	Oct 1695	3 songs, instr music
578	*The Comical History of Don Quixote, part iii*	D'Urfey	Nov 1695	1 song
584	*Oroonoko*	Southerne	Nov 1695	1 duet
585	*Pausanias, the Betrayer of his Country*	Norton	1695 or 96	1 song, 1 duet

SONGS FOR SOLO VOICE AND CONTINUO

This section includes all Purcell's songs for the stage and for other use: the two columns of Z numbers differentiate between these categories. Some stage works continue into a chorus.

Z number if single song	Title (author)	Z number of source stage work	Date of composition and/or first publication
359	A thousand several ways I tried	—	1684
—	A thousand, thousand ways	629	1692
—	Ah! Belinda	626	?1689
—	Ah! Cruel bloody fate	606	1680
352	Ah! Cruel nymph you give despair	—	1693
353	Ah! How pleasant 'tis to love	—	1688
—	Ah! How sweet it is to love	613	?1694
—	Ah me! To many deaths	586	1692
—	All our days and our nights	627	1690
355	Amidst the shades and cool refreshing streams	—	1687
356	Amintas to my grief I see	—	1679
357	Amintor heedless of his flocks	—	1681
423	Anacreon's Defeat — see 'This poet sings the Trojan wars'	—	1688
358	Ask me to love (A Hammond)	—	1694
360	Bacchus is a pow'r divine	—	?1687-9
—	Begon, curst fiends of hell	630	1695
382	Bell Barr – see 'I love and I must'	—	1693
—	Beneath the poplar's shadow	590	c1690
370	Bess of Bedlam – see 'From silent shades'	—	1683
361	Beware poor shepherds	—	1684
—	Britons, strike home	574	1695
362	Cease anxious world (G Etherege)	—	1687
—	Celia has a thousand charms	609	1695
364	Celia's fond, too long I've loved her	—	1694
—	Celia, that I once was blest	572	1690
—	Charon the peaceful shade invites	627	1690

Z number if single song	Title (author)	Z number of source stage work	Date of composition and/or first publication
—	Come all to me	632	1695
—	Come, all ye songsters of the sky	629	1692
—	Come away, do not stay	583	?1692
—	Come away, fellow sailors	626	?1689
—	Come ev'ry demon who o'ersees	575	?1685-95
—	Come if you dare	628	1691
—	Corinna, I excuse thy face	612	1691
365	Corinna is divinely fair	—	1692
367	Cupid the slyest rogue alive	—	1685
—	Cynthia frowns whene'er I woo her	592	1693
—	Dear pretty youth	631	1695
—	Dream no more of pleasures past	606	1680
—	Fairest isle	628	1691
368	Farewell all joys	—	1685
—	Fled is my love	571	1688
369	Fly swift ye hours	—	1692
—	For Iris I sigh	572	1690
—	From rosy bowers	578 iii	1695
370	From silent shades ('Bess of Bedlam')	—	1683
—	Genius of England	578 ii	1695
—	Great Diocles the boar has killed	627	1690
—	Great Love, I know thee now	628	1691
—	Hail to the myrtle shade	606	1680
—	Hang this whining way of wooing	612	1691
—	Hark, behold the heavenly choir	606	1680
—	Hark, how all things	629	1692
—	Hark, the echoing air	629	1692
—	Hear ye gods of Britain	574	1695
372	He himself courts his own ruin	—	1684
371	Hears not my Phillis ('The Knotting Song'), (C Sedley)	—	1695
—	Hence with your trifling deity	632	1695
—	Here's the summer, sprightly, gay	629	1692
—	Hither this way	628	1691
—	How blest are shepherds	628	1691
—	How happy is she	609	1695
—	How happy's the husband	582	1694
374	How I sigh when I think of the charms	—	1681
—	Hush no more	629	1692
—	I am come to lock all fast	629	1692
—	I attempt from love's sickness to fly	630	1695
—	I call you all from Woden's Hall	628	1691
375	I came, I saw and was undone (A Cowley)	—	1685
—	I come to sing great Zempoalla's story	630	1695
—	I look'd and saw within the book of fate	598	1692
382	I love and I must ('Bell Barr')	—	1693
381	I loved fair Celia (B Howard) (music same as mock song 'We now, my Thirsis')	—	1694
—	I sighed and I pin'd	571	1688
386	I resolve against cringing	—	1679
—	I see she flies me	573	?1692
—	I sigh'd and owned my love	595	1694
388	I take no pleasure in the sun's bright beams	—	1681
—	Ingrateful love	612	1691
378	If grief has any power to kill	—	1685
—	If love's a sweet passion	629	1692
379	If music be the food (H Heveningham) (1st setting)	—	1692
379	If music be the food (H Heveningham) (2nd setting = 1st setting decorated)	—	1693
379	If music be the food (H Heveningham) (3rd setting)	—	1693
380	If pray'rs and tears ('On the death of Charles II')	—	1685/6
—	If thou wilt give me back my love	571	1688
—	I'll mount to you blue coelum	571	1688
—	I'll sail upon the dog star	571	1688
383	Incassum lesbia, rogas ('The Queen's Epicedium'), (Herbert)	—	1695
384	In Cloris all soft charms (J Howe)	—	1684
385	In vain we dissemble	—	1685
—	In vain, Clemene, you bestow	588	1690
—	In vain, 'gainst love I strove	580	1692

A Performer's Catalogue of Purcell's Works

Z number if single song	Title (author)	Z number of source stage work	Date of composition and/or first publication
371	Knotting Song, The – see 'Hears not my Phillis' (C Sedley)	—	1695
—	Lads and lasses, blithe and gay	578 ii	1695
389	Leave these useless arts in loving – also as duet	—	c1693/4
390	Let each gallant heart (J Turner)	—	1683
391	Let formal lovers still pursue	—	1687
—	Let monarchs fight	627	1690
—	Let not a moon—born elf mislead ye	628	1691
—	Let the dreadful engines	578 i	1695
—	Let the graces and pleasures repair	627	1690
—	Let the soldiers rejoice	627	1690
—	Let us dance, let us sing	627	1690
392	Love arms himself in Celia's eyes	—	?1695
—	Love in their little veins	632	1695
393	Love is now become a trade	—	1685
—	Love quickly is pall'd	632	1695
396	Love thou can'st hear (R Howard)	—	1695
395	Love's power in my heart	—	1688
394	Lovely Albina's come ashore	—	?1695
—	Lucinda is bewitching fair	570	1695
—	Man is for the woman made	605	1695
—	Music for a while	583	?1692
399	My heart whenever you appear	—	1685
—	Next winter comes slowly	629	1692
—	No, no poor suffering heart	576	1692
400	Not all my torments can your pity move	—	?1693
—	Now, now the fight's done	606	1680
—	Now the night is chas'd away	629	1692
—	Nymphs and shepherds come away	600	?1695
—	O lead me to some peaceful gloom	574	1695
—	O let me weep	629	1692
406	O solitude (K Phillips translating St. Amant)	—	?1684-5
472	Ode on the death of Matthew Locke – see 'What hope for us remains'	—	1679
—	Oft she visits this lone mountain	626	?1689
402	Oh! Fair Cedaria, hide those eyes	—	?1688-95
—	Oh, how you protest	605	1695
404	Olinda in the shades unseen	—	?1694
—	One charming night	629	1692
405	On the brow of Richmond Hill (D'Urfey)	—	1692
407	Pastora's beauties when unblown	—	1681
408	Phillis I can ne'er forgive it	—	1688
409	Phyllis talk no more of passion	—	1685
410	Pious Celinda goes to prayers	—	1695
—	Pluto, arise	575	?1685-95
—	Pursue thy conquest love	626	?1689
—	Pursuing beauty	588	1690
383	Queen's Epicedium, The (Herbert) – see 'Incassum lesbia'	—	1695
411	Rashly I swore I would disown	—	1683
—	Retir'd from any mortal's sight	581	1681
—	Return, revolting rebels	632	1695
—	Sad as death at dead of night	606	1680
—	Saint George the patron of our isle	628	1691
412	Sawney is a bonny lad (P A Motteux)	—	1694
—	Say, cruel Amoret	612	1691
469	Scarce had the rising sun appear'd	—	1679
—	See, even night herself is here	629	1692
—	See, I obey	629	1692
—	Seek not to know	630	1695
—	See my many colour'd fields	629	1692
—	See where repenting Celia lies	603	1694
—	Shake the cloud from off your brow	626	?1689
413	She loves and she confesses too (Cowley)	—	1683
414	She that would gain a faithful lover	—	1695
415	She who my poor heart possesses	—	1683
—	Since from my dear Astrea's sight	627	1690
416	Since one poor view has drawn my heart	—	1681
—	Since the toils and the hazards	627	1690

Z number if single song	Title (author)	Z number of source stage work	Date of composition and/or first publication
—	Sing while we trip it	629	1692
—	Sound, fame	627	1690
417	Spite of the godhead, pow'rful love (A Wharton)	—	1687
—	Still I'm wishing	627	1690
—	Sweeter than roses	585	1695
420	Sylvia now your scorn give over	—	1688
—	Take not a woman's anger ill	609	1695
—	Tell me no more I am deceiv'd	601	1593
—	Thanks to these lonesome vales	626	?1689
—	The air with music gently wound	575	?1685-95
—	The cares of lovers	632	1695
—	The danger is over	595	1694
421	The fatal hour comes on apace	—	?1694/5
—	The gate to bliss does open stand	606	1680
—	There's not a swain	587	?1693
—	There's nothing so fatal as woman	571	1688
422	They say you're angry	—	1685
—	They tell us that your mighty powers above	630	1695
423	This poet sings the Trojan wars ('Anacreon's defeat')	—	1688
—	Thou doting fool	628	1691
—	Though you make no return to my passion	601	1693
—	Thrice happy lovers	629	1692
424	Through mournful shades and solitary groves (R Duke)	—	1684
—	Thus happy and free	629	1692
—	Thus the ever grateful spring	629	1692
—	Thus the gloomy world	629	1692
—	Thus to a ripe consenting maid	607	1693
—	Thy genius, lo! (2 settings)	604	1689
—	'Tis death alone can give me ease	571	1688
—	'Tis I that have warmed ye	628	1691
—	To arms, heroic prince	600	?1695
—	Trip it, trip it in a ring	629	1692
425	Turn then thine eyes – also as duet	—	c1692
—	'Twas within a furlong	605	1695
426	Urge me no more	—	?1682
—	Wake, Quivera	630	1695
381	We now, my Thirsis – music same as 'I loved fair Celia'	—	1694
428	What a sad fate is mine, 2 settings	—	?1692-4
429	What can we poor females do – also as duet	—	c1693
472	What hope for us remains ('Ode on death of Matthew Locke')	—	1679
—	What power art thou?	628	1691
—	What shall I do to show	627	1690
—	When a cruel long winter	629	1692
—	When first I saw the bright Aurelia's eyes	627	1690
431	When first my shepherdess and I	—	1687
432	When her languishing eyes said 'love'	—	1681
—	When I am laid in earth	626	?1689
—	When I have often heard	629	1692
434	When my Aemelia smiles	—	?1690-5
435	When Strephon found his passion vain	—	1683
—	When the world first knew creation	578 i	1695
437	While Thirsis wrapp'd in downy sleep	—	1685
438	Whilst Cynthia sung, all angry winds lay still	—	1686
—	Whilst I with grief	610	1694-95
440	Who but a slave can well express	—	?1683
441	Who can behold Florella's charms?	—	1695
—	Why should men quarrel?	630	1695
—	Ye blustering brethren	628	1691
—	Ye gentle spirits of the air	629	1692
441	Ye happy swains, whose nymphs are kind	—	1685
—	Ye twice ten hundred deities	630	1695
—	Yes Daphne, in your looks I find	629	1692
—	Your hay it is mowed	628	1691

A Performer's Catalogue of Purcell's Works

SOLO SONGS WITH 'CHORUS' (solo bass voice, usually only in final section)

Z number	Title (Author)	Date of composition or publication
461	Beneath a dark and melancholy grove	?1683
462	Draw near you lovers (T Stanley)	1683
463	Farewell ye rocks (D'Urfey)	1685
464	Gentle shepherds, you that know (Tate) ('On the death of Playford')	1687
465	High on a throne of glittering ore (D'Urfey) ('Ode to the Queen')	1690
373	How delightful's the life of an innocent swain	?1685
466	Let us, kind Lesbia, give away	1684
467	Musing on cares of human fate (D'Urfey)	1685
468	No to what purpose should I speak (Cowley)	?1683
470	See how the fading glories of the year	1689
471	Since the pox or the plague	1679
512	Sylvia 'tis true you're fair	1686
473	Young Thirsis' fate ('On the death of Thomas Farmer')	1689

MOCK SONGS (Songs with new words put to Purcell's tunes)

Z number	Title	Date of publication	Original source of melody
—	Honours may crown	c1691	Trumpet Tune, *Dioclesian*
376	I envy not a monarch's fate	1693	Birthday Ode for Queen Mary 1692
401	No watch, dear Celia, just is found	1693	Ode for St Cecilia 1693
403	O! How happy's he (W Mountfort)	1691	1st act tune of *Dioclesian*
427	We now, my Thirsis, never find (Motteux)	1693	I lov'd fair Celia
430	When first Amintas sued for a kiss (D'Urfey)	1687	lost instrumental piece

INCOMPLETE SONGS

354	Ah! what pains, what racking thoughts (Congreve) (bc lost)	
377	I fain would be free (bc lost)	

SONGS OF UNCERTAIN ATTRIBUTION TO PURCELL

—	A choir of bright beauties	Songs from The Tempest (Z631) previously attributed to but probably
—	Aaron thus proposed to Moses	not by Purcell
363	Cease, O my sad soul*	
—	How peaceful the days are	Aeolus, you must appear
387	I saw that you were grown so high*	Arise, ye subterranean winds
397	More love or more disdain I crave*	Come down, come down, my blusterers
444	Stript of their green our groves appear	Come unto these yellow sands
418	Sweet, be no longer sad*	Dry those eyes
s70	Sweet tyranness, I now resign*	Fair and serene
433	When I a lover pale do see*	Full fathom five
436	When Thyrsis did the splendid eye	Halcyon days
442	Why so serious, why so grave?	Kind fortune smiles
		See, see the heavens smile
		While these pass o'er the deep

* = probably by Henry Purcell (father)

SONGS FOR TWO OR MORE VOICES AND CONTINUO

This section includes all Purcell's songs for the stage and for other use: the two columns of Z numbers differentiate between these categories. Some stage works continue into a chorus.

Z number if single song	Title (author)	Z number of source stage work	Date of composition and/or first publication	Voices/instr.
481	A grasshopper and a fly (D'Urfey)	—	1686	SB
494	A Health to King James – see 'How great are the blessings'	—	1686	SB
D171	A poor blind woman	—	?	SSB
480	Above the tumults of a busy state	—	?	SB
—	Ah! How happy are we	630	1695	HT
482	Alas, how barbarous are we (K Philips)	—	?	SB
—	Art all can do, why then will mortals	578 i	1695	SSB
—	As Amoret and Thyrsis	607	1693	SB

Z number if single song	Title (author)	Z number of source stage work	Date of composition and/or first publication	Voices/instr.
—	As soon as the chaos was made	602	1692	SB
—	Behold the man ('Dialogue between a Mad Man and Woman')	608	1693	SB
—	Blow, Boreas, Blow	589	1681	SB
—	But ah! How much are our delights	632	1695	SSB
—	But ere we this perform	626	?1689	SS
—	Can'st thou, Marina, leave	606	1680	HTB
—	Celemene, pray tell me	584	1695	SS
—	Come away, no delay	627	1690	BB
483	Come, dear companions of th'Arcadian fields	—	1686	SB
184	Come, lay by all care	—	1685	SB
—	Come, let us agree	632	1695	SB
—	Come, let us leave the town	629	1692	SB, strs
—	Dialogue between a Mad Man and Woman – see 'Behold the man'	608	1693	SB
—	Dialogue between Corydon and Mopsa – see 'Now the maids and the men'	629	1692	AB, 2 vln
485	Dulcibella, when e'er I sue for a kiss (A Henley)	—	1694	SB
486	Fair Cloe, my breast so alarms (J Glanvill)	—	1692	SB
—	Fair Iris and her swain	572	1690	SB
—	Fear no danger	626	?1689	SS
487	Fill the bowl with rosy wine (A Cowley)	—	1687	SB
—	For folded flocks	628	1691	ATB
489	Go, tell Amynta, gentle swain (Dryden)	—	?	SB
—	Good neighbour, why do you look awry?	591	1694	SSHB
541	Hark, Damon, hark	—	?	SSB, 2rec, 2vn
—	Hark how the songsters	632	1695	SS, 2rec
542	Hark how the wild musicians sing	—	?	TTB, 2vn
—	Hark, my Damilcar	613	?1694	SB
491	Has yet your breast no pity learn'd?	—	1688	SB
490	Haste, gentle Charon	—	?	BB
—	Hear, ye sullen powers below	583	?1692	HTB, 2 vln
492	Hence, fond deceiver	—	1687	SB
493	Here's to thee, Dick (Cowley)	—	1688	SB
494	How great are the blessings ('A Health to King James')	—	1686	SB
543	How pleasant is this flowery plain	—	1688	ST, 2rec
495	How sweet is the air and refreshing	—	1687	SB
498	I saw fair Cloris all alone (W Strode)	—	1686	SB
499	I spy Celia, Celia eyes me	—	?	SB
544	If ever I more riches did desire (Cowley)	—	?	SSTB, 2vn
545	In a deep vision's intellectual scene (Cowley)	—	?	SSB
496	In all our Cynthia's shining sphere (E Settle)	—	?	SSB
497	In some kind dream (G Etherege)	—	1687	SB
—	Jenny, 'gin you can love	571	1688	ST
500	Julia, your unjust disdain	—	?	SB
—	Laius, hear!	583	?1692	HTB, 2 vln
—	Leave these useless arts in loving	579	1693	SB
—	Let all mankind the pleasures share	627	1690	SB
501	Let Hector, Achillles and each brave commander	—	1689	SB
—	Let the fife and the clarions	629	1692	AT
502	Lost is my quiet for ever	—	1691	SB
—	Love, thou art best of all human joys	596	1693	SS
—	Make room for the great god of wine	627	1690	BB, 2 obs
—	May the god of wit inspire	629	1692	HTB
—	My dearest, my fairest	585	1695	ST
503	Nestor, who did to thrice man's age attain	—	1689	SB
—	No more, Sir, no more	588	1690	SB
—	No, resistance is but vain	601	1693	SS
—	Now the maids and the men ('Dialogue between Corydon and Mopsa')	629	1692	AB, 2 vln
504	O dives custos Auricae domus ('Ode on the death of Queen Mary') (H Parker)	—	1695	SS
—	O, the sweet delights of love	627	1690	SS, 2 recs/obs
505	Oft am I by the women told (Cowley)	—	1687	SB
506	Oh! What a scene does entertain my sight	—	?	SB, rec, vn
507	Saccharissa's grown old	—	1686	SB
508	See where she sits	—	?	SB, 2vn

Z number if single song	Title (author)	Z number of source stage work	Date of composition and/or first publication	Voices/instr.
—	Shepherd, leave decoying	628	1691	SS
—	Since times are so bad	578 ii	1695	SB
—	Sing all ye muses	578 i	1695	HB
—	Sing, sing ye Druids	574	1695	SS, 2 recs
509	Sit down, my dear Sylvia (D'Urfey)	—	1685	SB
510	Soft notes and gently raised (J Howe)	—	1685	SB, 2rec
—	Sound a parley	628	1691	SB, 2 vln
511	Sylvia, thou brighter eye of night	—	?	SB
—	Tell me why my charming fair	627	1690	SB
513	There ne'er was so wretched a lover as I (Congreve)	—	?	SB
—	They shall be as happy	629	1692	SSB
514	Though my mistress be fair	—	1685	SB
546	'Tis wine was made to rule the day	—	?	SSB
—	To arms, your ensigns straight display	574	1695	AB
—	To Mars, let 'em raise	627	1690	ATB
515	Trip it, trip it in a ring	—	?1693	SB
—	Turn then thine eyes – also as solo song	629	1692	SS
—	Two daughters of this aged stream	628	1691	SS
516	Underneath this myrtle shade (Cowley)	—	1692	SB
547	We reap all the pleasure	—	?	STB, 2rec
517	Were I to choose the greatest bliss	—	1689	SB
518	What can we poor females do? – also as solo song	—	pre1693	SB
—	What flatt'ring noise is this	630	1695	HTB, 2 vln
519	When gay Philander left the plain	—	1684	SB
520	When, lovely Phillis, thou art kind	—	1685	SB
521	When Myra sings (G Granville)	—	1695	SB
522	When Teucer from his father fled (D Kendrick)	—	1686	SB
D172	When the cock begins to crow	—	?	SSB
523	While bolts and bars my day control	—	?	SB
524	While you for me alone had charms (J Oldham)	—	?	SB
525	Why my Daphne, why complaining?	—	1691	SB
—	With this sacred charming wand	578 i	1695	SSB, 2 vln
—	You say 'tis love	628	1691	SB

CATCHES

Z	Title (author)	Publication date	Voices
240	A health to the nut-brown lass (J Suckling)	1685	4vv
241	An ape, a lion, a fox and an ass	1686	3vv
242	As Roger last night to Jenny lay close	—	3vv
599	At the close of evening (from Beaumont & Fletcher: *The Knight of Malta*)	1691	BBB
243	Bring the bowl and cool Nantz	1693-4	3vv
244	Call for the reckoning	—	3vv
245	Come, let us drink (A Brome)	—	3vv with bc
246	Come, my hearts, play your parts	1685	3vv
247	Down, down with Bacchus	1693	3vv
248	Drink on till night be spent (P Ayres)	1686	3vv
249	Full bags, a brisk bottle (J Allestry)	1686	3vv
250	God save our sovereign Charles	1685	3vv
251	Great Apollo and Bacchus	—	3vv
254	He that drinks is immortal	1686	3vv
252	Here's a health, pray let it pass	—	3vv
253	Here's that will challenge all the fair (also known as Bartholemew Fair)	1680	3vv
256	I gave her cakes and I gave her ale	1690	3vv
255	If all be true that I do think	1689	3vv
257	Is Charleroy's siege come too?	?1693	3vv
574	Jack, thou'rt a toper (from Fletcher: *Bonduca*)	1695	3vv
101	Joy, mirth, triumphs I do defy	—	4vv
258	Let the grave folks go preach	1685	3vv
259	Let us drink to the blades	?1691	3vv
260	My lady's coachman, John	1688	3vv
594	My wife has a tongue (from E Ravenscroft: *The English Lawyer*)	1685	3vv
261	Now England's great council's assembled	1685	3vv

Z	Title (author)	Publication date	Voices
262	Now, now we are met and humours agree	—	3vv
263	Of all the instruments that are	1693	3vv
264	Once in our lives let us drink to our wives	1686	3vv
265	Once, twice, thrice I Julia tried	—	3vv
266	One industrious insect ('Insecta praecauta, alterius merda') (?R Thomlinson)	—	3vv
267	Pale faces, stand by (Mr Taverner)	1688	3vv
268	Pox on you for a fop	—	3vv
269	Prithee be n't so sad and serious (Brome)	—	3vv
270	Room for th'express	—	3vv
271	Since the duke is return'd	1685	3vv
272	Since time so kind to us does prove	—	3vv
273	Sir Walter enjoying his damsel	—	3vv
274	Soldier, soldier, take off thy wine	—	4vv
275	Sum up all the delights	1688	3vv
276	The Macedon youth (Suckling)	1686	4vv
277	The miller's daughter riding	1686	3vv
278	The surrender of Limerick	?1691	3vv
279	'Tis easy to force	1685	BBBB
280	'Tis too late for a coach	1686	3vv
281	'Tis women makes us love	1685	4vv
282	To all lovers of music (Carr)	1687	3vv
283	To thee, to thee and to a maid	1685	3vv
284	True Englishmen drink a good health ('Song on the 7 Bishops')	c1689	3vv
285	Under a green elm lies Luke Shepherd's helm	1686	4vv
286	Under this stone lies Gabriel John	1686	3vv
287	When V and I together meet	1686	3vv
288	Who comes there?	1685	3vv
289	Wine in a morning makes us frolic and gay (T Brown)	1686	3vv
290	Would you know how we met? (T Otway)	1685	3vv
291	Young Colin cleaving of a beam (D'Urfey)	1691	3vv
292	Young John the gard'ner	1683	4vv

INSTRUMENTAL

Z	Title, key	Scoring	Date	Comment
730	Chacony, g	2vn, vla, bc	?1680	
731	Fantasia upon a Ground, D/F	3vn/3rec, bc	c1680	
745	Fantasia upon One Note, F	5 viols	c1680	
732-4	3 fantasias, d, F, g	3 viols	c1680	
735-43	9 fantasias, g, B flat, F, c, d, a, e, G, d	4 viols	1680	
746	In Nomine, g	6 viols	c1680	
747	In Nomine, g Dorian	7 viols	c1680	
770	Overture, G	2vn, vla, bc	1681	version of overture to Ode 'Swifter, Isis'
771	Overture, d	2vn, vla, bc	?	
772	Overture, g	2vn, 2vla, bc	?	
—	Overture, B flat	2vn, vla, bc	?1675-8	the 'Staircase' overture
752	Pavan, g	3vn, bc	c1680	
748-51	4 pavans, A, a, B flat, g	2vn, bc	c1680	
N773	Prelude, g/d	vn	?	
850	Sonata, D	tpt, 2vn, vla, bc	?1694	
780	Sonata, g	vn, bc	?	reconstructed by T Dart for vn, b viol, bc
790-801	Twelve Sonnata's of III Parts	2vn, b viol, bc	c1680	publ. London, 1683
802-11	Ten Sonata's in Four Parts	2vn, b viol, bc	c1680	publ. London, 1697
770	Suite, G	4 str	?	inner parts incomplete
860	March and Canzona, c	4 flatt tpt	1695	For funeral of Queen Mary

HARPSICHORD

At the time of writing this repertoire is still awaiting an accurate catalogue; the list below should be used as a guide only.
(Some are arrangements by Purcell of pre-existing music)

The Second Part of Musick's Handmaid (London, 1687?)
Song Tune, C ('Ah! how pleasant 'tis to love')
Song Tune, C ('Sylvia, now your scorn give over')
2 marches, C

A New minuet, d
2 minuets, a, a
Minuet, d ('Raise, raise the voice')
A New Scotch Tune, G

A Performer's Catalogue of Purcell's Works

A New Ground, e ('Welcome to all the pleasures')
A New Irish Tune, G ('Lilliburlero')
Rigadoon, C
Sefauchi's Farewell, d
Suite, C
A Choice Collection of Lessons, hpd/spinet (London, 1696)
8 Suites, G, g, G, a, C, D, d ('The Married Beau'), F ('The Double Dealer')
March, C ('The Married Beau')
Trumpet Tune, C ('The Indian Queen')
Chaconne, g ('Timon of Athens')
Jig, g ('Abdelazer')
Trumpet Tune 'Cibell', C
Trumpet Tune, C ('Dioclesian')
7 airs: G; d ('The Indian Queen'); d ('The Double Dealer'); g ('Abdelazar'); d; d; F ('The Indian Queen')
4 grounds: Ground in Gamut, G; c ('Ye tuneful Muses'); c (possibly by Croft); d ('Celebrate this festival')
3 hornpipes: B flat ('Abdelazar'); d 'Round O' ('Abdelazar'); e ('The Old Bachelor')
4 overtures: c ('The Indian Queen'); D ('Timon of Athens'); D ('The Fairy Queen'); g ('The Virtuous Wife')
Suite, a: Prelude; Almand, Corant; Saraband
Suite, B flat: Almand, Corant, Saraband
Corant, G
Minuet, G

The Queen's Dolour, a
Canary, B flat ('The Indian Queen')
Prelude for the Fingering, C attrib. Purcell in The Harpsichord Master, 1 (London, 1697), anon in later vols
Voluntary, no 9 of Ten Select Voluntaries (London, c1780), 1 movt of which may be by Purcell

The recently discovered Purcell and Draghi manuscript sold at Sothebys, May 1994 contains
Prelude, C
Hornpipe (by Eccles)
Prelude, G (by O. Gibbons)
2 Preludes, Almand, Corant (from Suite in a)
Jig (?for Suite in a)
Prelude, C
Two movements (one a minuet?), C (possibly by Purcell)
Almand, Corant and Sarraband (from Suite in C)
keyboard versions of:
Minuet from *The Double Dealer*
Symphony to 'Thus happy and free' (*The Fairy-Queen*)
Hornpipe from *The Old Bachelor*
Air in C from *The Double Dealer*
Hornpipe from *The Fairy Queen*
Trumpet Minuet, Minuet and Air from *The Virtuous Wife*

ORGAN

716	Verse, F		721	Voluntary on the 100th Psalm, A
717-20	4 Voluntaries, C, d, d, (Double org), G			

THEORETICAL WORKS

'A Brief Introduction to the Art of Descant: or, Composing Musick in Parts', in J Playford: *An Introduction to the Skill of Musick* (London, 1694) (partly revision of earlier work by Campion, Simpson, Playford and others)

Selected Discography

There is a rich and ever-growing discography of Purcell's works of which this list represents only a small selection. Some works (especially *Dido and Aeneas*) are available in many different recordings. Where categories of works are available in "complete editions", it is these that have been selected.

OPERAS AND SEMI-OPERAS
Dido and Aeneas : von Otter, Varcoe, Soloists, The English Concert/Pinnock : Archiv 427624-2
The Fairy Queen : Soloists, The Sixteen/Christophers : Collins Classics 70132
King Arthur : Soloists, The English Concert/Pinnock : Archiv 435490-2
The Indian Queen : Soloists, English Baroque Soloists/Eliot Gardiner : Erato 2292-45556-2
Dioclesian : Soloists, Collegium Musicum 90/Hickox : Chandos CHAN0569/70

THEATRE MUSIC
The complete theatre music : Soloists, Academy of Ancient Music/Hogwood : Decca 425893-2 (6 CDs, not available separately)

CHAMBER MUSIC
Sonatas of three and four parts : The Purcell Quartet : Chandos CHAN 8591, 8663, 8763
Fantasias for viols : London Baroque/Medlam : EMI CDM 763066-2

ODES AND WELCOME SONGS
The complete odes and welcome songs : Soloists, The King's Consort/King : Hyperion CDS44031/8 (8 CD box set : also available separately on CDA66314, 66349, 66412, 66456, 66476, 66494, 66587, 66598)

SACRED MUSIC
The complete anthems and services : Soloists, Choirs, The King's Consort/King : Hyperion - only available separately on CDA66585, 66609, 66623, 66644, 66656, 66663, 66677, 66686, 66693, 66707, 66716

SONGS
The complete secular solo songs : Soloists, The King's Consort/King : Hyperion CDA66710, CDA66720, CDA66730
Airs and duets : Kirkby, Thomas, Rooley : Hyperion CDA66056
Countertenor duets and solos : Bowman, Chance, The King's Consort : Hyperion CDA66253
Songs and Ayres : Kirkby, Rooley, Hogwood : Decca 417123-2
Mr Henry Purcell's most admirable composures : Bowman, The King's Consort : Hyperion CDA66288

PURCELL SAMPLER DISC
The Essential Purcell : Soloists, Choirs, The King's Consort/King : Hyperion KING2

Selected Reading List

ASHBEE, Andrew (Ed.), *Records of English Court Music* (vols. I–V) (Aldershot, Scolar Press 1986-91)

BESANT, Walter, *Westminster* (London, Chatto & Windus 1925)

BLISS, Robert M., *Restoration England 1660-1688* (London, Methuen 1985)

BLOM, Eric, *Music in England* (Harmondsworth, Penguin 1942)

BRAUDEL, Fernand, *The structures of everyday life* (London, Fontana 1985)

CAMPBELL, Margaret, *Henry Purcell, glory of his age* (London, Hutchinson 1993)

COWARD, Barry, *The Stuart Age* (London, Longman 1980)

EDE, Mary, *Arts and Society in England under William and Mary* (London, Stainer & Bell 1979)

EVELYN, John, *Diary*, ed. E.S. de Beer (Oxford, Oxford Univesity Press, 1955)

FALKUS, Christopher, *The life and times of Charles II* (London, Weidenfeld 1972)

HARLEY, John, *Music in Purcell's London* (London, Dobson 1698)

HILL, Christopher, *Reformation to Industrial Revolution* (Harmondsworth, Penguin 1969)

———, *The world turned upside down* (London, Penguin 1975)

HODGEN, Margaret, *Early anthropology in the sixteenth and seventeenth centuries* (Pennsylvania, University of Pennsylvania Press 1971)

HOLMAN, Peter, *Four and twenty fiddlers* (Oxford, Clarendon Press 1993)

HOLLAND, A.K., *Henry Purcell* (Harmondsworth, Penguin 1948)

HOWARTH, Mary, *A plain man's guide to the Glorious Revolution* (London, Regency Press 1988)

HUTCHINGS, Arthur, *Purcell* (London, BBC Publications 1982)

HUTTON, Ronald, *The Restoration* (Oxford, Clarendon Press 1986)

JONES, J.R., *Country and Court, England 1658-1714* (London, Arnold 1978)

———, *The revolution of 1688 in England* (London, Weidenfeld & Nicolson 1972)

KENYON, J.P., *Stuart England* (Harmondsworth, Penguin 1978)

LAFONTAINE, H.C. de, *The King's Music* (London, 1909)

MACFARLANE, Alan, *The origins of English individualism* (Oxford, Blackwell 1978)

MILLER, John, *James II, A study in kingship* (London, Methuen 1978)

MORRAH, Patrick, *Restoration England* (London, Constable 1979)

NORTH, Roger, *Writings,* ed. John Wilson (London, Novello 1959)

———, *The Musicall Grammarian* (Cambridge, Cambridge University Press 1990)

OGG, David, *England in the reigns of James II and William III* (Oxford, Oxford University Press 1955)

OLLARD, Richard, *Pepys, a biography* (Oxford, Oxford University Press 1984)

PALMER, Tony, *Charles II, Portrait of an age* (London, Cassell 1979)

PARRY, W.H., *Thirteen centuries of English Church Music* (London, Hinrichsen 1946)

PEPYS, Samuel, *Diary*, ed. Latham, Robert and Matthews, William, (London, Bell & Hyman 1985)

PERKINS, Jocelyn, *Westminster Abbey* (Oxford, Oxford University Press 1940)

PRICE, Curtis, *Henry Purcell and the London Stage* (Cambridge, Cambridge University Press 1984)

SEAWARD, Paul, *The Restoration, 1660-1688* (London, Macmillan 1991)

STANLEY, Arthur, *Memorials of Westminster Abbey* (London, Murray 1867)

TANNER, Lawrence, *The story of Westminster Abbey* (London, Tuck & Sons 1932)

———, *Unknown Westminster Abbey* (Harmondsworth, Penguin 1948)

THOMAS, Keith, *Man and the natural world* (Harmondsworth, Penguin 1984)

TOOLEY, R.V., *Maps and map-makers* (London, Batsford 1949)

SADIE, Stanley, ed., *The New Grove Dictionary of Music and Musicians* (London, Macmillan 1980)

VAN DER ZEE, Henri and Barbara, *1688 Revolution in the family* (Harmondsworth, Penguin 1988)

———, *William and Mary* (Harmondsworth, Penguin 1973)

WESTERN, J.R., *Monarchy and Revolution* (London, Macmillan 1985)

WESTRUP, J.A., *Purcell* (London, Dent 1937, revised 1979)

ZIMMERMAN, Franklin B., *Henry Purcell, An analytical catalogue of his music* (London, Macmillan 1963)

———, *Henry Purcell, His life and times* (London, Macmillan 1967)

Acknowledgments

This book was conceived by mistake. Whether or not H.C. Robbins Landon's misdirection of a note from me to him into a tray at Thames and Hudson was accidental or not, it led to the birth of a new biography of Purcell. My fascination with Purcell and his music began when I was a twelve-year old chorister, standing next to the towering figure of James Bowman whilst recording the solos in the *Funeral Music* and the *Te Deum and Jubilate*. No music had ever had such an effect on me and, when the LP was issued, I completely wore out one track. More than twenty years later I have been fortunate enough to have performed and recorded much of Purcell's music: there has never been a day working on this extraordinary music that has not found me amazed at Purcell's genius. I am indebted to all my performing colleagues for their enthusiasm, their insights and their skill in bringing dots on the page into astonishing musical life. Singers including Rogers Covey-Crump, Charles Daniels, Gillian Fisher, Michael George, Susan Gritton and (now towering over me only by inches, rather than feet) James Bowman, wonderful instrumentalists including Jane Coe, Miles Golding, Helen Gough, David Miller, Jane Norman, David Woodcock and the irrepressible Crispian Steele-Perkins, the two finest choir trainers in the world, James O'Donnell and Edward Higginbottom and a series of marvellous boy choristers (including three astonishing soloists, Nicholas Witcomb, Mark Kennedy and Eamonn O'Dwyer) have taught me more than they can imagine. Without their collective musicianship this book could never have been written.

I am equally indebted to Robert Spencer for the generous loan of a vast amount of original musical and visual material, for his letting me loose on his unique library and for his kindness in checking my typescript. Professor Curtis Price, Tony Tweedale and James Bowman also read my first draft and made helpful comments. Susi Woodhouse compiled the index and additionally pointed out a number of inconsistencies. Tricia Yarwood and Margaret King lent me large numbers of books and gave advice on Purcell's psychological and medical state. Elizabeth Latimer carried out research into the wider field of post-Restoration history, Dr Roger Savage was generous in sharing his knowledge of Purcell's theatres, Curtis Price's research and writing on Purcell's theatre music was an example of clarity and wonderfully adventurous use of the English language, Dr Richard Luckett supplied information on Purcell's song texts, Dr Andrew Ashbee's researches into court records brought many insights into a colourful period of history, my technical guru Tim McNally showed me more computing tricks than I could have imagined and airline check-in staff all over the world generously turned a blind eye to the terrifying weight of my suitcase, invariably filled with computer gear, manuscripts and books. Ben Turner is not only the best and most supportive recording producer one will ever find but if anyone loves Purcell's music even more than I do, it is he. And finally my long-suffering PA Anne Willie has been, as ever, utterly invaluable: it was she who typed up the index of works (making sense of my chaotic notes), carried out initial picture research, co-ordinated with Thames and Hudson, and frequently and tactfully reminded me that I was overdue on every deadline. Without her I would never have finished the book in one lifetime, let alone nine months.

Despite all this help from so many kind and brilliant people, the numerous faults, omissions and failings of this book are entirely mine. In the end it is Purcell's music that matters and hopefully nothing I have written can harm that.

Robert King
London, June 1994

Sources of Illustrations

Index

Page numbers in *italics* refer to the illustrations.
Works by Purcell referred to in the text are indexed separately.

INDEX OF PURCELL'S WORKS MENTIONED IN THE TEXT

ODES AND WELCOME SONGS

ANTHEMS AND SERVICES

Index